Over Here, Over There

Over Here, Over There

Transatlantic Conversations
on the Music of World War I

EDITED BY
WILLIAM BROOKS,
CHRISTINA BASHFORD,
AND GAYLE MAGEE

UNIVERSITY OF
ILLINOIS PRESS
Urbana, Chicago, and Springfield

Publication of this book was supported in part by the Otto Kinkeldey
Endowment of the American Musicological Society, funded in part
by the National Endowment for the Humanities and the Andrew W.
Mellon Foundation.

Library of Congress Control Number: 2019945839

Contents

▩ Prelude: Beginnings   1
   William Brooks, Christina Bashford, and Gayle Magee

PART 1: INDIVIDUALS

1. Medium and Message: Frank Bridge's Lament for
   String Orchestra and the Sinking of the *Lusitania* (1915)   15
   Christina Bashford

2. "Every Man in New York": Charles Ives and the First World War   37
   Gayle Magee

3. Reflecting the Public Appetite in Text and Music:
   Debussy's Act of Wartime Propaganda   58
   Barbara L. Kelly

4. Profitable Patriotism: John Philip Sousa and the Great War   73
   Patrick Warfield

5. From the Great War to *White Christmas*: The Long Reach
   of Irving Berlin's *Yip Yip Yaphank*   97
   Jeffrey Magee

▩ Interlude: The Middle   115
    William Brooks, Christina Bashford, and Gayle Magee

PART 2: COMMUNITIES

6. Tommy Critics, an Unlikely Musical Community,
   and the *Longleat Lyre* during World War I   127
    Michelle Meinhart

7. Women at the Pedals: Female Cinema Musicians
   during the Great War   149
    Kendra Preston Leonard

8. Empire, Nation, and Music: Canada's *Dominion Songbook*   174
    Brian C. Thompson

9. Of Stars, Soldiers, Mothers, and Mourning   199
    William Brooks

10. The Beginning of the End of Something   224
    Deniz Ertan

▩ Postlude: Not an End   241
    William Brooks, Christina Bashford, and Gayle Magee

Contributors   245

Index   247

Over Here, Over There

Prelude: Beginnings

WILLIAM BROOKS, CHRISTINA BASHFORD, AND GAYLE MAGEE

The path to this volume has occupied nearly the full duration of the centennial of the Great War. The three collaborators and coeditors (who are still friends, amazingly) began by organizing a pair of international conferences: Over Here and Over There (University of York, England, February 27–28, 2015); and 1915: Music, Memory, and the Great War (University of Illinois, March 10–11, 2015). The first of these, conducted in tandem with an undergraduate module taught by William Brooks, included numerous performances, presentations, and exhibits by students and scholars, including Gayle Magee, Christina Bashford, and Deniz Ertan, each of whom has contributed to the present volume. The second conference included papers by many of the other authors represented here, with yet others in attendance; it included a performance by a Canadian troupe that re-created an entertainment given by Canada's legendary "Dumbells" at the western front during the war and a recital by tenor Justin Vickers and pianist Geoffrey Duce, who presented multiple settings by English and American composers of the iconic text "In Flanders Fields."

We offer this detail to demonstrate that from the start, this project was conceived to provide a transnational perspective on the ways music manifested the alliance among the Atlantic partners in the war: France and Britain, including the Dominion of Canada, and eventually the United States. Music expressed patriotic exhortation, privation, anxiety, and grief; above all, though, it affirmed commitment, the resolve to join with others to meet and overcome a perceived threat to world order. The conferences, the papers, the performances—and, yes, this volume—were meant to function similarly, to bring diverse voices into dialogue (multilogue, really) in a way that paralleled the interactions between these nations during the war years.

In so doing, the conferences also constituted a new alliance—a transnational community—formed of the individual voices of the presenters, performers, and other participants. The creation of this volume has entailed negotiating the relationships between individual responses and a collective understanding. So, too, the war itself generated musical responses that ranged from those by single individuals on through responses that were communal, local, regional, national, and global. The organization of this volume reflects that spectrum: the five essays in part 1 are about five individuals; the five essays in part 2 discuss communities that range from the very local to the entirely transnational.

After the initial conferences, subgroups of authors continued to collaborate somewhat independently (not unlike the various national armies during the war). Brooks and Ertan, for example, coauthored a presentation at a conference organized by Barbara L. Kelly, Music and Nation, 1918–1945 (Royal Northern College of Music, England, November 23–24, 2016), and various pairs or trios met, presented, and paneled at academic conferences in England, Canada, and the United States. Perhaps the most enduring collaboration was undertaken by Brooks, Magee, and Bashford, representing their nationalities (the United States, Canada, and Britain) and joined by Scottish pianist Duce accompanying American singers Vickers and Laurie Matheson, in a series of jointly authored and presented lecture-performances that began in November 1915 and culminated on May 18, 2017, in an annual AMS/Library of Congress lecture and podcast.[1]

All this work, and all the contributions to this volume, are thus a kind of extended conversation—not an authoritative statement but an ongoing process of inquiry. Consistent with that, much of the introduction that follows is written alternately by the three editors, each with a distinct voice that is represented by a distinct icon at the head of each section:

Christina Bashford, speaking for Britain, is indicated by a crown

Gayle Magee, speaking for Canada, is indicated by a maple leaf

William Brooks, speaking for the United States, is indicated by an eagle

Our collective voice, speaking transnationally, is indicated by a composite icon

We offer this device as more than a literary conceit: it really does capture the way this work has been conceived and created—and, we would suggest, the way the alliance itself was negotiated, developed, and affirmed by musical individuals and communities in transatlantic countries during the Great War.

■ ■ ■

On August 3, 1914, Germany declared war on France, which responded with its own declaration of war. On August 4, 1914, Germany invaded Belgium, and Great Britain declared war on Germany. On August 5, the French composer Théodore Dubois wrote in his *Journal*, "Behind every Prussian truly hides a barbarian."[2] Two weeks later, he was in despair: "My music is sadly neglected. I have neither the heart nor the courage to return to it."[3]

The United States entered the war thirty-three months later, on April 6, 1917. On April 7, 1917, German American musician Charles Greinert was copying a score for composer Charles Ives. "He was all discouraged and cast down, almost in tears—that his fathers' country and his [had] come to make war," Ives reported. "[He] was so troubled and discouraged [that] he couldn't seem to work at all, made mistakes by the mile, and finally gave up."[4]

From one perspective, contemporaneous responses to the Great War are a collection of distinct, often irreconcilable experiences by millions of individuals. Some individuals responded with despair, some with creativity, some with opportunism. Each person's story is a part of the whole; in part 1 of the present volume, five authors explore the responses of five English, French, and American composers. There are many more stories that could be told, and the vast bulk of them concern ordinary people, not statesmen or generals or celebrated composers. To understand the war, surely, we need do no more than to give these voices a hearing.

Yet, from another perspective, the Great War is equally understood by means of collective responses that transcended the individual. On August 5, 1914, the French liner *La Lorraine* left New York, taking eleven hundred French reservists, who had been resident in the United States, back to Europe. The front-page headline in the *New York Evening Post* read "War Songs on La Lorraine," and the story continued: "While the Vessel [was] getting ready to sail . . . the martial notes of the 'Marseillaise' floated over the river, and 5,000 French men and women on the pier sang back at the reservists who lined the vessel's sides. But through it all there was scarcely a note of hysteria. The feeling seemed to be too deep and earnest for that. . . . [A]mong those who actually took part in these scenes there was a lack of surface demonstration that spoke volumes." On the next page, the story continued with an account of the departure of the liner *Lusitania*, a few berths away, which was departing for Liverpool escorted by British cruisers: "As the vessel left her pier, several of the crew sang 'God Save the King,' and the refrain was taken up by the passengers."[5]

Music was part of World War I from the very beginning, and it bound individuals into communities constituted by geography, occupation, and nationality. These communities—and their musical manifestations—were linked through transnational exchanges of people, goods, and ideas. Indeed, music was essential to those exchanges: it played a crucial role not only in expressing national integrity and resolve but also in gathering very different peoples into the Allied force that eventually prevailed. Part 2 of this volume offers five case studies of collective responses to the war. These reveal the adjustments made by social classes, industries, and nations, as new constituencies appeared and new alliances were formed, together with new cultural bonds created among France, Britain, Canada, and the United States.

 When Britain entered the war on August 4, 1914, the country was not only aligning itself with France and Russia as the major players in the bid to quell German and Austro-Hungarian aggression, but also creating the crux of the association that would eventually become known as the Allied forces. At the same time, it was defending its position as the world's preeminent imperialist power, while dragging its colonized possessions (Canada, South Africa, Australia, New Zealand, and India) into the fray. In the course of the war, a staggering 2.7 million men from the colonies would serve the British army, fighting for a tiny island thousands of miles away, making significant contributions that—as in the case of the enormous number of Indian soldiers who fought—have only recently begun to be recognized.[6] As historians are prone to remind us, one of the signal features of the so-called Great War is that it was not one conflict but many, fought in several regions of the world, both on land and at sea, by different nations with different agendas. By way of example: fewer than three weeks after Britain declared war, Japan entered on the side of the alliance, pushing back against German naval ships in the Pacific and Indian Oceans. Even so, at the start of the war, with the British military underresourced and the Allied pact still in its infancy, the only support that Britain could count on to defend its territorial and strategic interests was its colonial armies. As yet the United States was neutral (though looking on with interest), and the idea of a special relationship between the French- and English-speaking "Allies" of the Northern Hemisphere, with their historic and political linkages, was by no means clear—at least not in terms that histories of the Great War typically recognize.

But in terms of cultural exchanges, the ground was being prepared. Transnational relationships can be detected in the popular music that was rushed out in Britain in the early phase of the war. "For King and Country," a rousing recruitment song expressing loyalty to Britain's monarch, was written and published by Robert Harkness, an Australian living in London, in August 1914 and issued a few months later by Gordon V. Thompson in Toronto.[7] An American recording, meanwhile, was issued by Victor, sung by Brooklyn-born Reinald Werrenrath.[8]

A recruitment song better known today is British composer and lyricist Paul Rubens's "Your King and Country Want You," which was published in London by

Chappell and Company in late 1914—just weeks after the British government had declared war on Germany and kicked off a major recruitment campaign, based on the slogan "Your King and Country Need You," which Rubens's song refers to and subtly manipulates.[9] Billed by Chappell as a "woman's recruiting song," it was immensely popular, including in British music halls, and, with its teasing sexual undertones and the declared guarantee that profits would be devoted to the "Queen Mary's Work for Women Fund," it surely helped establish a role (and implied duty) for women in the bid to enlist young men—a role that would become highly visible in Britain by the spring of 1915 and also in Canada.[10] By this time, Chappell and Company was distributing sheet music with war themes in Toronto, Melbourne, and New York, even running to a "Colonial edition" of Rubens's recruitment song and a piano version with red, white, and blue coloring.

A further apt example from Chappell's stable is Francesco Paolo Tosti's one and only overtly political song, "The Allies March to Freedom," which the émigré Italian singer and prolific composer of drawing-room ballads wrote shortly after Italy entered the war on the Allies' side in May 1915. Chappell published it with Italian and English words and a lavish color cover that depicted the flags of the major Allies (Britain, France, Belgium, Russia, and Japan), with gleaming finials that look like stand-ins for bayonets, which for now at least were still the soldier's quintessential weapon of war.[11] Beyond its appeal to the nearly twenty thousand Italians then living in London, there was the possibility of its reaching the far-greater number of Italian Americans across the Atlantic (we know, for instance, that it was sold in the United States). So as the war that was supposed to have been over by Christmas 1914 looked set to become a longer-term nightmare, music was feeding—if not whipping up—interest in the fight for king and country way beyond Britain's shores.

Since the 1920s, the Great War has been portrayed as a defining moment in Canada's emergence from its British colonial past to an independent and unified nation on the world stage. Yet recent scholarship has questioned these long-held beliefs, suggesting that the war proved highly problematic for relations between two distinct populations: the majority Anglophones and the minority Francophones. Seen from the distance of a century, the war did less to unite the country than to divide it along linguistic, cultural, religious, and political fault lines, deeply dividing approximately half of the country's population that was English-speaking from the roughly quarter of the nation that claimed French as its main language.

Apart from the differences between these populations, the country faced significant challenges in raising the army that would be known as the Canadian

Expeditionary Force, or CEF. In the early part of the war, most "Canadian" officers were not from Canada at all, in the sense of having been born and raised there. Instead, many were British military veterans, reservists, or retirees who had fought in the Boer War or expatriates from France, Switzerland, Belgium, and Francophone colonies who felt allegiance to their European origins.

The composition of the armed forces in the first year of the war explains in large part the character of many of the songs issued in Canada. These songs had to be approved by the government's censorship office, which under the War Measures Act allowed for complete control over sheet music publication and reissues for the entirety of the war. A slew of songs dedicated to King George V and the Union Jack appeared through Canadian publications and reissues of British songs, aimed at British Canadian enlistees and the country's Anglophone population that identified with the empire: "Will the King Be Proud of Canada," "Hats Off to the Flag and the King," "The Call of the King," "God Bless Our Empire," and "The Best Old Flag on Earth."[12] Moreover, Canadian World War I songs made common use of imported British imagery and melodies, liberally quoting *Rule Britannia*, "God Save the King," and "It's a Long Way to Tipperary" within fairly formulaic patriotic songs.

While reservists, veterans, and expatriates filled the first encampments at the Valcartier training grounds outside Quebec City in August 1914, regular citizens registered to fight for a distant country in foreign lands, creating the first substantial Canadian army. Through the late summer and fall of 1914, men from most parts of the country rushed to enlist: within one year, thirty-five thousand troops were fighting in Europe.

The United States would remain neutral for much of the war, but individual Americans expressed partisan sentiments within a few months. The United States' alliance with France harked back to the War of Independence, which would be famously evoked in words ascribed (wrongly) to General Pershing in 1917: "Lafayette, we are here!"[13] But in 1914, the alliance to come was intimated mostly by hybrid Americans such as Natalie Townsend, born in Paris and a Belgian resident for six years, who set a text by her daughter Yvonne, "Belgium Forever!" Recorded by Herbert Stuart, it enjoyed considerable success and was a forthright attempt to rouse support for intervention:

There's a weeping and a wailing
For the brave men who have died,
For the homes all lying wasted,
Devastation far and wide,
Why must little Belgium suffer
Such appalling agony?[14]

America's sizable Francophone population, centered in Lowell, Massachusetts, also rallied around their European forebears. A steady stream of war-inspired music appeared from two Lowell publishers, E. L. Turcot and Eusèbe Champagne. Turcot was first, with "Marche l'humanité" (1914) and "Le 41eme Battalion R.C.F." (1915), both written by Georges Milo.[15] Milo's real name was George Marchant de Trigon; he was born in France, published in America, enlisted in Canada on July 14, 1915, died on November 16, and was buried in an English cemetery.[16] It's hard to imagine a more transnational identity.

In general, though, the country viewed the "European war" from a comfortable distance. For many Americans, the overriding political objective was to keep Wilson's presidency on track. After decades of work, American progressives finally had a president and a climate that supported their reform agenda; the war threatened to deflect attention and resources from the domestic tasks at hand, and they wanted no part of it. Much American music, too, was resolutely neutral, from the witty "Neutrality Rag" to the polemical (and controversial) "I Didn't Raise My Boy to Be a Soldier."[17] Such productions were, of course, largely insular and isolationist, though a few titles enjoyed some controversial success in Britain.

But other songwriters were very aware of European political and national differences, sometimes deploying them for humorous effect. "Alsace Lorraine" converted France's rallying cry into a lament about "a big bound'ry line in my heart" from a narrator whose father is in Berlin, mother in Paris, and sweetheart in Alsace Lorraine; his solution, in the final line, is to "bring them all over here."[18] A very similar story is told in "The Fatherland, the Motherland, the Home of My Best Girl," except the sweetheart is in England.[19] These two songs, written immediately after the war started, cleverly weave in quotations of the German and French national anthems; as in Canada, musical quotations served as icons that could be manipulated to express conflict or alliance.[20]

In any case, national differences were of immediate concern to American politicians; even in its early stages, the war threatened to set ethnic groups against each other, fracturing the progressive community. German Americans wanted strict neutrality, English Americans favored support for Britain, and Irish Americans were with the Germans, since anti-British feelings were running high. Wilson's administration steered a very careful course through the swamp of opinion, protected by the country's sense that the problems were "over there" and that American soldiers would stay at home.

That sense began to shift in 1915, as trenches were dug, chemical warfare introduced, and submarines unleashed and it became clear that the war would continue indefinitely. And it changed dramatically on May 7, 1915, when the *Lusitania* was sunk by a German submarine. The British luxury liner was on the final leg of its journey from New York to England and was carrying nearly two thousand people when the torpedo struck; less than an hour later, nearly twelve hundred were dead. The Anglophone countries of the Atlantic Seaboard—Canada, Britain, and the United States—were united in shock and mourning.

The tragedy was too great and the grief too deep to be successfully addressed by popular songwriters in the three countries. But composers of concert music responded with some of their finest works. In chapter 1, Christina Bashford discusses the genesis, style, and implications of Frank Bridge's Lament, dedicated to a *Lusitania* victim, with particular attention to the medium Bridge chose. She illuminates not only the musical and cultural threads that came together in the "lullament" that Bridge wrote but also the relationship between his composition and the place of women in Britain's wartime music making.[21] In chapter 2, Gayle Magee explains the background and implications of Charles Ives's "From Hanover Square North at the End of a Tragic Day, the Voice of the People Again Arose," which was conceived in the immediate aftermath of the tragedy. She goes on to explore Ives's other wartime work—in business as well as music—to draw out threads of memory, idealism, and practicality that have resonated to the present day.

Other composers, on both sides of the ocean, were more or less compelled to redefine themselves in response to the war. France responded to German militarism not only with an effort to secure its own integrity but also with a burning sense of grievance, an urgent desire to regain its territories and to retaliate for the events of the past half century. Much French music from the war expresses that urgency; within a year after the war began, Théodore Botrel had published *Les chants du bivouac*, with a song that called for "expelling the Kaiser and his troops from our territory" and concluded, "France! We need victory to avenge our flag; it's your glory that we need!"[22] Major figures were drawn into the cause, shaping the rhetoric to suit both their own and the nation's purposes. In chapter 3, Barbara L. Kelly explores the trajectory of Debussy's wartime compositions, focusing in particular on his *Noël des enfants qui n'ont plus de maison*. She skillfully demonstrates the ways in which this "little carol" adapts and refines Debussy's musical language in response to the national climate of revenge, together with the factors that made it important at the time and neglected thereafter.

John Philip Sousa, like Debussy, was a cultural icon when the war began. In chapter 4, Patrick Warfield traces the interconnected evolution of American politics and Sousa's career, from neutrality through preparedness to Sousa's late setting of "In Flanders Fields." Like so many others caught up in the wartime excitement, Sousa attempted (more successfully than most) to reposition himself to take advantage of new interests and motivations while remaining at least somewhat true to his own musical taste and persona—though he did shave off his beard.

Irving Berlin also followed a winding course through the war years, from his early acerbic "Stay Down Here Where You Belong" to the jingoist "For Your Country and My Country."[23] But his most lasting wartime song was "Oh! How I Hate to Get Up in the Morning," written with heartfelt feeling after he was drafted in 1918 and had to confront—briefly—an early-morning reveille. In chapter 5, Jeffrey Magee explores the "long reach" of *Yip Yip Yaphank*, the soldiers' show that introduced that song, explaining not only the show's genesis and structure but also its extensive postwar revivals and adaptations.

Yip Yip Yaphank links World War I to World War II and beyond; indeed, all five chapters in part 1 demonstrate the extent to which compositions endure beyond the immediate circumstances that gave them life. Wars are always, in a sense, revivals: just as the music of World War I reframed the songs and sentiments of the American Civil War, the Boer War, and the Franco-Prussian conflict, so World War I has been echoed in wartime films from the 1940s and in responses to perceived threats from the Falklands crisis of 1982 to the destruction of the World Trade Center in 2001.

Notes

1. Portions of the text of that lecture have been adapted and revised for inclusion in this introduction. A video recording of the presentation at the Library of Congress is available at https://www.loc.gov/item/webcast-8147. Additional papers by two of the three editors were presented at the Society for American Music Annual Conference (Sacramento, 1915) and in a special issue of *American Music* (Winter 2016), edited by Gayle Magee.

2. "Sous tout Prussien se cache décidément un barbare." Théodore Dubois, *Journal*, ed. Charlotte Segond-Genovesi and Alexandre Dratwicki (Lyon: Symétrie, 2012), 95. Here and elsewhere, translations are by the editors.

3. "La pauvre musique est bien délaissée. Je n'ai ni le coeur ni le courage de m'y remettre." Ibid., 100.

4. Charles Ives, *Memos*, ed. John Kirkpatrick (New York: W. W. Norton, 1972), 65.

5. "War Songs on La Lorraine," *New York Evening Post*, August 5, 1914, 1, 2. Portions of these opening paragraphs are adapted from an unpublished paper, "From . . . to . . . *in* Flanders Fields," available at https://www.academia.edu/3408335/from_._._._to_._._._in_Flanders_Fields.

6. George Morton-Jack, *The Indian Army on the Western Front: India's Expeditionary Force to France and Belgium in the First World War* (Cambridge: Cambridge University Press, 2014); Shrabani Basu, *For King and Another Country: Indian Soldiers on the Western Front, 1914–18* (New Delhi: Bloomsbury, 2015).

7. Harkness wrote both words and music, registering copyright in the United States on August 26, 1914. Thompson's Canadian edition, published in Toronto, was hugely popular, selling more than a hundred thousand copies. See Helmut Kallmann, "Gordon V. Thompson," *The Canadian Encyclopedia*, http://www.thecanadianencyclopedia.ca/en/article/gordon-v-thompson-emc/, digitized copy available at https://archive.org/details/CSM_00838.

8. Victor 17711 (mx B-15378, recorded November 11, 1914). For this title, Werrenrath recorded under the pseudonym Edward Hamilton.

9. Paul Rubens, "Your King and Country Want You" (London: Chappell, 1914), was copyrighted in the United States on September 28; digitized copy available at https://digital .library.illinois.edu/items/fb171da0-c556-0134-2373-0050569601ca-e.

10. More notable still in terms of sexual innuendo was "I'll Make a Man of You," with words by Arthur Wimperis and music by Herman Finck (London: Francis, Day, and Hunter, 1914), copyrighted in the United States on October 23. This was popular throughout the British Empire; a digitized copy of an Australian imprint, for example, can be found at http://nla .gov.au/nla.obj-165514537.

11. A digitized copy can be found at http://digital.lib.uiowa.edu/cdm/compoundobject/ collection/sheetmusic/id/189/rec/1; note the US import stamp.

12. Frank Eberoll (music) and S. G. Smith (words), "Will the King Be Proud of Canada" (Toronto: Whaley Royce, 1915), copyrighted in the United States as "The King Will Be Proud of Canada" (February 21, 1916), digitized copy available at https://archive.org/ details/CSM_00537; Will J. White, "Hats Off to the Flag and the King" (Toronto: Musgrave Bros., 1916), US copyright September 28, 1916, digitized copy available at https://archive .org/details/CSM_002257; Mary Gilmour (music) and James A. Ross (words), "The Call of the King" (Toronto: Whaley Royce, 1915), US copyright September 28, 1916; Bert Berry and Lester Berry, "God Bless Our Empire" (Winnipeg: Berry, 1916), digitized copy available at https://repository.library.brown.edu/studio/item/bdr:90813/; Charles F. Harrison, "The Best Old Flag on Earth" (Vancouver and Toronto: Charles F. Harrison, 1914), digitized copy available at https://archive.org/details/CSM_00865.

13. The sentence closed a speech actually given by Colonel Charles E. Stanton at Lafayette's tomb in Paris, July 4, 1917. See Albert H. Gilmer, "When a Soldier Spoke Effectively: 'Lafayette, We Are Here!,'" *Quarterly Journal of Speech* 29, no. 3 (1943): 298–300.

14. Townsend's song was copyrighted in manuscript on November 11, 1914; the publication by G. Schirmer (New York) was copyrighted December 8; digitized copy available at https://repository.library.brown.edu/studio/item/bdr:99957/. Stuart, using the pseudonym Albert Wiederhold, recorded Townsend's song on April 10, 1915, on Columbia A1766 (mx 45543, take 1); on July 11, the *Chicago Daily Tribune* listed it third among Columbia's bestselling records (2).

15. "Marche l'humanité" was copyrighted December 28, 1914; "Le 41eme Battalion R.C.F." a year later, on December 31, 1915.

16. See http://www.veterans.gc.ca/eng/remembrance/memorials/canadian-virtual -war-memorial/detail/2758013.

17. Jack [Harold G.] Frost, "Neutrality Rag" (Chicago: Frank K. Root, 1915), digitized copy available at https://www.loc.gov/item/ihas.200203315; Al Piantadosi (music) and Alfred Bryan (words), "I Didn't Raise My Boy to Be a Soldier" (New York: Leo Feist, 1915), digitized copy available at https://www.loc.gov/item/ihas.100008457/.

18. Lewis F. Muir (music) and L. Wolfe Gilbert (words), "Alsace Lorraine" (New York: F. A. Mills, 1914), copyright September 1, 1914, digitized copy available at http://digital.lib .niu.edu/islandora/object/rbsc%3A3002.

19. Harry Carroll (music) and Ballard MacDonald (words), "The Fatherland, the Motherland, the Home of My Best Girl" (New York: Shapiro, Bernstein, 1914), copyright September 2, 1914, digitized copy available at https://digital.library.illinois.edu/items/4780bfc0-c0e6-0134-2373-0050569601ca-a#.

20. Later American songs would express national unity similarly, by, for instance, bringing together snippets of "Dixie" and "Marching through Georgia." See, for example, M. Witmark's great success, "For Dixie and Uncle Sam" (music by Ernest R. Ball, words by J. Kiern Brennan, copyrighted May 9, 1916), digitized copy available at https://digital.library .illinois.edu/items/f65ac370-c556-0134-2373-0050569601ca-b.

21. Women's roles during the war are also discussed in chapters 4, 7, 8, and 9.

22. "France! Il nous faut la victoire / Pour venger notre drapeau / . . . / C'est ta Gloire qu'il nous faut!" Théodore Botrel, "C'est ta Gloire qu'il nous faut!," in *Les chants du bivouac* (Paris: Payot and Cie, 1915), 26. In another instance of transatlantic influence, Botrel's book was the starting point when John Jacob Niles began collecting songs sung by African American soldiers. See John Jacob Niles, *Singing Soldiers* (New York and London: Charles Scribner's Sons, 1927), [i].

23. "Stay Down Here Where You Belong" (New York: Waterson, Berlin, and Snyder) was copyrighted October 20, 1914, digitized copy available at https://digital.library.illinois.edu/items/be1e7780-e8ed-0135-4ad8-0050569601ca-1; "For Your Country and My Country" (New York: Waterson, Berlin & Snyder) was copyrighted May 8, 1917, digitized copy available at https://digital.library.illinois.edu/items/b8cda1f0-e8ed-0135-4ad8-0050569601ca-6.

PART 1

Individuals

CHAPTER 1

Medium and Message

Frank Bridge's Lament for String Orchestra and the Sinking of the *Lusitania* (1915)

CHRISTINA BASHFORD

> We saved all the women and children we could,
> but a great many of them went down.
>
> Eyewitness account, "Survivors,"
> *New York Times*, May 9, 1915

In Britain during the first eighteen months of the war—the period before despondency and despair started to set in on the home front—most artistic responses to the conflict that came to public attention were in the domain of popular song. Sheet music, live performances, and recordings of numbers—famously, Paul Rubens's "Your King and Country Want You" (1914), Ivor Novello's "Keep the Home Fires Burning" (1915; lyrics by Lena Gilbert Ford), and "Pack Up Your Troubles" by George Powell and Felix Powell (1915)—poured forth, capturing and contributing to the upbeat atmosphere of the war's opening phase.[1] In sharp contrast, few responses to the conflict by British composers of "serious" music reached the public sphere. Of the ones that did, the most obviously successful works tapped into the general mood of patriotism or into support for the emerging notion of the Allies in Europe. Elgar's melodrama *Carillon*, for narrator and orchestra, composed in 1914 both in defiance of the recent destruction of Belgium's cities and in solidarity with the Belgian people, is a case in point. The score, a setting of poetry by the exiled Emile Cammaerts ("Chantons, Belges, chantons!"), makes clever, symbolic play on pealing bells and ends in a blaze of imagined eventual triumph. Quickly translated into English ("Sing, Belgians, Sing!"), *Carillon* premiered in December 1914 and was heard in concerts across the country well into 1916, demonstrating its popular appeal.[2] Elgar's *Polonia*, composed for a London Symphony Orchestra charity concert for the Polish Victims Relief Fund (July 6, 1915), directed attention to the suffering on the eastern front; nevertheless, the piece creates an uplifting mood, using melodies from Polish patriotic songs alongside quotations from Chopin and Paderewski in a more ambitiously "symphonic" work.[3] Meanwhile, Francesco Paolo Tosti's ballad "The Allies March to Freedom," composed on Italy's entrance to the war in May 1915, presented a fervent anthem of defiance and solidarity; it was published in 1915 by Chappell with both Italian and English texts.

Even at this stage of the war, not all conflict-inspired compositions were fashioned in a patriotic vein.[4] Elgar attempted a notably reflective and critical response to events in his second melodrama, *Une voix dans le désert*, begun in summer 1915 and premiered in London in January 1916 at the Shaftesbury Theatre.[5] The work (also to poetry by Cammaerts) is set in a desolate landscape and narrates the awfulness of the "rape" of Belgium and the cost to both humanity and nation, while seemingly lacking hope for an end to the conflict.[6] But as Lewis Foreman points out, it failed to achieve "the impact or popular success of *Carillon*";[7] recognition of its significance came almost a century later.[8]

A similarly contemplative tone comes across in another work from 1915: Frank Bridge's Lament for string orchestra (H. 117), a short five-minute piece written in memory of a child who lost her life in the infamous sinking of the RMS *Lusitania* by a German torpedo in May that year.[9] Performed in London at the Promenade Concerts in the Queen's Hall on September 15, 1915, and reprised the following year (October 14) at the Queen's Hall Symphony Concerts (Bridge conducted both performances of his piece),[10] the work represents a public statement of raw grief in the aftermath of the atrocity and one that stands apart from the existing war-related pieces of British classical music that had come to public attention by this point. Its acceptability for public performance is perhaps explained by its function as an expression of mourning for civilian, as opposed to military, losses (the latter being typically bathed in a glow of patriotic valor), along with the absence of a sung text that could drive home a potentially problematic message. Repeat professional performances, however, did not ensue, despite its being a remarkable gem of string orchestra repertoire and despite its publication by Goodwin and Tabb in 1915, along with a piano transcription that Bridge himself made.[11] The orchestral version attracted limited critical comment at the time of the first performances, and the work subsequently disappeared from the repertoire until commercial recordings began to become available in the 1970s.[12] One cause of that subsequent neglect may be the meager scholarly interest in Bridge's music for much of the twentieth century, stemming not only from a relative dearth of manuscript materials with which to document the composer's life and work but also from the marginalization of British music within musicology. Within the past ten years, however, as the study of the "Vaughan Williams generation" has claimed attention and validity, that situation has changed: witness the recent research of Paul Hindmarsh, Kevin Salfen, Fabian Huss, Mark Amos, and Ciara Burnell. While all these writers consider the Lament and its musical language in passing,[13] the most substantial treatment comes in a compelling recent essay by Byron Adams. His work places the music and Bridge's heartfelt memorialization of a life lost at sea in the context of Milton's poem "Lycidas" of 1637, an elegy for a friend who drowned on a ship that went down during a voyage from England to Ireland (likely not far from the waters that would claim the *Lusitania*).[14]

This essay will take a somewhat different and complementary tack, exploring the Lament in its historical context and asking two interrelated questions: first, why Bridge should have lighted on the string orchestra as the medium for this particular expression of grief and, second, what contemporary cultural meanings a lament that was scored in this fashion might have had in the context of wartime Britain and the aftermath of the *Lusitania* tragedy—a tragedy that yoked Canada, the United States, and Britain together in grief and an event that would eventually be construed in the popular imagination as the turning point for bringing the United States into the war.[15]

The *Lusitania*, War at Sea, and May 1915

The *Lusitania*, the Cunard Company's massive luxury liner, had been in service since its maiden voyage from Liverpool to New York in 1907. Although later eclipsed by the *Titanic* and other commercial steamships, at the time the *Lusitania* was considered one of the largest, fastest transatlantic ships of the day.[16] It was also the subject of much press attention for its opulent accommodation—"more beautiful than Solomon's temple," as one contemporary commentator apparently put it— while its matching lifestyle on board offered those individuals who traveled in first or even second class enviable social prestige.[17] Quite simply, the liner was the talk of the town when it arrived in New York in 1907, its celebrity translating into all manner of commercial goods: crockery, fans, badges, and even sheet music (Florence Fare's piano intermezzo "*Lusitania*," published in London, and F. A. Fralick's "*Lusitania* Two-Step," published in Toronto, both 1907). The Liverpool–New York crossing became popular, and when the ship went down in May 1915 it was on the return leg of its 101st round trip. On board were a number of regular travelers, including British citizens returning from visits to the United States. Also traveling were people with Canadian addresses, as well as American doctors and nurses who had volunteered to serve in military hospitals in France and Belgium.[18]

The Americans' medical missions were particularly timely, for the war had, since January 1915, begun to escalate, and casualty figures were starting to mount (in April came reports of poison gas being used by the Germany Army on the battlefield at Ypres). Meanwhile, fears on the British home front were surfacing: in early 1915, the first zeppelin raids occurred over England (though not over London until May, just weeks after the *Lusitania* was sunk). In addition, anxiety about British civilian safety at sea was starting to develop.

The nature of the fears for travelers is worth stating. From the very start of the war, Germany had struggled with the British blockade of the North Sea, the intention of which was to starve the country of vital imports and disrupt its economy. In February 1915, however, Germany retaliated, declaring the waters around Britain a war zone and beginning a period of unrestricted submarine warfare, launching torpedoes at Allied shipping. The move created the possibility that any ship, commercial or naval, that sailed close to the British coast (including the coast of Ireland—the country was still under British rule) could be attacked and sunk simply on suspicion of carrying war cargo.[19] This quickly became a serious political worry for Britain, not only because its military prowess and imperial pride had long been tied to its command of so much of the world's waters, but also because of the reliance of the British wartime economy on imported goods, both food and weaponry, which had to arrive by ship. Moreover, with American industry eagerly supplying arms and munitions to Britain, often by concealing them in commercial passenger liners, civilian sea travel was starting to look like a highly risky undertaking from the American perspective as well, since any loss of its own people would surely threaten US neutrality. The risk became especially evident when an American tanker traveling from Texas to France was attacked in April 1915.[20] Anxiety for German immigrants at the Imperial German Embassy in Washington, DC, led to the publication of a warning to passengers of the potential dangers of traveling to Britain in the *New York Times* the day before the *Lusitania* left the city on its final voyage.[21] Few people, however, heeded it.

The *Lusitania* sank in a mere eighteen minutes, in calm waters close to the south coast of Ireland, after being struck in the side by a German torpedo on the afternoon of Friday, May 7. The terror experienced by the passengers and crew on the listing ship can only be imagined, though survivors' testimonies, from which the standard histories quote, make the horrors and chaos of the situation all too real and dreadful, even at a century's distance. Leslie Morton, one of the crew, described "the turmoil of passengers and life belts, many people losing their hold on the deck and slipping down and over the side, and a gradual crescendo of noise building up as the hundreds and hundreds of people began to realise that, not only was she going down very fast[,] but in all probability too fast for them to get away."[22] Just under 1,200 people perished; fewer than 770 survived.[23] When the news reached Britain via the morning papers, there was deep shock, which only intensified as the identity of victims became concrete. Whether the ship was carrying munitions or not, why the ship's captain had changed course twice in the area of danger, and what had caused a second explosion on the ship were questions for the future. What stunned people was the number of civilian deaths in a war that had so far, despite the zeppelin attacks, barely affected the home front. Meanwhile, a sense of déjà vu prevailed, since it was only three years since British newspapers had reported the sinking of the *Titanic* (operated by the White Star Line) with the loss of some 1,500 lives, an equally awful disaster with an even higher death toll. Yet there were salient differences between the tragedies. The *Titanic*'s end had elements of natural catastrophe about it (for all that it lacked adequate lifeboats), but in the *Lusitania*'s case the mass deaths of innocents had come about through an act of wartime aggression. In addition, unlike the *Titanic* disaster, when the ship had sunk over a period of hours and evacuation was instituted in an orderly, albeit socially hierarchical, fashion, with the result that many first-class passengers were saved, the events on the *Lusitania* were characterized by pandemonium and by mortalities right across the social board, including many glitterati of the day who had not balked at traveling.[24] Among the high-profile fatalities were Alfred Vanderbilt, one of the richest men in America; Elbert Hubbard, founder of the Roycroft artistic colony (East Aurora, New York); Hugh Lane, director of the National Gallery of Ireland; and British explorer J. Foster Stackhouse, who had been planning to lead an expedition to the Antarctic.[25] Many well-heeled wives and daughters also drowned since, on this occasion, women and children were not helped off first, as was the traditional code of conduct in maritime emergencies and as had happened on the *Titanic*. Furthermore, most of the children perished—a shocking 94 out of 129.[26] This figure included all six children of Gladys and Paul Crompton; a prominent English businessman in his midforties, Paul was relocating his family to London, having lived and worked in Philadelphia for several years. It was to the memory of the Cromptons' second-eldest daughter, Catherine, that Bridge inscribed his Lament.

Frank Bridge and Catherine Crompton

Frank Bridge was thirty-five when Britain entered the war. Unlike several other British composers such as Ivor Gurney, George Butterworth, and Cecil Coles, he did not volunteer for active service. Nor did he play a part in noncombat duties behind the lines, as Vaughan Williams did. Rather, he continued to work as a professional musician in London, mostly as a viola player and a conductor, and when conscription was introduced (1916) he took on the mantle of "conscientious objector."[27] As a young man, he had studied the violin and composition (as a pupil of Charles Villiers Stanford) at the Royal College of Music (RCM), and he subsequently ground out a good career as a conductor and string player, demonstrating particular skill on the viola and becoming a member of the high-profile English String Quartet.[28] By the time war broke out, he was starting to gain recognition as a composer, with a growing corpus of distinctive chamber music to his name. Like many musicians and artists, he became profoundly troubled by the conflict; according to cellist Antonia Butler, he was "in utter despair over the futility of war and the state of the world generally and would walk round Kensington [where he lived] in the early hours of the morning[,] unable to get any rest or sleep."[29]

The origins of Bridge's relationship with the Crompton family and how he came to know Catherine (and how well) are somewhat obscure. That the Catherine whom the work memorializes—its epigraph reads "Catherine, aged 9 'Lusitania' 1915."—was Catherine Mary Crompton is confirmed by the names of the children in the ship's passenger lists, which feature only one appropriately aged Catherine (of that, or any other, spelling). A retrospective account of the Lament's premiere, published in the February 1919 *Musical Times*, by Edwin Evans, a prominent London critic and promoter of contemporary English music, states that Catherine was a "well-loved child-friend" of Bridge's;[30] it echoes the opening of the program note for the 1915 concert, which was penned by Rosa Newmarch: "This brief pathetic piece was composed on June 14th, 1915, in memory of a dear child friend, 'Catherine, aged 9,' who, together with her whole family, went down with the 'Lusitania,' and it is well that this musical tribute should help British men and women to keep in mind the manner of her death."[31] Meanwhile, the passenger lists report the child was in fact ten, not nine, years of age (a fact confirmed by Catherine's birth certificate, as Adams shows),[32] indicating that Bridge's awareness of her age was slightly hazy.

How the family came into Bridge's orbit is largely a matter of educated guesswork. Paul and Gladys Crompton were both English and of the same generation as Bridge; after marrying in 1900, they lived in London for a few years, initially at Paul's home in Mecklenburg Square, to the east of Bloomsbury.[33] Whether the couple was known to Bridge at this time is not established. In the first years of their marriage, with Paul an employee of Alfred Booth's steamship and leather company, the Cromptons traveled internationally for Paul's business responsibilities, and many of their children were born abroad, though Gladys gave birth to Catherine in London during a visit "home." By 1906 the family had relocated to the United

States, settling in a wealthy suburb of Philadelphia, where Paul soon became vice president of the Surpass Leather Company, which specialized in kid and patent leather and which the Booth firm had bought. Paul is nevertheless said to have traveled back to England regularly, typically taking the entire family with him,[34] and it may well be that on those occasions Bridge encountered the Cromptons, since they were associated with the same locality. As Adams explains, by 1915 Bridge and his wife resided at 4 Bedford Gardens, in the affluent district of Kensington (also home to the RCM and an area favored by musicians), about a mile from the Crompton family home at 29 Gilston Road;[35] the lease on the Gilston Road house, on the Chelsea side of Kensington, was in the name of Paul's mother and was presumably where Paul's family stayed when they visited.[36] For all that, no evidence has so far emerged to indicate that the Cromptons had musical interests or social or musical connections with the Bridges (who incidentally had no children), though these possibilities cannot be discounted. Besides, it is conceivable that Bridge, who did a certain amount of violin teaching, gave the young Catherine occasional lessons on the instrument during these trips; learning the violin was, as we shall see, a much-favored social endeavor for wealthy middle-class girls in this period, competing with the parlor piano among desirable accomplishments for women both in Britain and in the United States.[37]

In May 1915, Paul's work was taking the Cromptons back to London for good. The entire family, including a baby, was traveling first class on the *Lusitania* and had their own dining room aboard.[38] When the ship sank, all the Cromptons, as well as the children's nanny, perished—the only complete family so lost. The American press, outraged at the act of war, was swift to pick up on their tragedy, with the *Harrisburg Telegraph* in Philadelphia publishing on May 10 a short notice of the Cromptons' demise ("A Whole Family Wiped Out by a German Torpedo"), along with a poignant photograph of Gladys surrounded by all her children that was reprinted fairly widely, including in the *New York Times* and the shoe- and leather-trade press (see figure 1.1).[39] Catherine is standing at the back of the group, behind her mother.[40] Back in Britain, the reporting of their deaths was less sensational and the coverage limited;[41] given the family's now American identity, theirs was apparently not as newsworthy a story. However, a short report of the funeral of Crompton's eldest son in Queenstown and a notice of the entire family's fatalities was run in the *Times* on May 14. If he had not known that the Cromptons were traveling on the *Lusitania*, Bridge would surely have learned of their deaths from the English papers fairly soon after the sinking. Evans, in 1919, stated that Bridge composed the Lament in one day, on June 14, 1915. That information is uncorroborated, yet even if that date merely indicates the day on which Bridge completed the score, the Lament's composition was still fast work and likely cathartic, too.

Figure 1.1. Gladys Crompton with her six children; Catherine (*standing*) is the second child from the right of the picture. Photograph published in the *Harrisburg (PA) Telegraph,* May 10, 1915, and later in the *New York Times.* Image reproduced from Logan Marshall, *Horrors and Atrocities of the Great War* ([Philadelphia]: [G. F. Lasher], 1915), facing 73.

The Lament and Lamentation

Press reactions to the public performances of 1915 and 1916 seem to have been relatively few and cursory. One critic described the music as "duly pathetic and simple," implying that it made a fitting memorial for a child; another considered it "expressive, if rather too tearful."[42] On the whole, at a time when the public face of the war effort was generally upbeat and patriotic, no writer seems to have been prepared to dwell on the inward sorrow of the Lament, to reflect on the atrocity of war that spawned it, or to comment on audience reaction. But four years later (1919), Evans recalled publicly that "there lingers in the memory an impression of the effect it [the Lament] made when first heard at Queen's Hall. The audience was too spell-bound for a noisy demonstration of favour, but the eloquence of the music had achieved what a more ambitious or studied composition could not have effected."[43] Such a muted response may indicate how powerfully the music had hit home. There was, after all, much in Bridge's score that would have made the music speak so eloquently. There was also the power of suggestion: the work's very title signaled generic grief and mourning, emotions intensified by the epigraph, which named "nine-year-old" Catherine and made reference to the *Lusitania*. Both pieces of information were reported in the program note, as mentioned. There was also this description of the music:

> The Lament begins *Adagio con molto espressione*, the strings being muted, with a few introductory bars foreshadowing the theme and ending on a long pause. The first violins, still *con sordini*, then present the elegiac melody, which forms the principal material of the miniature work. The music broadens in character, and solo violin, viola, and 'cello now make themselves heard in sad, regretful phrases above the rest of the strings. An expressive passage, starting in the 'cello and finishing in the higher registers of the violin, leads to a recapitulation of the theme, *dolcissimo*; the solo-instruments still remaining more or less prominent. After another prolonged pause, the introductory figures are recalled, and the music dies away very quietly *un poco più adagio*.[44]

Specifically, the modal, quasi-pentatonic flavor of the prominent, repetitive violin melody and the work's straightforward ternary form may have encouraged the comments about simplicity, which followed likewise from the slow tempo, soft dynamic, and compound duple meter that is emphasized by the bass line's pedal points. Salfen has suggested that these latter features fix the work's genre as lullaby, that is, a mother's song as she pushes the cradle regularly from side to side, soothing her baby to sleep.[45] We might develop this point further by spelling out the analogy between the awake-sleep transition and the life-death one, for musical laments for the dead that integrate elements of lullaby, though not universal, are found in several cultures.[46] In such a reading, the piece may be understood to reference not only Catherine Crompton but the many children who died that day. Certainly, the use of compound meter seems to have been deliberate: the three laments that Bridge had already composed ("Lament: Fall Now My Cold Thoughts" for voice and orchestra, H. 40, 1904; Elégie for cello and piano, H. 47, 1904; and the Lament from the Two Pieces for two violas, H. 101, 1911–12) were all in triple meter (with occasional triplet movement). A second possibility is that the compound meter can be heard as the rocking, and ultimate listing, of the ship, an idea that is enhanced by what can seem like a constant feeling of sinking. A good deal of chromatic motion in the inner parts has a descending contour, and in the opening measures (figure 1.2), Bridge builds two six-note chords downward, preceding them with a triadic anacrusis and luxuriating in their sonority with fermatas; meanwhile, the resonance of the low pitches in the double basses draws the ear's attention to that deep register, as if to evoke the bottom of the sea. By way of confirmation, the

Figure 1.2. Frank Bridge, *Lament*, mm.1–3

pulsating open fifths between cello and bass that punctuate the ensuing measures emphasize the sensation of depth.[47]

At the same time, the uneasy dissonant bite of the harmonies in the divided second violin and viola lines—especially the clashing major seconds against the modal melody—do much to conjure up the exacting pain of those who grieve. There is also agony in the emphatic, falling semitones (like sobs or cries) on the accented anacruses of the opening chords (which return toward the end) and in the abundance of sliding linear chromaticism.[48] The ending, too, is notable for how the cello line traces a short, slow chromatic descent followed by a diatonic one; descending bass lines are gestures firmly associated with the lament in classical music (Dido's Lament by Purcell is a case in point). Also, Bridge deliberately withholds a diatonic E-flat major chord until the last four measures, when the chord sounds three times.[49] This moment serves, if not to resolve the emotional pain of the bereaved, to suggest the finality of the ship reaching its resting place on the seabed and to hint at a droplet of consolation for those left to process the event on shore.

But only a droplet. After all, in reality, consolation is rarely immediately achieved. As Thomas M. Carr explains, according to classical thought, consolation for the mourner involves the acceptance of loss, making it the end point in a grieving process that takes time.[50] That process is what Sigmund Freud and his followers described as "grief work" for the survivor, or what might be described in modern popular psychology as the stages of mourning, which are not necessarily experienced linearly. The idea of grieving as a process to be executed by mourners takes on particular significance when brought into dialogue with Bridge's composition and its overlaying of the genre of lament with lullaby. In an article in the *American Journal of Hospice & Palliative Medicine*, music therapist Clare O'Callaghan coins the term *lullament* for melodies that combine lullaby and lament, and she argues through clinical studies for the inherently therapeutic and positive qualities of "lullament" when used to negotiate situations of loss and bereavement.[51] This finding not only helps explicate the observation that lullaby-inflected laments for the dead are found in several cultures but also links to other therapeutic aspects embodied in Bridge's piece.

The String Medium and Therapeutic Grieving

Why Bridge initially scored the Lament for strings and envisioned its public performance in that medium is a question worth pondering, not least because Stanford, Bridge's teacher, is said to have insisted that musical compositions should suit the medium for which they are written.[52] It was not unusual for Bridge to write for strings; he was a masterful violinist and violist, and he knew how to score effectively for the string family. At the time of the Lament's composition, he had produced a series of successful works for string quartet (three bespoke quartets, one of which was completed only in March 1915; a Phantasie in F minor; and several miniatures). He had also written a Suite for string orchestra (1908; premiered 1910).

In the 1910s, music for string orchestra represented a new medium that many English composers—among them Elgar, Vaughan Williams, and Holst—were exploring, a phenomenon that may be understood as a particular expression of Englishness and the quest for a lost artisanal past.[53] Much of this repertoire, which had begun to emerge in the 1890s, favors relaxed, upbeat modes of expression in melody-driven pieces of short duration that are easy to grasp aurally. A full list would include many sets of dances, often with an antique flavor or drawing on English folk dances, such as Parry's *An English Suite* (1890–1918), Rutland Boughton's *Three Folk Dances* (1911), and Holst's *St. Paul's Suite* (1912–13); there would also be character pieces with descriptive titles and other self-standing miniatures. Much of this music has a pastoral or nostalgic tinge, or both, though with some exceptions. A few compositions, such as Elgar's *Introduction and Allegro* (first performed by the London Symphony Orchestra in 1905), draw on traditions of development

or timbral sophistication more associated with symphonic music. Other pieces—
and this is significant for understanding the lineage for Bridge's Lament—take on
a serious, elegiac tone. Of these, the landmark work is Vaughan Williams's dark
and compositionally complex *Fantasia on a Theme by Thomas Tallis* of 1910 (revised
in 1913 and again in 1919), a fifteen-minute piece based on Thomas Tallis's tune
for the funereal hymn of penitence "When Rising from the Bed of Death." There
was at least one precedent in the sphere of shorter pieces too: Elgar had written an
Elegy in 1909 on the loss of a friend, which had been published by Novello. Bridge
almost certainly knew both these works.

What underlay this trend to write string orchestra repertoire—especially the
numerous short suites and character pieces—was new market demand for such
music from the growing number of amateur string bands that were flourishing in
Britain, especially among middle- and upper-class women. The backdrop here is
that, beginning in the 1880s, string instruments were taken up by a large and new
slice of the population, thanks to a nexus of cultural causes, one of which was the
demise of the social taboos that had previously prevented women from playing
the "ungainly" instruments of the violin family and that had insisted that string
playing was gendered male.[54] While surely an exaggeration, the comment from one
journalist in 1894 that "every other girl you meet in the street now-a-days carries
a fiddle-box!" sums up the strength of the new craze.[55] Moreover, by 1914, as the
market for supplying instruments and lessons grew, a glut of well-trained female
string players emerged. Some of them managed to work professionally, although
their employment was typically limited to teaching or performing in tea-shop
ensembles—the more illustrious orchestras and solo careers being out of bounds
to all but a few. Far more of them ended up as accomplished musicians who played
as a hobby, especially before marriage, and many eagerly joined amateur string
orchestras (as did some professional female players).[56]

Such ensembles looked to existing music, playing anything from string quartet
movements (as string orchestra versions) to baroque *concerti grossi*, many of which
were being rehabilitated, published, and brought into the concert repertoire. But
groups also performed new works that were being written for the medium, sometimes even for specific ensembles. Hubert Parry composed his *Lady Radnor's Suite* of
1894 for the Countess of Radnor's amateur string band—a notable group of well-
heeled women of leisure—and Elgar tried out his Serenade for strings (written in
1892) with the Ladies Orchestral Class in Worcester. Another well-known ensemble from the late Victorian period was the Reverend Moberley's String Orchestra,
made up of some ninety women from the South of England.[57] There were many
others, less well known, such as the Ladies String Orchestra in Dundee and the
all-women Mignon String Orchestra in Newcastle; traces of their activities can be
found in the violin and orchestral press of the time.

Through the 1910s, including the Great War, amateur orchestras continued to attract women, and bespoke ladies' ensembles attracted public attention: for instance, the Glasgow Ladies' String Orchestra[58] and, in London, the all-women Orchestra of Queen Alexandra's House (mostly students at the RCM), which performed in the Thomas Dunhill Chamber Concerts at Steinway Hall.[59] Similarly, in their day, both Moberley's and Radnor's groups gave high-profile charity concerts at fashionable London venues such as St. James's Hall, placing advertisements in newspapers (sometimes listing all the women players),[60] receiving favorable reviews in the press and, on one occasion, a striking illustration (see figure 1.3). All of this is worth bearing in mind, for it indicates that, even twenty years before the *Lusitania* went down, the string orchestra (and by extension its repertoire) was gendered female in the public imagination and associated with a privileged social class.[61] More specifically, it suggests that an orchestra of strings might have had pointed appeal for Bridge when he began composing a musical response to the death of a young girl from a wealthy family, herself symbolizing the many women and child victims who had enjoyed the *Lusitania*'s first-class luxuries. (The sensibility would not have been lost on Bridge, who conducted the women's orchestra that Audrey Chapman founded and funded during the war years; the strings were mostly women amateurs.)[62] The resulting musical lamentation would thus have

Figure 1.3. Lady Radnor's ladies orchestra performing at Prince's Hall, London (*Graphic*, July 26, 1884, 80). Image reproduced from the collections of the University Library, University of Illinois at Urbana-Champaign.

carried broad gendered and class-ridden meanings for its wartime audience—meanings that do not strike us today.

An objection to this interpretation might be that Bridge's Lament was premiered by a professional ensemble, not an amateur one, and that the major British orchestras were still considered bastions of masculinity. Yet a further fact to consider here is that, from 1914, with male musicians going into military service, some of the seats in professional orchestras were temporarily opening up to women.[63] The concert programs for the two Lament performances did not print lists of players, but we know that Henry Wood admitted some women to the string section of the orchestra for the Promenade Concerts in the summer of 1916 (conscription had been introduced that March), and it seems highly likely that all or many of them were retained for the Symphony Concerts orchestra in the Queen's Hall and thus performed in Bridge's piece that year. Their presence on the platform of London's major concert hall would have been striking.[64] In addition, although the circumstances of the two London concert performances suggest an ultimately limited size of audience for the string version of the Lament, there remains the possibility that the work was taken up by amateur string orchestras more widely in Britain. More research is needed, but the parts were published by Goodwin and Tabb, which ran a rental library, meaning that many women may have played the work well beyond the capital and thus contributed both to statements of grief and to growing Anglo-American solidarity.

In any event, Bridge's compositional choices go beyond these contemporary cultural associations. By choosing to use Lament as the work's title, Bridge was signaling the vocal genre that both expresses grief and is traditionally sung by women, adding further gendered signification. At the same time, Bridge eschewed setting a text to music, producing instead a wordless lament, as if to insist that this particular grief defied meaningful verbal expression. Considered in these terms, scoring for string instruments appears to have been a way for Bridge to articulate the raw distress and bewilderment that arose from so many innocent (and many female) lives being lost. (Also, as suggested earlier, to have created a texted vocal work for concert performance in 1915—when the public mood in Britain favored unrelenting upbeat patriotism and the mourning of military deaths as noble sacrifice—might have simply made the message unacceptably direct.)

What is more, Bridge chose to score his piece for instruments closely associated with the expressivity of the human voice and their ability to "sing." This decision is significant because the composer was a skilled orchestrator (who had already written some short orchestral works) and could easily have extended the timbral palate to full orchestra, writing poignant solos for the oboe or clarinet and underpinning the music with warm brass or wind chording. But instead he used strings (mostly muted) alone. His choices seen thus, it seems possible he was seeking to capture the grain of multiple pained human voices expressing emotions of loss. At the same time, Bridge elected not to compose the work for string quartet, despite having already written short character pieces for that medium (for example, *Three Idylls* [1905] and *An Irish Melody* [1908]): given that the Lament scoring favors eight (even nine) individual parts and close harmonies, a quartet version would have limited its expression in harmonic, textural, and timbral terms, thus weakening it. In sum, Bridge seems to have wanted nothing less than the full string orchestra resonance, complete with double-bass sonorities and the muted color that results from the key of E flat (which favors stopped, rather than open, strings) and from the division of the string section into several parts.[65]

Of course, this scoring gave Bridge the tools with which to convey a sense of the overwhelming power of the sea and of the huge liner sinking (with the moment of Catherine's passing perhaps conveyed in the upward rhapsodic fragments for solo viola, cello, and violin—sending her spirit on its journey?—at the halfway point). But it also enabled him to express, by requiring multiple performers onstage, a collective grief for the large body of humanity lost in the disaster. The consequent sharing of this grief with a large listening audience at a concert in central London positioned the piece to create a moment of shared public mourning.

Yet Bridge's use of strings may have still more implications for such a line of reasoning, if his Lament is contextualized against the contemporary stirrings of what was then termed *musicotherapy*. Although a clinical approach to music therapy is said to have coalesced only in the mid-twentieth century,[66] ideas about the beneficial effects that music could have on the nervous system were emerging during World War I and were gaining some currency in the medical community.[67] By way of an example, Margaret Anderton, an English-born pianist who had undertaken music-therapeutic work with Canadian soldiers, became an active proponent of the emerging discipline, having gained exposure to ideas about music therapy while pursuing her piano studies in Paris. Anderton, who taught a course at Columbia University on the healing power of music in 1919, believed that the timbre of instruments was an important factor in creating positive circumstances for healing. In particular, she proposed that instruments made of wood—strings, of course, are an obvious example—were the most effective, arguing that their vibrations affected the nerve centers in the spine of listeners more so than other instruments, even the human voice. In 1919 she even put her thesis in these terms: "Wood instruments are particularly potent for a certain kind of war-neurosis because of their penetrating, sustained tone."[68] We have no idea whether Bridge was aware of, or even interested in, such ideas, though we might note that ideas about music therapy's value had gained some exposure in Victorian medical journalism.[69] Regardless, it seems that there was for Bridge—not to mention other English composers who wrote string orchestra music in a similarly elegiac mode—something inherently attractive about the string orchestra's soundscape that drew him to the medium, particularly during wartime. Frederick Septimus Kelly, while serving in Gallipoli, wrote an Elegy for string orchestra on the death in 1915 of his close friend, poet Rupert Brooke. In 1917 Herbert Howells would respond similarly when a viola player he had known at the RCM, Francis Warren, was killed in action; he modeled his work, Elegy for viola, string quartet, and string orchestra, on Vaughan Williams's *Fantasia on a Theme by Thomas Tallis*.

Earlier, I suggested that while the advanced harmonic language of Bridge's Lament placed it in the expressive category of grief and anguish (the final cadence notwithstanding), the music retained a therapeutic quality, resulting from the generic imprint of "lullament" that stood to aid the processes of mourning. A second, equally important, ingredient in its therapeutic properties was arguably the resonance of massed strings, which enabled the work to both communicate a communally vocalized grief and heighten the beneficial effect of its lamentation. By offering a means of counterpointing its overt expression of sorrow, the Lament seems to have been poised to play an active part in the catharsis of grieving. In broader terms, Bridge's decision in the summer of 1915 to use a string orchestra, an ensemble with strongly gendered associations, as the vehicle for a piece that would publicly and communally mourn a young girl of Anglo-American identity (and symbolically hundreds of other women and children—including several from the North American continent, with which Britain was developing an increasing wartime affinity) appears to have been opportune, suggesting that at root the medium was intrinsically linked to the music's message.

Notes

1. Popular song is the subject of John Mullen's recent book, *The Show Must Go On! Popular Song in Britain during the First World War* (Farnham and Burlington, VT: Ashgate, 2015).

2. The premiere was on December 7. For discussion of *Carillon*, see Glenn Watkins, *Proof through the Night: Music and the Great War* (Berkeley: University of California Press, 2003), 38–41; and Lewis Foreman, "A Voice in the Desert: Elgar's War Music," in *Oh, My Horses! Elgar and the Great War*, ed. Lewis Foreman (Lower Broadheath: Elgar Foundation Enterprises, 2014), 263–77.

3. For more, see Joseph A. Herter, "Solidarity and Poland: Elgar's Opus 76," in *Oh, My Horses!*, ed. Foreman, 327–45.

4. Some music composed at the time embodied a retreat to reassuring pastoral notions of England: examples include Ernest Farrar's *English Pastoral Impressions* (1915) and Frank Bridge's orchestral pieces *Summer* (1914–15) and *Two Poems* (1915). The trend continued throughout the war, as shown in some of the songs that Ivor Gurney wrote while serving in France.

5. Foreman, "Voice in the Desert," 277. The premiere was on January 29, 1916, and served as a curtain raiser between *Cavalleria Rusticana* and *I Pagliacci*.

6. For an especially insightful discussion of this work, see Eric Saylor, "'It's Not Lambkins Frisking At All': English Pastoral Music and the Great War," *Musical Quarterly* 91 (2008): 39–48.

7. Foreman, "Voice in the Desert," 277. The same is said of Elgar's follow-up setting of lines by Cammaerts in *Le drapeau Belge*, a melodrama celebrating the nobility of dying for Belgium (written in spring 2016). It was not premiered until April 14, 1917, by which point the public mood had changed.

8. For somewhat parallel developments in France, see Barbara L. Kelly's discussion of Debussy in chapter 3 of this volume.

9. In the United States, Charles Ives was composing his own response at about the same time; see Gayle Magee's chapter in this volume.

10. Henry Wood was the principal conductor at the Promenade Concerts. Printed programs for these concerts were consulted at the British Library (Promenade Concert) and the library of the Royal Academy of Music, London (Symphony Concert). Concert reviews provide further documentation and a sampling of critical opinion; see *Daily Telegraph*, September 16, 1915, 11; *Musical Standard* (September 25, 1915): 231; *Musical Times* (October 1, 1915): 619; *Strad* (October 1915): 163; *Monthly Musical Record* (December 1, 1916): 317; *Musical Times* (November 1, 1916): 513; and *Times*, October 16, 1916, 11. Contrary to what the *Musical Times* states, Bridge did conduct the Lament in 1916 (Wood, who had instigated this second performance, directed the rest of the program); see the printed concert program and the *Monthly Musical Record* and *Times* reviews.

11. As Byron Adams (see note 14 below) points out, the piano version offered the possibility of the music serving for moments of private mourning in intimate performance spaces.

12. The first of these dates from 1976. Paul Hindmarsh, *Frank Bridge: The Complete Works* (Poynton: PHM, 2016), 137, lists all recordings. The most recently released version is by the BBC National Orchestra of Wales, conducted by Richard Hickox, in 2004.

13. Ibid., 137–38; Kevin Salfen, preface to *Lament for String Orchestra*, by Frank Bridge (Munich: Musikproduktion Höflich, 2013); Fabian Huss, *The Music of Frank Bridge* (Woodbridge: Boydell Press, 2015), 97–98. See also Ciara Burnell, "The Anxiety of Memory: Frank Bridge's Late Works and Inter-war British Modernism" (PhD, Queen's University, Belfast, 2009), 135–36; and Mark Amos, "'A Modernist in the Making'? Frank Bridge and the Cultural Practice of Music in Britain" (D. Phil., University of Oxford, 2009), 173.

14. Byron Adams, "Sea Change: A Meditation upon Frank Bridge's *Lament: To Catherine, Aged 9, "Lusitania' 1915*," in *The Sea in the British Musical Imagination*, ed. Eric Saylor and Christopher M. Scheer (Woodbridge: Boydell, 2015), 51–66.

15. On the problems with this "cause-and-effect" argument, see David Ramsay, Lusitania: *Saga and Myth* (London and New York: W. W. Norton, 2001), 253–65. He writes, "In reality, the United States declared war for reasons which had little to do with the torpedoing of the great liner" (253).

16. The *Mauritania*, also a Cunard liner, was one of these.

17. Cited (without source) in Diana Preston, *Wilful Murder: The Sinking of the* Lusitania (London: Doubleday, 2002), 44; published in America as Lusitania: *An Epic Tragedy* (New

York: Walker, 2002). This book, along with Ramsay's Lusitania: *Saga and Myth* (2001), has provided the information for much of the historical overview that follows.

18. The number, profiles, and birth origins of those traveling from Canada is murky. Ramsay (Lusitania: *Saga and Myth*, 194) indicates 345 people with addresses in Canada; many likely had family in the UK. How many were British-born male immigrants returning to the UK, with their families, to enlist, is unclear. Canadians traveled on British passports.

19. There were long-standing rules of engagement for Europeans at war on the seas, especially regarding commercial ships. Those rules meant that private vessels could be stopped and searched and that if they were found to be carrying any form of contraband, they would become a legitimate target of war (in which case, they could be destroyed only once every person had been let off the vessel). But in 1915, warfare was different: taking passengers onto submarines was simply not possible, and this heightened fears for civilian safety at sea. Private ships began to paint out their names and to fly the flags of neutral nations, but suspicion alone that a ship might be carrying war cargo (including food) became a reason for the German Navy to launch an attack. See Preston, *Wilful Murder*, 64–67; and Ramsay, Lusitania: *Saga and Myth*, 43.

20. See Ramsay, Lusitania: *Saga and Myth*, 54–55. There was no loss of life.

21. Reproduced in Preston, *Wilful Murder*, 89 (see also 90).

22. Quoted ibid., 221.

23. According to Ramsay, Lusitania: *Saga and Myth*, 94, 296, quoting Cunard's archives, 1,962 people were on board, 764 survived (of whom 474 were passengers, not crew), and 1,198 died. Slightly different numbers are given at http://www.rmslusitania.info/lusitania/ and http://www.rmslusitania.info/people/statistics/.

24. The papers, in contrast, typically reported calm and stoicism at this desperate moment of crisis. Adams describes press accounts of "general calm" as a "preposterous lie" ("Sea Change," 52). See also his compilation of survivors' accounts of the panic on board and the mishandling of the evacuation (52–53).

25. These and other prominent passengers are discussed by Preston (*Wilful Murder*, 92–103).

26. According to ibid., 299 (see also 124); a slightly different count can be found at http://www.rmslusitania.info/people/statistics/.

27. According to Karen R. Little, *Frank Bridge: A Bio-bibliography* (New York: Greenwood Press, 1991), 8–9, during the war years and up to 1924 Bridge's professional viola playing declined, but his work as a conductor increased, and he supplemented his earnings through teaching. Hindmarsh (*Frank Bridge*, 7) corroborates this view, suggesting that by 1918, "Bridge had all but given up playing professionally." For more details, see the discussion of Bridge's career in Amos, "'Modernist in the Making,'" 37–166.

28. The group participated in a performance of Ravel's Introduction and Allegro, conducted by the composer, at the Bechstein Hall in 1913. Published sources conflict about the length of time Bridge served in the quartet, many suggesting that he left in 1915. However, W. S. Meadmore, "British Performing Organizations: (2) Present-Day Organizations," in *Cobbett's Cyclopedic Survey of Chamber Music*, comp. and ed. Walter Willson Cobbett (1929; reprint, Oxford: Oxford University Press, 1963), 1:205, indicates that the group disbanded

in 1925, having latterly given mostly private performances. This view is endorsed by Amos ("'Modernist in the Making,'" 67–70), who notes that the group was performing in 1919 and 1920 and making recordings in 1923, and also by the description of the quartet at http://sounds.bl.uk/Classical-music/Chamber-music. This online source notes that while the musicians began playing together in 1902, they did not adopt the name English String Quartet until 1908, that Bridge was sometimes replaced by Alfred Hobday, and that from ca. 1916 the quartet gave mostly private performances. The earliest recording appears to date from 1915. See Nicholas Travers Morgan, "The National Gramophone Society" (PhD diss., University of Sheffield, 2013), 145. I am grateful to the author for his help in documenting the English String Quartet.

29. Quoted in Hindmarsh, *Frank Bridge*, 144. Adams ("Sea Change," 59–60) provides a sage discussion of the extent to which Bridge can be considered to have been a pacifist and scrutinizes the limited evidence for this claim, much of which stems from Benjamin Britten's remarks of 1964, some years after Bridge's death. Adams describes Bridge's only other war-related work from the period, "Blow Out, You Bugles" (1918), a song that sets a Rupert Brooke sonnet and celebrates the nobility of sacrifice, as a "robustly public response to the war" (58).

30. Edwin Evans, "Modern British Composers: 1.—Frank Bridge," *Musical Times* (February 1, 1919): 59.

31. Program book for the Queen's Hall Promenade Concerts, 1915 season.

32. She was born in Chelsea on August 23, 1904 (Adams, "Sea Change," 56).

33. Paul was born in 1871, Gladys in 1878. See http://www.rmslusitania.info/people/saloon/paul-crompton/ and http://www.rmslusitania.info/people/saloon/gladys-crompton/. Bridge was born in 1879.

34. Stated in the biography of Gladys Crompton at http://www.rmslusitania.info/people/saloon/gladys-crompton/. The family is said to have usually traveled on the *Lusitania*.

35. See discussion in Adams, "Sea Change," 57–58. In 1909 Bridge was living in Foster Road, Chiswick (about four miles away from Gilston Road); the date of his relocation to Kensington is unknown, but it seems not to have taken place before 1914 (post office directories place him there only in 1915). However, as Adams's argument suggests, Bridge's association with the RCM would have placed him frequently in the Kensington and Chelsea area, and there was a real possibility that neighborhood connections had brought him into contact with the Crompton family.

36. The 1911 census and the quinquennial valuation lists for Kensington, 1900–1901 to 1911–16 (which are held in Kensington Central Library), indicate that Lucy Henrietta Crompton (Paul's widowed mother) moved to 29 (formerly 11) Gilston Road between 1905 and 1911. In 1901 she had been living in Bloomsbury. Catherine Crompton was born (1904) in the Royal Hospital Chelsea.

37. A further possibility, suggested by Fabian Huss (*Music of Frank Bridge*, 98, 232), is that Crompton and Bridge knew one another through Bridge's links with members of the Booth family, proposing Henry (not Alfred) Booth as the father of the children who were associated with Bridge's 1921 ballet for piano duet or piano solo, *In the Shop*. More research is needed

on this point, since A. H. John, *A Liverpool Merchant House, Being the History of Alfred Booth and Company, 1863–1958* (London: George Allen and Unwin, 1959), does not list a Henry as a living Booth relative or descendent at this time, and Hindmarsh (*Frank Bridge*, 165, and in his preface to his adaptation of the work *Dance Suite* [n.p.: Thames, 1999]) does not identify the Booths definitively, either. I am grateful to Dr. Huss for answering questions relating to this issue.

38. In addition to running his own steamship business, Alfred Booth was chairman of the Cunard Line. This may have given Crompton privileges for travel.

39. The photograph was published in the *New York Times* on May 16, 1915 (picture section); in *Shoe and Leather Reporter* (May 13, 1915): 18; and in *Shoe and Leather Facts* (June 1915): 35–36. (It had first appeared in Washington papers on May 9, 1915.) Other arms of the leather-trade press published obituaries: *Boot and Shoe Recorder* (May 15, 1915): 21; and *Hide and Leather* (May 15, 1915): 16. Adams reports ("Sea Change," 55) that the photographer was Mathilde Weil (1871–1918), of Philadelphia.

40. Her position in the photograph is identified in the *Harrisburg (PA) Telegraph*, May 10, 1915, 10; and *Shoe and Leather Facts* (June 1915): 36. The poignancy of the image is discussed by Adams ("Sea Change," 55), who suggests that the composition of the photograph echoes Renaissance paintings of Madonna with Child, surrounded by saints.

41. Thus, for instance, the *Daily Graphic,* May 8, 1915, 5; the *Daily Express*, May 8, 1915, 1; and the *Daily Sketch*, May 8, 1915, 1, simply listed Mr. and Mrs. Paul Crompton as among the passengers, without any photographic illustration. This is noteworthy given that many papers published photographs of the deceased or lost. I have not seen evidence that the Harrisburg photograph was reproduced in the British press.

42. *Musical Times* (November 1, 1916): 513; *Monthly Musical Record* (December 1, 1916): 317. See also the *Musical Times* (October 1, 1915): 619, which opined that the piece was "born of a private grief" and noted its "ring of pathos and sincerity," and the *Times*, October 16, 1916, 11, which said it had "immediate and intimate appeal." Less favorable was the *Musical Standard* (September 25, 1915): 231; it referred to the work as a dirge and "a poor-spirited, gentle little thing" that puzzled its writer, Wat Tyler.

43. Evans, "Modern British Composers," 59. See also the review in the *Daily Telegraph*, September 16, 1915, 11, which admired the work's sincerity and noted that it "struck a responsive chord in those who heard it." (Conversely, the *Strad* [October 1915]: 163 indicated that the "novelties" presented so far that Proms season had not "made much stir.")

44. Program book for the Queen's Hall Promenade Concerts, 1915 season; reprinted in the program book for the 1916 Queen's Hall Symphony Concert.

45. Salfen, preface to *Lament for String Orchestra*, by Bridge.

46. For discussion, see James Porter, "Lament" and "Lullaby," in *The New Grove Dictionary of Music*, ed. Stanley Sadie, 2nd ed. (London: Macmillan, 2001), 14:181, 15:291–92. For a parallel attempt to relate musical styles and expressions of grief, see William Brooks's analysis of "gold-star mother" songs in chapter 9 of this volume.

47. The fifths might equally be felt to hint at the drone in a bagpiper's lament, an interpretation influenced by Hindmarsh's suggestion (on page 27 of the liner notes to *Bridge Orchestral Works: The Collector's Edition*; CHAN 10729 [6] X, 2012) that the melody is "like a Scottish lament."

48. Adams ("Sea Change," 64) points out that the downward semitonal sighing gesture that Bridge uses was a well-known device for indexing pain, as well as a common baroque *Affekt,* with which the composer would have been familiar.

49. Salfen (preface to *Lament for String Orchestra,* by Bridge) makes a parallel here with the ending of Samuel Barber's *Adagio for Strings* (1936).

50. Thomas M. Carr Jr., "Separation, Mourning and Consolation in *La Route d'Altamont,*" *Québec Studies* 31 (Spring–Summer 2001): 97–98, 109. Note too that Burnell ("Anxiety of Memory," 135–36) hints that Bridge's harmonic language in the body of the Lament, clearly anticipating his later style, was an indication that he was becoming resistant to expressing consolation.

51. Clare O'Callaghan, "Lullament: Lullaby and Lament Therapeutic Qualities Actualized through Music Therapy," *American Journal of Hospice & Palliative Medicine* 25, no. 2 (April–May 2008): 93–99.

52. Little, *Frank Bridge: A Bio-bibliography,* 4, perhaps drawing from Stanford's *Musical Composition: A Short Treatise for Students* (New York: Macmillan, 1911), which places much emphasis on the facility for knowing the "medium of sound-production" that is to perform a composer's music and on being able to hear sound colors in one's head as one composes (175). I am grateful to Paul Rodmell for help identifying likely sources for Stanford's pedagogy.

53. As explored in my "English String Orchestra Repertoire as Cultural Phenomenon" (unpublished paper given at the Ninth Biennial Conference on Music in Nineteenth-Century Britain, Cardiff University, June 25, 2013).

54. For discussion, see Paula Gillett, *Musical Women in England, 1870–1914: "Encroaching on All Man's Privileges"* (New York: St. Martin's Press, 2000), 77–108.

55. "The Resin Club," *Strings* (March 1894): 30. The article is an imagined conversation between Tartini, Spohr, and other celebrated violinists of the past.

56. For an overview, see Christina Bashford, "Art, Commerce and Artisanship: Violin Culture in Britain, c. 1880–1920," in *The Idea of Art Music in a Commercial World, 1800–1930,* ed. Christina Bashford and Roberta Montemorra Marvin (Woodbridge: Boydell Press, 2016), 178–99.

57. Programs for the String Orchestra's concerts at prominent venues in London, 1892–95, are preserved in the British Library, London. The *Orchestral Times* carries favorable reports of the group and their impressive standard of playing.

58. See reports in the *Strad* (June 1915): 36, noting membership increasing from twenty-eight to forty players, and in the *Musical Herald* (June 1915): 280, noting five concerts given during the season. The band was conducted by Hilda Bailey (Royal Academy of Music, London).

59. Concert on March 16, 1915 (program in RCM Library, London), conducted by Dunhill, who taught at the Royal College of Music. The repertoire included Parry's *Lady Radnor Suite* and Elgar's Serenade. See reviews in the *Strad* (April 1915): 380; and the *Musical Standard* (April 10, 1915): 280. Queen Alexandra's House was a hall of residence for women students. See http://www.queenalex.com/about-us/.

60. See the *Standard,* June 22, 1896, 1 for an advertisement for Lady Radnor's orchestra.

61. In a similar vein, the *Gentlewoman* in 1895 published striking photographic collages of the women members of the English Ladies' Orchestral Society (an amateur symphony

orchestra); see the pages pasted in one of Edward Heron-Allen's scrapbooks (Edward Heron-Allen Collection, vol. 21, RCM Library, London).

62. As recounted by Daphne Oliver in her memoirs of Bridge (1978–79), published in Hindmarsh, *Frank Bridge*, 21. Whether Bridge's association with the orchestra predated the Lament is not made clear. The ensemble was known as the Audrey Chapman (later Melville) Orchestra. See also Hindmarsh, *Frank Bridge*, 10.

63. Much the same happened across the ocean after the United States entered the war. See, for example, Kendra Preston Leonard's account of female professional advancement among theater organists in chapter 7.

64. On the numbers used in the Promenade Concerts orchestra, see Leanne Langley, "Building an Orchestra, Creating an Audience: Robert Newman and the Queen's Hall Promenade Concerts, 1895–1926," in *The Proms: A New History*, ed. Jenny Doctor and David Wright, with Nicholas Kenyon (London: Thames & Hudson, 2007), 51. Some women had been playing in the venue's main orchestra (Queen's Hall Orchestra) since 1913, when Wood hired six women for the upper strings.

65. Two of the three laments mentioned above (H. 47 and H. 101) are scored for strings and favor key signatures with three and six flats, respectively.

66. Leslie Bunt, "Music Therapy," in *New Grove Dictionary*, ed. Sadie, 17:539.

67. This is a topic on which Jillian Rogers, who has studied the phenomenon in relation to French medicine and musicians, has spoken publicly, to demonstrate the growing scientific interest in music's ability to heal the psyche. Her paper "*La plus grande consolatrice*: Music as Therapeutic Corporeal Practice in World War 1–Era France," given at the American Musicological Society conference in Milwaukee on November 7, 2014, was the impetus for developing this line of argument. See also her "Grieving through Music in Interwar France: Maurice Ravel and His Circle, 1914–1934" (PhD diss., University of California at Los Angeles, 2014) and her "Mourning at the Piano: Marguerite Long, Maurice Ravel, and the Performance of Grief in Interwar France," *Transposition: Musique et Sciences Sociales* 4 (2014): 1–33.

68. "Columbia University to Heal Wounded by Music," *Literary Digest*, March 1, 1919, 62.

69. See William B. Davis, "Music Therapy in Victorian England," *Journal of British Music Therapy* 2, no. 1 (1988): 10–16.

CHAPTER 2

"Every Man in New York"

Charles Ives and the First World War

GAYLE MAGEE

The attack occurred on an ordinary weekday morning, as bankers, traders, and brokers headed to work in New York's financial district. The initial impact released a wall of fire, loosening rivets and dislodging steel plates. As windows exploded and dishes shattered, frightened people took to the stairwells, avoiding the now useless elevators. Later that day, a group of shaken Americans wrestling with the scope of the tragedy, the loss of life, and the likelihood of war joined together in an impromptu, tearful chorus, in an expression of collective mourning.[1]

The similarities between the sinking of the *Lusitania* by a German submarine on May 7, 1915, and the terrorist attacks of 9/11 may not seem obvious, especially given the revolutions in technology and media coverage over the intervening decades. Streaming news and images on the Internet and through cable broadcasts allowed for real-time coverage of the latter calamity. By comparison, although the *Lusitania* was torpedoed off the shore of Ireland at 9:10 a.m. New York time and sank in less than twenty minutes, rumors circulated throughout the day in the city about the extent of the disaster before the Cunard Line confirmed the loss of vessel and life twelve hours later. Yet both events changed the course of American history. The *Lusitania* tragedy moved the United States closer to entering World War I, while 9/11 sparked what became the wars in Afghanistan and Iraq. Most important, both events provide a lens through which to view representations of "American" identity as defined by ethnic, racial, gendered, economic, regional, and national characteristics, as well as the shifting connections between the United States and the greater world.

This crucible of emerging nationalism within an increasingly global economy informs several of Charles Ives's works that originated in the period surrounding America's entry into World War I. For this chapter, I will consider several significant works within the larger context of Ives's changing business environment between 1915 and 1918, particularly "From Hanover Square North at the End of a Tragic Day, the Voice of the People Again Arose," from the Second Orchestral Set. Along with the war songs "In Flanders Fields," "Tom Sails Away," "He Is There!," and "The Things Our Fathers Loved," these works reflect the journey of a country determined to remain neutral to one fully engaged in the "war to end all wars." Contemporary sources drawn from industry and government documentation provide new insights into the intellectual and professional context surrounding these remarkable works, while informing a deeper understanding of Ives's unique position as a modernist composer and a New York–based life insurance executive working amid the travails faced by that industry—and Ives himself—as a result of the conflict.

"From Hanover Square North" and the *Lusitania*'s American Connections

For "From Hanover Square North," Ives provided a remarkably detailed anecdote concerning its inspiration involving a motley group of strangers on an elevated train in New York, on the day that the *Lusitania* sank. As Ives recalled, the news stunned everyone:

> I remember, going downtown to business, the people on the streets and on the elevated train had something in their faces that was not the usual something. Everybody who came into the office, whether they spoke about the disaster or not, showed a realization of seriously experiencing something. (That it meant war is what the faces said, if the tongues didn't.) Leaving the office and going uptown about 6 o'clock, I took the Third Avenue "L" at the Hanover Square Station. As I came on the platform, there was quite a crowd waiting for the trains, which had been blocked lower down, and while waiting there, a hand-organ, or hurdy gurdy was playing on a street below. Some workmen sitting on the side of the tracks began to whistle the tune, and others began to sing or hum the refrain. A workman with a shovel over his shoulder came on the platform and joined in the chorus, and the next man, a Wall Street banker with white spats and a cane, joined in it, and finally it seemed to me that everybody was singing this tune, and they didn't seem to be singing for fun, but as a natural outlet for what their feelings had been going through all day long. There was a feeling of dignity all through this. The hand-organ man seemed to sense this and wheeled the organ nearer the platform and kept it up fortissimo (and the

chorus sounded out as though every man in New York must be joining in it). Then the first train came and everybody crowded in, and the song eventually died out, but the effect on the crowd still showed. Almost nobody talked—the people acted as though they might be coming out of a church service. In going uptown, occasionally little groups would start singing or humming the tune.

Now what was the tune? It wasn't a Broadway hit, it wasn't a musical comedy air, it wasn't a waltz tune or a dance tune or an opera tune or a classical tune, or a tune that all of them probably knew. It was (only) the refrain of an old Gospel Hymn that had stirred many people of past generations. It was nothing but—"In the Sweet Bye and Bye." It wasn't a tune written to be sold, or written by a professor of music—but by a man who was but giving out an experience. . . . This third movement [of Orchestral Set No. 2] is based on this, fundamentally, and comes from that "L" station. It has secondary themes and rhythms, but widely related, and its general makeup would reflect the sense of many people living, working, and occasionally going through the same deep experience, together.[2]

For Ives, the strangers' singing of this hymn tune, "In the Sweet Bye and Bye" (also known as "In the Sweet By and By"; see figure 2.1), vindicated the work against long-remembered criticisms uttered decades earlier by his music professor at Yale Horatio Parker, who had inveighed against this very tune, and the "Moody and Sankey" gospel hymn in general, as overly sentimental and vulgar.[3]

Beyond the specifics of the hymn tune and its significance to Ives's personal history, this recollection can provide an entry point for considering Ives's own multivalent roles as documentarian, narrator, musician, Yale alumnus, and New York "everyman" who worked in the heart of the nation's financial district. In the weeks, months, and even years that followed, the sinking of the *Lusitania* took on a new significance that echoes through Ives's detailed portrayal and later commemoration of impromptu hymn singing in a moment of shared grief.

Given the enormous loss of life, a comparatively small number of Americans perished when the *Lusitania* sank in 1915: an estimated 128 out of nearly 1,200 total casualties, with the majority traveling in first class. Yet by this time, the *Lusitania* had become a mainstay in New York Harbor, and it occupied a unique role in American consciousness. Since its inception, the ship served as a symbol of increasingly global economic interests amid American corporate expansion. Christened and launched on June 7, 1906, the *Lusitania*, as well as its sister ship, the *Mauritania*, existed due to a new public-private partnership between the British government and Cunard. The unprecedented subsidies were an urgent response in the face of increased competition from American financiers such as J. P. Morgan, whose new multinational corporation International Mercantile Marine Company merged smaller British and European lines with Morgan's American-based shipping companies in 1902. As reported in the *North American Review* that December,

Figure 2.1. S. Filmore Bennett and Joseph P. Webster, "In the Sweet By and By." Reproduced from *The Service Hymnal* (Chicago: Hope, 1935).

the "newspapers of England and America for the last few days have been replete with discussion of the action of the British Government . . . [and] the re-subsidizing of the Cunard Line, in order to keep it out of the hands of the so-called Morgan Merger and to retain it under purely British control and capitalization."[4] Cunard's two new subsidized steamships were heralded for their speed, for their luxurious first-class accommodations, and for the company's remarkable safety record.[5]

The increase in transatlantic shipping routes from the end of the nineteenth century and through the first decade of the twentieth brought new energy to the United States, introducing "rapid transit between the two great English-speaking nations" amid "universal demand . . . for the shortest possible sea passage for travelers and the quickest delivery of the mails between the two great distributing cities, London and New York."[6] The two Cunard ships were nicknamed "flyers" and "Atlantic greyhounds" for their remarkable speed. In the United States, the vessels were promoted based on the unprecedented crossing time of less than four days from New York to Queenstown.[7]

While other steamers brought millions of immigrants in steerage across the Atlantic through the processing centers at Ellis Island, after which many settled in New York's Lower East Side and other locales, Cunard preferred an upper- and middle-class clientele. Additionally, all transatlantic crossings limited travel to mostly white passengers and crew, with few (or no) passengers of color. Wealthy passengers traveled between New York, Britain, Europe, and beyond for international business and pleasure via luxury suites. Although the *Lusitania* and similar vessels sailed to and from other North American cities on a regular basis, it was New York that served most often as the crossroads for the passengers and crew members. Accommodating the massive *Lusitania* and its contemporaries required the construction of a new shipping channel into New York Harbor; in fact, the Ambrose Channel was still under construction when the *Lusitania* arrived on its maiden voyage in September 1907.[8] Thus, despite its British origins, the *Lusitania* was deeply connected to New York, through the upper- and middle-class residents who patronized the ship as well as through the physical presence of the vessel in the city's harbor.

Not surprisingly, the ship's sinking had an immediate impact on individuals throughout the city, and it is worth connecting the participants in Ives's reminiscence to larger sectors of New York. First, Ives recalled the anxiety shown by "the people on the streets and on the elevated train" as well as "everybody who came into the office" showing "a realization of seriously experiencing something." At the time, the Ives and Myrick agency was located at 38 Nassau Street with an entrance at the corner of Liberty Street, just over three blocks from the New York Stock Exchange building; the livelihoods of most people that Ives witnessed in his office as well as on the train and streets would be deeply impacted by the tragedy. Ives and Myrick's parent company, Mutual of New York, faced tens of thousands of dollars in unexpected losses due to the sinking, so it is no surprise that visitors to Ives's workplace were particularly shaken by the event on a professional as well as a personal level.[9] Markets witnessed "an avalanche of selling orders" amid "a violent decline in both the stock and cotton markets" that directly impacted one of the figures at the Hanover train station, the "Wall Street banker with white spats and a cane."[10]

Apart from documenting the milieu of the financial district on the day of the sinking, Ives likely realized within hours of the announcement that he knew at least a few of the victims personally, as the media began to profile specific victims of the tragedy.[11] Of the six passengers who were "Yale men," Ives had at least an acquaintance with two. Justus Miles Forman was in Ives's own class of '98 and a successful author and playwright. Forman's recent play, *The Hyphen*, centered on "hyphenated" Americans, including, in the parlance of the times, German-Americans whose loyalty to the United States had been publicly challenged by such high-profile figures as former president Theodore Roosevelt. *The Hyphen* had debuted the previous month at the Knickerbocker Theatre in New York, while a silent film based on Forman's 1902 novel, *The Garden of Lies*, premiered shortly after his death, in late June or July 1915.[12] At Yale, Forman studied with legendary professor William Lyon Phelps, who taught a controversial course on the modern novel in his first year on the faculty in 1895. Phelps served a crucial role in Ives's education as well by introducing him to American and European literature, so much so that Ives sent a copy of his *Essays before a Sonata* to Phelps decades later, in 1920, and it was warmly received.[13] And Phelps certainly remembered Forman from his time at Yale, recalling in his 1939 autobiography that Forman had written to him only a few months before the sinking of the *Lusitania*.[14] Forman's death was covered in the New York press, and it seems reasonable that Ives would have had some memory of his deceased classmate.[15]

Perhaps the most famous *Lusitania* fatality graduated from Yale the year after Ives, and the two men had crossed paths at least once through their joint selection to an exclusive society. Alfred Gwynne Vanderbilt (1877–1915, Yale '99) drowned in the *Lusitania* tragedy after reportedly aiding in placing children in lifeboats and giving his life vest to a female passenger despite his inability to swim, as was widely reported in the media. Two decades earlier, he had been a mainstay of the campus's social scene due to his family's fame (which included Yale's Vanderbilt Hall) and his own colorful personality. Alfred became the primary heir to the Vanderbilt fortune shortly after graduation, following the death of his older brother William (while a student at Yale in 1892) and the disinheriting of his second-oldest brother, Cornelius Vanderbilt III, another Yale graduate, after marrying against his parents' wishes in 1895. A younger brother, Reginald Claypoole Vanderbilt, graduated from Yale in 1903, further reinforcing the close connections between this high-profile family and Ives's alma mater.[16]

Alfred Vanderbilt's career paralleled that of Ives in several ways, with both men belonging to the same elite sophomore club, Hé Boulé, a year apart (1895–96 for Ives and 1896–97 for Vanderbilt). As was standard, the outgoing Hé Boulé members selected the incoming sophomores, in which case Ives would have been part of the group that admitted Vanderbilt. The club chose only seventeen members per year, and, according to a contemporary account from 1894, this organization and its competitor, Eta Phi, were "the most powerful cliques in the college, since the high place of society membership in the Yale mind cannot be overestimated, and since initiation into one of these two clubs practically insures admission to those of the Junior and Senior years."[17] Indeed, both men followed their admission to Hé Boulé with selection to fraternities and secret societies in their junior and senior years, respectively (Delta Kappa Epsilon in 1896–97, which inspired the piece *Calcium Light Night*, and Wolf's Head in 1897–98 for Ives, Psi Upsilon in 1897–98 and Skull and Bones in 1898–99 for Vanderbilt).[18]

Vanderbilt was the wealthiest person to perish on the *Lusitania*. In the United States, coverage of his heroic death, his family's response, and the many entanglements surrounding his vast estate dominated headlines in New York papers for months. Despite Ives's retreat to Redding the day after the disaster, the death of one of the most prominent students at Yale whom he knew—at least tangentially—was unavoidable.

In "From Hanover Square North," Ives used the hymn tune "In the Sweet Bye and Bye" as the main theme, gradually assembling the tune in a cumulative form until the full melody emerges at the movement's apex. The tune would have had additional resonance in memorializing the *Lusitania* victims, as the chorus's main images bring together the metaphors of the afterlife ("the sweet bye and bye"), and the meeting of departed loved ones in eternity, depicted as "that beautiful shore." Moreover, for Ives and his contemporaries, there would have been a clear memory of the *Titanic* disaster only three years earlier, and the sheer horror of a shipwreck would have been well known. The hymn tune brought together images of death and the ocean, the resting place of men such as Forman and Vanderbilt, who despite their differences were in many ways like Ives: educated white male New Yorkers who lost their lives to a global conflict in which they believed they were not engaged, on an average workday.

"The Conscience of America": Patriotism and Insurance

The economic and legal implications of American deaths on the *Lusitania* impacted Ives's profession deeply over the next several years. First, Alfred Vanderbilt's estate filed a lawsuit against Travelers Insurance in October 1916, claiming both the $50,000 original policy plus an additional rider for $100,000 purchased shortly before Vanderbilt's passage on the *Lusitania*. The suit was covered in insurance industry media, in which readers were reassured that "there should be nothing in the suit that Travelers had to fear" and that "there is nothing that can be used as a suit against the company."[19] After the war, Vanderbilt's widow filed a petition as part of the Mixed Claims Commission that was pursued by the federal government against Germany on behalf of American citizens lost in the *Lusitania*; it was resolved only in March 1925, nearly a decade after her husband's death.[20] Cunard, in the meantime, petitioned for and was granted limited liability based on a detailed account of the ship and the actions of its crew and captain prior to and during the attack, essentially nullifying the life insurance policies carried by the passengers.[21]

In fact, insurance factored as a significant concern from both federal and private sectors in the United States and internationally from the outset of the war. The War Risk Insurance Bureau was approved by the House and Congress in early September 1914, mere weeks after the outbreak of hostilities in Europe. The bureau issued government-sponsored policies providing additional support for maritime shipping by insuring goods as well as the lives of the sailors and seamen who faced increased risk as a result of the war. Because of taxpayer subsidies for the minimal overhead of the organization, federal marine insurance proved to be a profitable business while the United States remained neutral.[22]

However, the *Lusitania* was a passenger ship with a British registration and not covered by the war-risk insurance in the United States. Moreover, many of the passengers on board, including Vanderbilt, held US-issued life insurance policies that carried a so-called wartime exemption. These were based on the norms of peacetime insurance rates, in which the likelihood of an unexpected fatal illness, accident, and untimely death was factored into mortality statistics on which the policies were priced and issued. Put another way, if the United States was at war, none of the insurance policies (including that of Vanderbilt) would need to be paid, since they would have been null and void as a result of the wartime exemption. If the country was at peace, however, the insurance industry, of which Ives and his company were a vital and successful part, faced an enormous, unexpected payout.[23]

The complicated relationship between publicly subsidized wartime insurance and for-profit private policies is well documented in government records from the period. Read in tandem with industry publications, these sources illustrate the conundrum of placing monetary value on the lives of soldiers in the nation's service as well as on those of noncombatants such as the *Lusitania* victims. And as the United States edged closer to entering the war, with the expected participation of thousands of US soldiers who carried peacetime-based life insurance policies, Ives's profession faced an unprecedented crisis that pitted patriotism against fiscal responsibility.

Patriotism took precedence in the public arena, with the industry as a whole stepping forward to play a role in the preparedness campaign of 1916. Just over a year after the *Lusitania* sank, a massive Preparedness Parade took place in New York, with more than one hundred thousand participants marching from Wall Street to midtown on May 13. An account circulated by the Associated Press described the event as follows: "Twenty abreast, filling the streets from curb to curb, keeping in step to the patriotic tunes of two hundred bands, the parade that began this morning will last for twelve hours or longer."[24] Onlookers were impressed not only by the number of marchers but also by the sight of men from diverse backgrounds marching together, in another manifestation of patriotic democracy on the streets of New York that echoed the Hanover "L" moment: "Men from the offices of millionaires and manual laborers walked almost literally side by side."[25] Like "the workmen sitting by the side of the tracks" and the "workman with a shovel over his shoulder," those manual laborers would find themselves "offer[ing] their services to our country" by working for the war effort, building training camps and other military infrastructure in league with the federal government.[26]

Ives was not at the parade, since he and his family had left for Redding two weeks earlier, on April 29. Yet he may have heard details about the event and particularly the participation of the insurance delegation, which included his own business partner, Julian Myrick. According to a report in the *Eastern Underwriter*, eighty-five hundred members of the insurance industry turned out as "the answer of the insurance district to pacifists everywhere in the nation": "For several weeks there has been the greatest enthusiasm prevailing from one end of the insurance district to the other, and it has reached every type of person, from office boys to presidents. . . . For days five great American flags, carrying suitable captions, have been flying in streets near insurance offices, and red, white and blue posters have been found in nearly every office on William street, Maiden Lane and Broadway."[27] The sea of New Yorkers surging along Maiden Lane passed less than a block from Ives and Myrick's office at 38 Nassau Street, and it seems plausible that this location featured the same posters in the lead-up to the parade.

While patriotism carried the day publicly, in private insurance representatives mobilized to protect their business interests against competition from Uncle Sam. Less than a year after the Preparedness Parade, in April 1917, insurance executives in New York held meetings to discuss how to move forward as the United States entered the war. Discussions with industry representatives focused on how best to protect their shareholders, through such means as new disability clauses that would apply to returning soldiers and adding surcharges to existing and new policies.[28]

Within this profit-centered discussion, Ives arranged to have his setting of "In Flanders Fields" performed publicly at one insurance luncheon by professional musicians, a rarity for the composer during this time. With Myrick's help, baritone McCall Lanham and pianist William Lewis performed the work, although in a later recollection Lanham stated that they worked "for countless weeks, really never making head or tail" of the song, and that "the dissonance was unbearable."[29] Indeed, Myrick seems to have been unusually involved in this work, as it was his suggestion that led Ives to set the text by Canadian John McCrae.[30] McCrae was serving as a military physician after working for Mutual Life—Ives and Myrick's parent company—in Montreal and wrote the poem after the bloody Second Battle of Ypres in May 1915.[31]

Ives's setting is, as Lanham recalled, heavily dissonant, in keeping with the bleak tone of McCrae's poem. Both text and music struggle to reconcile the ugly reality of death with lofty goals of heroic sacrifice. Ives portrays the military back-drop of McCrae's text using brief quotations from Civil War and other patriotic tunes, from an opening reference to "Columbia, the Gem of the Ocean" and pass-ing excerpts from "The Battle Cry of Freedom" and "America." The impressionistic second verse remembers the soldiers' lives and loves and is the most tonal, at times even Romantic in the rolling left-hand piano accompaniment—an appropriate look back for Ives at an earlier musical era. While the poem and Ives's setting remain somewhat circumspect through the first two verses, McCrae's admoni-tion from the deceased to the living, to "take up our quarrel with the foe," is set to an extended, defiant quotation in the voice from "La Marseillaise" to portray the French battlefield and cemetery, combined with "America" in the piano to embody what J. Peter Burkholder describes as "the passing of the torch from dead French soldiers to the Americans."[32] Ives's incorporation of a markedly French quotation seems especially curious when heard against the increasingly contentious backdrop of Anglophone and Francophone (or Quebecois) cultures within contemporary Canadian discourse. McCrae, who had fought with British forces in the Boer War, wrote the poem in part as a response to the death of his friend Lieutenant Alexis Helmer, another Anglophone Canadian, and in part as a tribute to the high number of casualties from the overwhelmingly British-Canadian soldiers who fought at Ypres.

Given the context of the song's premiere, it is tempting to see the work as a reminder from Ives to his fiscally minded colleagues of the human cost of war. Most likely, the performance of Ives's setting at the insurance meeting in April 1917 had no impact whatsoever, as representatives of the industry prepared to make their voices heard in the development of a government-sponsored insurance plan that would cover all US soldiers. In advance of a planning meeting that July with insurance executives, Secretary of the Treasury William G. McAdoo argued passionately on behalf of fighting soldiers:

> No organized effort ever has been made by any government to provide this sort of protection and comforting assurance to its fighting men. . . . Why should not America take the lead in this noble and humane action? I earnestly hope that as a result of the measures thus initiated, a great system of insurance will be devised which will give to every officer, soldier and sailor in the military and naval service of the United States the assurance that some provision is made for the ones he leaves behind if he is called upon to make the greatest sacrifice that a patriot can make for his country.[33]

The meeting saw the approval of a general plan for insuring active-duty soldiers for up to $4,000.

Yet only a few weeks later, the "old-line insurance companies [had] declared war on Secretary McAdoo's plan of insurance," with "open threats of strong opposition" sent to members of the House and Senate committees reviewing the legislation.[34] What changed in the meantime was the introduction of two points within the insurance bill that threatened private insurers: a maximum amount of insurance of $10,000 in the coverage offered to combatants and the option for soldiers to continue government-issued policies after the conclusion of the war, regardless of their physical condition.[35]

Through the fall of 1917, a coordinated letter-writing campaign and in-person statements from insurance professionals before the congressional committee reviewing the legislation strongly argued against overinsuring US soldiers and insisting that the government avoid competing with private insurers after the end of the conflict.[36] The committee's records show that the lobbying from heads of insurance companies navigated a tricky path between patriotic sentiment and, at times, blatant self-interest and appallingly mercenary sensibilities. The most vocal representative was George E. Ide, president of Home Life Insurance, whose in-person statement to the committee emphasized that while "it is the patriotic duty of the Nation to provide, and to provide in advance, for the vicissitudes of war so that the fighting man may go to the front with a clear conviction that the Nation is to stand behind him, protecting him and his dependents against the fearful risk he is undertaking from a patriotic sense of duty," nonetheless the "patriotism of the insurance men of the country is no less, because in this discussion we have not indulged in glittering generalities nor allowed our sober judgment to be blinded." Part of the discomfort from the industry emanated from the sheer volume of life insurance that would be handled by the government, an estimated $10 billion in policies, "or about twice the outstanding insurance of the Mutual Life, the Equitable Life, and the New York Life combined." Later, in discussion with committee members, Ide recommended a flat, no-cost insurance plan of between $1,000 and $3,000 per soldier to be paid "in the event of death from any cause at any time prior to 5 years or 10 years after the war is over," rather than term life insurance of up to $10,000.[37] Had the committee agreed, altering the legislation would have given soldiers a very basic payout within a decade at most after the war and would not have competed with private insurance interests, while significantly reducing the assumed value of the lives of American soldiers.

Other leaders expressed concern that the government would socialize insurance following the war. In the words of F. A. Howland, president of National Life Insurance, the "continuance of the life-insurance service after the close of the war . . . may furnish an opening wedge for those who may be inclined to favor

Government insurance generally" and cautioned that "the danger of the Government embarking in the life insurance business [should be] quite largely avoided." Howland similarly recommended reducing the amount of coverage to as little as $2,000 per soldier. Yet another industry spokesman, Thomas W. Blackburn, opined that the Wilson "administration certainly has enough difficult problems to solve without taking up the life-insurance business as a Government function" and blasted the bureau's intention to "enter the field of life insurance because we regard it as impolitic, unwise, and unnecessary," since private companies represented "the greatest single form of successful fiduciary enterprise in the land." Proposals by others recommended that the military focus be on recruiting young single men with no dependents who might decline optional insurance coverage, debated whether marriages entered into after the war should qualify for widow's benefits, and suggested that the government should enter into a public-private partnership with the industry by appointing "a commissioner to go and negotiate with one of the big companies, any one of the companies having a large insurance in force," that would use their resources to administer the policies instead.[38]

In the face of these objections, McAdoo embarked on a de facto media campaign blasting the insurance industry, which he frequently described as "selfish," "monstrous," "callous," and "visionless." In speeches, statements, and published writings between August and November 1917, as the legislation moved through both houses, McAdoo reinforced his position in the most patriotic of terms, stating that government-subsidized insurance was "an insignificant sum as compared with what these men do for their country and for the world."[39] In his most extensive and eloquent statement, McAdoo argued against the insurance industry's lobbying in no uncertain terms:

> Who with blood in his veins, patriotism in his heart and justice in his soul can deny to the men and their families who must suffer, more than any other class of our people, the horrors of this world carnage and war, these poor compensations? . . . Humanity and justice cry out against such monstrous indifference as that would be. It has been intimated that the organized insurance companies of the United States may oppose this legislation. I do not believe it. It is not conceivable that in a time like this men would be so callous and visionless. Men of vision and humanity will get behind this bill and not in front of it. But if any such effort should be made, who is willing to listen to the selfish cry of organized insurance companies that their interests may suffer if the Government dares to be humane and just to its heroes? Can we for one instant permit any selfish interest, however organized and wherever existent, to stand in the way of humanity and justice? Shall we subordinate the interests of the nation, shall we imperil the cause of liberty in the world . . . in order that the selfish interests of any private corporations or organizations be conserved? . . . [I]f such an attempt should be made, we should welcome the opportunity to arouse the conscience and soul of America against any such selfish

purpose or demand. . . . Let us not hesitate to go forward in this fight for America's right, for liberty and justice with all the might and power and courage of the nation . . . by setting an example to the world of what a mighty, just, humane and courageous nation can do for its own people who are called upon to make supreme sacrifices in order that the world shall be free.[40]

The plan created low-cost insurance for up to $10,000 that would continue indefinitely after the end of the war and ensured that policies covered death or disability occurring during and after discharge from the service.[41] Eventually, the program insured more than four million soldiers and sailors with an average policy of $8,700, resulting in payouts of more than $1 billion.[42]

In support of the government-funded program, and under strong encouragement from McAdoo, the Treasury Department, and other government agencies, the private insurance industry mobilized on an unprecedented scale to support the third and fourth Liberty Loan drives, in April and October 1918.[43] Ives marched in lockstep with thousands of insurance workers in New York committed to buying and selling bonds. The industry reported the kickoff of the third drive in April 1918, noting that "2,500 life insurance agents began a canvas of the lower end of Manhattan Island on a Liberty Loan drive which is $10,000,000 in subscriptions. . . . Five of the life insurance men making large personal subscriptions were L. A. Cerf, Charles Jerome Edwards, Charles E. Ives, J. F. Myrick and J. G. Batterson."[44] During this drive, Ives and Myrick went so far as to install two large signs on the outside of their building (as shown in figure 2.2, taken from a profile of the firm published

Figure 2.2. The Ives and Myrick offices at 38 Nassau Street, with Red Cross workers. Photo from the *Eastern Underwriter* (June 1918).

in the *Eastern Underwriter* in June 1918). According to the article, "Messrs. Ives and Myrick took an active part in the Liberty Loan drive, and both believe that it is essential for the Government to let the public know what the loan subscription quota of each citizen should be. The signs on the building give punch arguments for the loan, saying that the soldier gives his life, if necessary, and pointing out what others should do in proportion to their income."[45]

In the conflict between patriotism and profit, Ives left no doubt as to his position: he sided as an artist with McAdoo against his own self-interest as a successful insurance man. The collage of memories in "Tom Sails Away" offers a series of bucolic vignettes of an average white working- or middle-class soldier's childhood that refuted the crass focus on profit voiced by insurance leaders. "He Is There!" is the most insistently patriotic work, redefining the "old campground" of the Civil War as the "new campground" of American might, using a textual and musical quotation from the famous Civil War song "Tenting on the Old Camp Ground," by Walter Kittredge and first published in 1864 by Oliver Ditson of Boston. As Clayton Henderson notes, the song's "boisterous march rhythms" portray "unabashed enthusiasm for taking on the enemy, and its citations from 'Yankee Doodle,' 'Tenting on the Old Camp Ground,' and George M. Cohan's 'Over There,' among others, strike the contemporary listener with its wide-eyed, naive, and optimistic spirit."[46]

And in his song "The Things Our Fathers Loved," Ives refers to the word that was nearly ubiquitous throughout these years as a symbol for US involvement in the Great War: *liberty*, "the greatest of these" values espoused by American forefathers. *Liberty* was used by Secretary McAdoo as a direct refutation of the avarice of the insurance executives, in the bonds that Ives and his fellow workers bought and sold in the financial district, in the posters hanging on the outside of the office, and in the street name within view of Ives's workplace.[47] Although the word is not used in Ives's own text, the subtitle ("And the greatest of these was Liberty") pervades the setting as the counterargument to neutrality and pacifism. The verse's combination of tunes with regional implications suggests a motley group of soldiers from throughout the United States has come together in the service of the nation and a shared goal ("Dixie," "My Old Kentucky Home," "On the Banks of the Wabash," and "The Battle Cry of Freedom").

At the chorus, Ives presents a nearly complete statement of the hymn tune "In the Sweet Bye and Bye" with fresh vigor, at the words "Now! Hear the tune! I know not what are the words" (see example 2.1, with the hymn's text superimposed above the vocal line). Indeed, the hymn's original text, its later context, and its musical contours reimagine "that beautiful shore" unreached by the *Lusitania* victims now as the destination for US soldiers: the "everyman" humanized in "Tom Sails Away," celebrated in "He Is There!," and mourned in "In Flanders Fields." By linking the hymn with a new vision of fighting for the liberty of the world, the humble

Figure 2.3. Ives, "The Things Our Fathers Loved," mm. 14–17, with Bennett's original text for "In the Sweet By and By" superimposed above the staff. Renotated from Ives, *114 Songs* (Redding, CT: C. E. Ives, 1922), 92.

hymn tune sung at Hanover Square station triumphantly reappears, (re)uniting the cross-section of New Yorkers on the "L" platform that day in 1915 with the two musicians present at the performance: the humble hurdy-gurdy player, who first introduced the hymn tune, and Ives himself, who later immortalized the scene.

Conclusion

The group of men standing on the Hanover Square North platform on May 7, 1915, may or may not have realized that their world was already changing irrevocably. Apart from the looming war and its impact on the nation, the city's landscape viewed from that "L" station would alter beyond recognition, and very quickly. In July 1916, city planners passed an innovative zoning law that required setbacks on new buildings that would reshape the New York skyline, resulting in such iconic structures as the Chrysler Building and the Empire State Building. Tiered "wedding-cake" skyscrapers brought light and air once again into the canyons of the financial district and dominated the city's architecture through the 1950s. While we think of these buildings as classic Art Deco styles, that skyline represented a drastic renovation for Ives and his peers.

Along the way, the Hanover Square North station closed in 1950, in response to real estate concerns over noise and blight and the consolidation of the subway system. In 1961 the zoning laws were revised, phasing out tiered buildings in favor of more modernist styles and the floor-area ratio rule, in which glass and steel skyscrapers balanced unprecedented height with open, airy public plazas. The next year saw the unveiling of a plan for the World Trade Center to be built between Church, Liberty, West, and Vesey Streets—three blocks from the former Ives and Myrick office at 38 Nassau Street and within sight of the previous Ives and Myrick offices at 37 Liberty Street. The World Trade Center's signature buildings, the Twin Towers, officially opened in 1973: they collapsed less than thirty years later on September 11, 2001. One of the many memorials to 9/11 victims in the area is the British Memorial Garden at Hanover Square Park, just below the former "L" station; it is dedicated to the sixty-seven British fatalities of the attacks.

While many musical works have commemorated the tragedy, the one most closely associated with Ives is John Adams's *On the Transmigration of Souls* (2002). In creating the memorial work, Adams consciously drew directly and indirectly from Ives's *The Unanswered Question*, claiming that the preexisting composition is "a ghost in the background, and every once in a while it peeks through this screen of activity. . . . And, of course, 9/11 and the loss of all those people . . . from a sudden violent act is an unanswered question"—a statement that could, arguably, apply to the sinking of the *Lusitania*, or even to war in general.[48]

Unlike Ives's "From Hanover Square North," Adams's work embraces a more diverse image of New York by reading victims' names—themselves representing a wider range of ethnicities, nationalities, and classes than the victims of the *Lusitania*—in male and female voices. This "litany" (as Adams described it) is integrated with select readings of missing persons signs posted in the area after the attacks, creating deeply personal portraits set against the larger context of a national tragedy. Yet both *On the Transmigration of Souls* and "From Hanover Square North" capture through music a shared experience of grief, of a coming together at a moment of crisis, of the breaking down of barriers between New Yorkers in an urban and ever-changing environment: in Ives's words, "the sense of many people living, working, and occasionally going through the same deep experience, together."

Notes

1. This evocative summary draws on sources about both tragedies to illustrate what might be unrecognized commonalities. For a detailed discussion of the sinking of the *Lusitania*, I have relied on Erik Larson, *Dead Wake: The Last Crossing of the* Lusitania (New York: Crown, 2015), including his use of oral histories to document the elevators on the vessel (150, 257) as well as communications with the United States concerning the disaster. For a video of members of Congress spontaneously singing "God Bless America" on the steps of the Capitol building on the evening of 9/11, see https://www.youtube.com/watch?v=Izb459vJ-8Q.

2. Charles E. Ives, *Memos*, ed. John Kirkpatrick (New York: W. W. Norton, 1972), 92–93. The recollection begins with this statement: "We were living in an apartment at 27 West 11th Street. The morning paper on the breakfast table gave the news of the sinking of the *Lusitania*." However, as has been well documented elsewhere, in this recollection Ives appears to have conflated Friday, May 7—the date of the sinking and singing on the elevated train—with Saturday, May 8, which is when the newspaper with the headline about the disaster would have been on the breakfast table. Ives and his family left for their vacation home in Redding, Connecticut, on May 8. Cited in James B. Sinclair, "Appendix 4: Chronology of Significant Events in Ives's Life," in *A Descriptive Catalogue of the Music of Charles Ives, MSS 14,* revised version from 2012, 779, available online at https://elischolar.library.yale.edu/ivescatalogue/1/.

3. See Gayle Sherwood Magee, *Charles Ives Reconsidered* (Urbana: University of Illinois Press, 2008), 51–54.

4. Charles H. Cramp, "British Subsidies and American Shipping," *North American Review* 175, no. 553 (1902): 829–30.

5. The focus on speed and ostentatiousness represents a reversal of the values of the Cunard company at the time of its founding in 1840, as discussed in Crosbie Smith and Anne Scott, "'Trust in Providence': Building Confidence into the Cunard Line of Steamers," *Technology and Culture* 48, no. 3 (2007): 471–96. Regarding Cunard's safety record, see Larson, *Dead Wake*, 19–21. For discussion of the elegance of the *Lusitania*, see Christina Bashford's chapter in this volume.

6. Austin Corbin, "Quick Transit between New York and London," *North American Review* 161, no. 468 (1895): 513.

7. See, for example, "Special Dispatch: To Cross Ocean within Four Days," *San Francisco Chronicle*, March 16, 1906, 1; and "Latest Atlantic Greyhounds," *San Francisco Chronicle*, March 17, 1906, 6.

8. "*Lusitania* Will Open It," *New York Tribune*, August 3, 1907, 7; "New Channel for Liners," *Washington Post*, August 3, 1907, 4.

9. See William F. Gephart, *Effects of the War upon Insurance*, Preliminary Economic Studies of the War, ed. David Kinley, no. 6 (New York: Oxford University Press, 1918), 111, which summarizes the losses of Mutual Life Insurance Company from July 1, 1914, until October 1915. It lists nearly $64,000 and more than 20 percent of its expenses related to life insurance payments as "accidents to noncombatants (including *Lusitania* losses)."

10. "Friends Besiege Cunard Offices," *Louisville (KY) Courier-Journal*, May 8, 1915, 1. The piece originated with the Associated Press and was distributed throughout the country.

11. See ibid.; and "Many Noted New Yorkers on *Lusitania*," *New York Tribune*, May 8, 1915, 1, which mentions both Vanderbilt and Forman. Two victims worked in the insurance industry: Thomas Bloomfield, an underwriter for Prudential Casualty, and Ogden Hammond, a Yale graduate (class of 1893) who ran his own insurance company as well as working in real estate. However, it isn't clear whether Ives would have crossed paths with either. For Bloomfield, see http://www.rmslusitania.info/people/saloon/thomas-bloomfield/.

12. See the record of this lost film at the Library of Congress Performing Arts Database, http://memory.loc.gov/diglib/ihas/loc.mbrs.sfdb.5546/default.html. A digital reproduction of the novel is available at https://archive.org/details/gardenofliesroma00formiala.

13. As J. Peter Burkholder notes, "While there are other sources for Ives's tastes in literature, including his family and his wife, Phelps's literary interests and preferences exercised a strong influence on Ives, and he probably learned more in Phelps's courses than in any other subject he took at Yale outside music." Burkholder, "Ives and Yale: The Enduring Influence of a College Experience," *College Music Symposium* 39 (1999): 30. For the 1920 correspondence between Phelps and Ives, see Ives, *Selected Correspondence of Charles Ives*, ed. Tom C. Owens (Berkeley: University of California Press, 2007), 70–72. Owens notes that Phelps "had been one of Ives's favorite professors at college and was probably instrumental in awakening the interest in American literature that manifested itself most conspicuously in the *Concord* Sonata and *Essays*" (70).

14. William Lyon Phelps, *Autobiography with Letters* (New York: Oxford University Press, 1939), 621. Interestingly, Phelps does not mention Ives in the volume.

15. See, for example, "Many Noted New Yorkers on *Lusitania*," 1, which describes Forman as "the author, whose first play 'The Hyphen,' a war drama, was produced in New York a few weeks ago."

16. Cornelius (Neily) also attended Yale and overlapped with Ives's time there, graduating in 1895 with a BA and completing a B.Phil. in 1899.

17. Rupert Hughes, "Secret Societies at Yale," *Munsey's Magazine* 11 (April–September 1894): 288.

18. Vanderbilt's membership in these organizations is documented in *The Scroll of Phi Delta Theta* 24 (1900): 329.

19. "Vanderbilts Sue," *Eastern Underwriter* (October 27, 1916): 18.

20. For the Mixed Claims Commission documents, see http://legal.un.org/riaa/cases/vol_VII/32-44.pdf. The commission ruled against Vanderbilt's widow, Mary Emerson Vanderbilt Baker, and she received no additional compensation. See http://www.rmslusitania.info/primary-docs/mcc/alfred-vanderbilt/.

21. "The *Lusitania,*" *American Journal of International Law* 12, no. 4 (1918): 862–88.

22. Bureau of War-Risk Insurance, Committee on Interstate and Foreign Commerce, House of Representatives, May 4, 1917, 8. According to a member of the bureau's advisory committee, William N. Davey, "The business was profitable at first, but, of course, that was at a time when we were a neutral. Now we are a belligerent and the profits accrued before the unrestricted submarine warfare was put in force."

23. Even in his early forties, Ives and his business partner, Julian Myrick, were considered "young men" within the industry, according to a 1917 notice in *Eastern Underwriter,* an industry magazine, which stated, "Both Mr. Ives and Mr. Myrick are young men, hustlers, and have succeeded in making their agency one of the greatest in the country." "Ives and Myrick Record," *Eastern Underwriter* (February 9, 1917): 7.

24. "Unusual Preparedness Parade in New York," *Cornell Daily Sun* (Ithaca, NY), May 15, 1916, 6.

25. "The Great Preparedness Parade," documents of the Assembly of the State of New York, 18:206. The same document indicates that out of an estimated 140,000 marchers, a few thousand women participated, and thus the parade consisted almost entirely of men.

26. AFL [American Federation of Labor] Proceedings, 1917, quoted in Grace Palladino, *Skilled Hands, Strong Spirits: A Century of Building Trades History* (Ithaca, NY: Cornell University Press, 2007), 63.

27. "8,500 Insurance Men Ready to March in Preparedness Parade," *Eastern Underwriter* (May 12, 1916): 15, which lists Myrick as a participant. A photo of the parade in the Library of Congress from farther north on the route suggests how the flags with captions and bunting may have appeared. See "5th Ave. decorated for Preparedness Parade," Library of Congress Prints and Photography Division, Bain Collection, Lot 10853, https://www.loc.gov/resource/ggbain.21741/.

28. See Magee, *Charles Ives Reconsidered,* 131.

29. Cited ibid., 204n36.

30. Ibid.

31. McCrae's poem was first published in the British magazine *Punch* in December 1915 and appeared throughout the Western world over the next years. After McCrae's death in 1918, the insurance bimonthly the *Indicator* republished the poem noting that "Col. McCrae was Alternate Medical Referee of the Mutual Life at Montreal." "In Flanders Fields," *Indicator* 44 (1918–19): 251. For other settings, and for McCrae's poem in the context of Canada's response to the war, see Brian C. Thompson's chapter in this volume.

32. J. Peter Burkholder, *All Made of Tunes: Charles Ives and the Uses of Musical Borrowing* (New Haven, CT: Yale University Press, 2004), 313.

33. Quoted in "Soldier Insurance Confab Called," *Detroit Free Press*, June 28, 1917, 11. The results of the meeting are summarized in "U.S. May Issue Own Soldier Insurance," *Washington Post*, July 3, 1917, 2.

34. "McAdoo Insurance Plans Opposed by Old Companies," *Wall Street Journal*, August 18, 1917, 7.

35. The committee meetings quoted throughout this essay concern H.R. 5723, which introduced amendments to the original September 2, 1914, bill establishing the Bureau of War-Risk Insurance as the terms and conditions were ironed out. The full bill is reproduced in War-Risk Insurance Hearing Before the Subcommittee of the Committee on Finance, 3–12. The insurance industry's objections pertained mostly to material in Article IV, Section 400, involving insurance up to $10,000, and Section 404, which ensures continuation of the policies postwar "without medical examination" (12).

36. References to the meeting are found throughout the media and within the War-Risk Insurance Hearing Before the Subcommittee of the Committee on Finance, United States Senate, Sixty-Fifth Congress, available online through the HathiTrust Digital Library at http://hdl.handle.net/2027/nnc1.cu56150903, which mentions, "A conference of insurance men was called by the Secretary of the Treasury on July 2 and was largely attended. At this conference a general plan of compensation proposed for soldiers and sailors was outlined by the Secretary of the Treasury and by Mr. Sweet, the Assistant Secretary of Commerce" (26–27). McAdoo, in fact, had ties to the insurance industry, having turned down the presidency of Metropolitan Life in 1914. Douglas B. Craig, *Progressives at War: William G. McAdoo and Newton D. Baker, 1863–1941* (Baltimore: Johns Hopkins University Press, 2013), 105.

37. War-Risk Insurance Hearing, 14, 16, 22.

38. Ibid., 12–13, 35, 58–59, 66–68.

39. "Insurance for Soldiers," *Nashville Tennessean and the Nashville American*, August 28, 1917, 4. See also "'Insure Men,' His Plea," *Washington Post*, August 19, 1917, 7; and "McAdoo Advocates War Insurance," *New York Times*, August 19, 1917, 4.

40. William G. McAdoo, "William G. McAdoo Explains War Insurance and Allowances," *Baltimore Sun*, October 28, 1917, B10.

41. A promotional pamphlet from January 1918 issued with an introduction by McAdoo encouraged enrollment and clearly explained the advantages of the program. Treasury Department, *Uncle Sam's Insurance for Soldiers and Sailors: Answers to Questions You Will Ask* (Washington, DC: Department of the Treasury, 1918), 5. A sample insurance contract is reproduced in William F. Gephart, *Effects of the War upon Insurance, with Special Reference to the Substitution of Insurance for Pensions* (New York: Oxford University Press, [1918]), 129–37.

42. Craig, *Progressives at War*, 177. Craig notes as well that McAdoo campaigned to have the Bureau of War Insurance placed under the authority of the Treasury Department, contrary to its more logical placement within the Commerce Department (107). McAdoo planned to pay for the insurance program using funds raised in the second Liberty Loan campaign. "Insurance Terms Out: McAdoo Announces Conditions in Soldiers' Contracts," *Washington*

Post, October 15, 1917, 3; "McAdoo Gives Detailed Plan to Insure Army," *New York Tribune*, October 15, 1917, 2.

43. See Thomas R. Weddell, "Insurance News in All Branches East and West: Treasury Department Made a Call on the Life Companies," *Chicago Daily Tribune*, October 20, 1918, 16, which states that McAdoo "during the closing days of the Liberty loan campaign called upon the life insurance companies of the country to borrow substantially and thus anticipate their incomes, in order to subscribe more largely to the Liberty loan," a call that was seconded by the "governor of the federal reserve bank in each district." The insurance companies had a new challenge as well, through the impact of the War Revenue Act of October 1917, which levied increased taxes on the industry, including specific taxes on company profits and newly written life insurance policies. *Insurance and Pensions*, 98–104. Liberty Loans were introduced by the federal government to help raise funds through public and private investment to pay for the war: a total of $21 billion was raised in four Liberty Loan drives and one Victory Loan drive. For a general introduction to Liberty Loans, see Lawrence D. Schuffmann, "The Liberty Loan Bond," *Museum of American Finance*, https://www.moaf.org/exhibits/checks_balances/woodrow-wilson/materials/LibertyBonds.pdf.

44. "New York Agents Start Bond Drive," *Eastern Underwriter* (April 19, 1918): 3.

45. "Where $15,000,000 Was Paid for Last Year," *Eastern Underwriter* (June 28, 1918): 9.

46. Clayton Henderson, *The Charles Ives Tunebook* (Bloomington: Indiana University Press, 2008), 90.

47. Liberty Tower was even the name of the building opposite the Ives and Myrick office, at 55 Liberty Street. Liberty Tower housed the E. V. Gibbons company, a sham organization behind which German operatives involved in the infamous "Zimmermann Telegram" plotted the New Jersey "Black Tom" explosions of July 30, 1916. See "Plotted Black Tom, Says Von Rintelen," *New York Times*, January 3, 1940, 7; and Barbara Wertheim Tuchman, *The Zimmermann Telegram* (New York: Random House, 1985), 70. For a discussion of the word *liberty* and anti-German sentiments, see Magee, *Charles Ives Reconsidered*, 129.

48. Daniel Colvard, "John Adams Discusses *On the Transmigration of Souls*," in *The John Adams Reader: Essential Readings on the American Composer*, ed. Thomas Robert May (New York: Amadeus Press, 2006), 198.

CHAPTER 3

Reflecting the Public Appetite
in Text and Music

Debussy's Act of Wartime Propaganda

BARBARA L. KELLY

Claude Debussy's little carol *Noël des enfants qui n'ont plus de maison* is often dismissed as a blatant piece of propaganda.[1] The choice of a work by Debussy in a volume devoted to music during the Great War is fitting both because he was regarded as the leading experimental composer in France at this time and because of his own personal struggle with terminal illness and death in March 1918. His letters show the private man struggling to compose, acutely aware of his own frailty, mourning the conflict and loss of life, but eager to contribute artistically to the war effort. Building on the important work of Glenn Watkins and Marianne Wheeldon on Debussy and the First World War, the present chapter will look at the issue of public and private expression, the timeliness and significance of the work, and the extent to which Debussy was able to benefit from his prominent position and his creative work to comment on and reflect the circumstances of his time through music and text.[2]

The year 1915 was Debussy's final productive one and followed a year of compositional inactivity; despite suffering from rectal cancer, he found he was able to compose again. At the outbreak of the war and the invasion of Belgium, he wrote *Berceuse héroïque* as a contribution to *King Albert's Book*, to which many prominent public figures contributed as a sign of international solidarity. In novelist Hall Caine's view, this volume revealed a "new spirit of brotherhood."[3] There were contributions from writers, including Thomas Hardy and Arnold Bennett, and from politicians and public figures, such as Winston Churchill and Andrew Carnegie. Other composers included André Messager, Charles Stanford, and Edward Elgar, who wrote the rousing *Carillon*. Debussy's *Berceuse* was initially written for piano, but Debussy also orchestrated it in December 1914. The following summer he composed several works, the first of which was an occasional piece, written for charity: *Pièce pour piano pour l'Œuvre du "vêtement du blessé"* (June 1915).[4] This was followed by a number of his most significant late works: *En blanc et noir* for two pianos (June–July), *Douze études* for piano (July–September), Sonata for cello and piano (July–August), and the Sonata for flute, viola, and harp (September–October). This body of work signaled a distinctive late style, which included a new preoccupation with more abstract titles and traditional forms (sonata, cyclic form) and a conscious engagement both with the past (Rameau, Couperin, and Chopin) and with contemporaries, particularly Stravinsky. Debussy finished the year by writing both the *Élegie* for piano and the *Noël* for voice and piano, the latter of which he also arranged for two-part children's chorus and piano. He completed *Noël* just before a debilitating operation put an end to this run of late-life creativity.

Debussy's works from 1915 fall into a number of categories. First, there are works written explicitly in response to war: *Berceuse* and *Pièce pour piano*, which was composed for wartime charity fund-raising. Second, there are compositions framed by allusions to war: *Berceuse* and *En blanc et noir*, both of which contain unobtrusive musical references to national anthems. *Noël* also belongs to this category but is more blatant in its message than the other works because it contains a text. Third, there are compositions reinforcing tradition: two of the three sonatas (out of a projected set of six) pay homage to French baroque traditions but are also very much about the present. And finally, there are works with no evident connection to war or extramusical ideas: the *Études*. In the context of this repertoire, the *Noël* may appear to be insignificant. It is seen as problematic because it is not experimental musically and lacks subtlety of meaning. It is also one of the few works for which Debussy wrote both the text and the music.[5] However, *Noël* enables us to explore a number of important themes: the overt and implicit meaning in Debussy's writings, in contrast to his music; his musical discretion; the carol in performance; Debussy in relation to his audiences; and the composer as an elite or popular national figurehead.[6]

Debussy's Texts and Paratexts

There are striking differences between Debussy's often forthright statements about French music—the role of music in national culture—and his often understated and delicately expressed musical works. Jane Fulcher bases her assessment that

Debussy was a nationalist with right-wing leanings on his occasional outbursts in the press and his private letters, but even she recognizes that his musical outputs do not bolster this claim; there was a mismatch between Debussy's writings and his compositions.[7] In the guise of Monsieur Croche, Debussy expressed outspoken views about contemporary music: notable and frequent were his comments that Wagner had infiltrated and threatened French music.[8] His fear that French music was in crisis intensified during the war, and his comments frequently appear chauvinistic. On March 11, 1915, he published an article on the front page of the paper *L'Intransigeant* titled "Enfin seul," in which he linked the fate of France on the battlefield with a similar musical conflict and urged composers to return to the French "classics" of Rameau and Couperin to retrace and rediscover a French musical tradition.[9] His wartime letters are full of references to the "Boches," and they express anger about the enemy and loss of life and deep fear for the uncertain future of his nation. Louis Laloy commented in 1928 that many seemingly chauvinistic expressions were in the air and were exacerbated by the context of war. He also testified that Debussy was completely dejected and obsessed by the events, to the point that "our conversations . . . had no other subject than the country's suffering."[10] In Laloy's view, the intensity of Debussy's feeling exacerbated his illness and infused his music: "The *Noël des enfants qui n'ont plus de maison* and the *Berceuse héroïque* bore witness, right from the beginning of the war, to Debussy's feelings." The next, more substantial, work was to have been *Ode à la France*, on the subject of Joan of Arc "as an image of France in its sufferings, a victim offered up to the injustice of fate."[11]

Debussy used text to frame and orient some of his wartime works. There are some notable examples from the list above. In *En blanc et noir*, Debussy prefaced each of the three movements with literary quotations. The second movement is prefaced by a quotation from François Villon's *Ballade contre les ennemis de la France*, which includes the lines "For whoever wishes to harm the kingdom of France / Does not deserve to have virtues."[12] Jonathan Dunsby has carried out a fascinating study of the paratexts in this otherwise enigmatic piano duet.[13] The meaning of this movement is highly dependent on the associated poetry; it enables the listener to detect a musical battle and an ultimate, if tentative, French victory.

Debussy achieved something comparable when he set out to write a set of six sonatas in the French baroque tradition. The title page of the Durand edition adopts an antique calligraphy and describes the composer as "Claude Debussy, musicien français," thus reinforcing his link to the French past.[14] Debussy's letters show that he was determined to avoid the incongruity of "gothique allemande" script, preferring to imitate the title pages of eighteenth-century editions of Couperin and Rameau.[15] Debussy's nod to the French baroque period worked: various scholars have searched for baroque stylistic elements.[16] The most plausible musical reference is the dotted rhythms in the magisterial opening to the Sonata for cello and piano. Marianne Wheeldon argues that composers during the war were discouraged from experimental writing and were expected to conform to "a new cultural conservatism."[17] I argue in *Music and Ultra-Modernism in France* that these sonatas were not quite what they seemed; despite the framing, they are indeed experimental and show Debussy's engagement with new sonorities, experimentation with instrumental combinations, and acute awareness of the younger Stravinsky.[18] To some extent, he succeeds in misleading us.

Debussy's Musical Discretion

Some of Debussy's wartime works contain narratives that reflect the views and sentiments that he expressed with considerable abandon in his texts and letters, but they are striking in their musical discretion. The second movement of *En blanc et noir* is a case in point. Here Debussy enacts a battle between the Germans and French. The opening is full of rising fourths, suggesting bugle or clarion calls. At measure 53, the relative consonance gives way to rhythmically turbulent and more dissonant writing, with superimposed seconds undermining a sense of tonal center. We hear the unambiguous and strident melody of the Lutheran chorale *Ein feste Burg* in the midst of the turbulence, between measures 79 and 88. The bugle calls and opening melodic fragments return at measure 129, and the marking "Joyeuse" suggests a victory. In the midst of the rising fourths, however, only those paying the greatest attention will hear the "Marseillaise" (measures 163–70), marked "pp leggierissimo" and "à peine" (scarcely) and stripped of its rhythmic identity, announcing a faint but decisive French victory. But without these paratexts, would we be able to follow this discreet musical narrative about the as yet far from resolved military conflict? The response is probably yes—but only after reference to the score, most likely not in the moment of listening.

Noël is unique in Debussy's output in being an explicitly emotional response to the war. Glenn Watkins describes it as an "unabashed piece of heart-tugging propaganda."[19] Marianne Wheeldon regards it as a reaction to the reception of the orchestral version *Berceuse héroïque*, which took place on October 26, 1915, during the opening concert of the Concerts Colonne-Lamoureux (1915–16 series).[20] The *Berceuse* was programmed alongside Berlioz's *Symphonie fantastique* and Beethoven's *Eroica* Symphony. Inevitably, the four-minute piece was completely overpowered by these mightier works. Debussy was only too well aware of this, as his letter to the critic Vuillermoz on January 25, 1916, indicates:

> The dimensions of the *Berceuse*, which you are being kind enough to concern yourself with, are precisely those of an Estampe. . . . Now an "Estampe" is not a fresco, which I certainly didn't have in mind. Anyway, do we need another 375 pages in order to get our feelings down on paper?

This lullaby is melancholy and modest and the "Brabançonne" doesn't make a racket. If you don't hear enough of the ravaging of Belgium in it, let's say no more on the subject.

. . . I was asked to contribute to a book dedicated to the King of Belgium; you know me sufficiently well to know that I don't like to be indiscreet.[21]

Debussy was right to point to the work's discreet expressivity. The Belgian national anthem, which appears in measures 35–42, is to be played "calmly, proudly but quietly" by the solo horn. Debussy's ending was typical of him but hardly rousing. Although he changes the ending in the orchestral version by adding a final clarion call and a snippet of the anthem, he makes them fade ambiguously into the distance, pianissimo.

Debussy's letter indicates that he was aware that his work did not constitute "war music" in the traditional sense.[22] It seems that *Noël* was his riposte. The text is crucial to the work's impact, and it is more in keeping with the anguished and emotional tone evident in Debussy's private letters from this period. The song is small-scale and written for solo voice and piano. The singer adopts the perspective of the child who tells of the atrocities of losing parents, home, possessions, and even Christmas presents. The full text reads as follows:

We have no more house nor home!
Enemies took all we had; all gone, all gone, even our own little beds!
The school they burnt; they burnt our teacher too.
They burnt the church and Mister Jesus-Christ,
The poor old beggar too who could not get away!
We have no more house nor home!
Enemies took all we had; all gone, all gone, even our own little beds!
Surely, Daddy to fight has gone;
Poor Mummy is in Heaven; died and did not see all this.
O! what shall we do now?
Jesu! Infant Jesu! do not go to them; don't go back to them ever!
Punish them all!
Avenge the children of France!
The little Belgians! the little Serbians! and the Polish children too!
And the Polish children too!
Yet should we some forget, forgive us.—Noel! Noel!
No toys! We want no toys!
But may we please get back again our daily bread?
We have no more house nor home!
Enemies took all we had; all gone, all gone, even our own little beds!
The school they burnt; they burnt our teacher too;
They burnt the church and Mister Jesus-Christ;
The poor old beggar too who could not get away!

Jesu! listen to us! our wooden shoes we have no more;
So please give Victory to the Child[ren] of France![23]

As Wheeldon observes, the singer takes on the persona of the child except for two crucial lines: "Vengez les enfants de France!" (Avenge the children of France!) and, at the end, "Mais donnez la victoire aux enfants de France!" (So please give victory to the children of France!).[24]

Vengeance and victory are appropriate wartime cries. Debussy uses another word—the key word *Noël*—as another cry, as Ravel had used "Asie" in the *Shéhérazade* songs of 1903. Children and Christmas were important preoccupations of wartime popular songs and poems. Debussy evokes these, but he turns a word with Christian associations into a rousing war cry. He exploits the Christian element further by paraphrasing the Lord's Prayer: "But may we please get back again our daily bread?"[25] The connection to Debussy's private utterances is clear when he complains about the lack of daily bread in his own life in a letter to Godet;[26] it was not just the children who were suffering deprivation. Debussy had garnered all the ingredients to elicit an emotional response.

The song stands out from Debussy's *mélodies* in its treatment of text setting. It does not follow the rhythmically subtle contours of his characteristic and, by 1915, famous songs. The rhythms here are more regular and clear-cut. The writing is not exactly melodic but has a wider range, more in keeping with his earlier songs. The musical treatment takes on the simplicity and directness one might expect of a child. There are parallels with Fauré's *En prière* and Ravel's writing for the child in the opera *L'Enfant et les sortilèges* (1925). In terms of Debussy's own works, the musical writing is closest to Yniold in *Pelléas et Mélisande*. Like Yniold, the child is a victim who observes the adult world with both clarity and innocence. Debussy remarked on a melodic similarity to act 2, scene 1, of *Pelléas* in a letter to Jane Bathori. Lesure and Herlin note the similarity in text between the lines "Qu'est-ce que l'on va faire?" (*Noël*, m. 34) and "Qu'allons-nous faire maintenant?" (*Pelléas*, act 2, scene 1), but the melody is somewhat different.[27] However, Debussy creates the same sense of urgency in the face of danger through fast-paced writing in both the melody and the instrumental parts.

Debussy was troubled and preoccupied by the audience's emotional response to this carol. His letters are full of unease about the work's immediate success. In a letter to Robert Godet, he asked, "Should I thank [Debussy] the poet or the musician?"[28] His answer seems to favor the poet, because in a letter to Dukas from April 1917 he highlighted some of most emotive parts of the text, observing, "It's not more cunning than that? It is only that it goes straight to the heart of the citizenry."[29] Debussy showed a certain disdain for audiences who would be so moved by this carol. Writing to Godet on several occasions, he spoke about the need to give multiple encores (*trisser*, not *bisser*): "This took place in the world of the rich bourgeoisie, whose hearts are usually hardened. They cried, dear friend, to the point where I asked myself if I should not apologize to them!"[30] He asked for Godet's advice about how to extricate himself from this "bad/false step." Debussy, who was used to setting contemporary writers, including the self-consciously complex Stéphane Mallarmé, was a rarefied and elite taste; he was not accustomed to writing in order to elicit a predominantly emotional response from his audience. It was a rare moment when his own musical expression embodied a popular national sentiment; *Noël* stems from the feeling he shared with many of his countrymen. Laloy comments that "the fracas of the war, waking him [Debussy] as from a dream, forced him to turn his thoughts back to the external world. . . . Neither Claude Debussy nor I at that time had the serenity of mind necessary to reach [a] level of impartiality, above the mêlée."[31]

Struck by the vengeful tone of the phrase "Punish them!" Annette Becker explains that Debussy, along with other artists and intellectuals, was caught in a wave of worldwide reprobation against German atrocities in the summer of 1914. Drawing parallels with Raoul Dufy's engraving *La fin de la Grande Guerre*, which was published in Cocteau's journal, *Le Mot*, in 1915, she concurred with Laloy that it was only much later that people could stand back from the propaganda and distinguish between the "rumours and myths" and the facts.[32] When they expressed their outrage through art, both Dufy and Debussy were caught up in the moment.

The issue of scale is important when considering how Debussy communicated the collective mood. He had offers from two composer friends, André Caplet and Henry Busser, to orchestrate the work, making it suitable for bigger venues. Debussy declined both in favor of a version for children's voices and piano. He replied to Busser, "I want this piece to be sung with the most discreet piano accompaniment. We mustn't lose a word of this text, which has been inspired by the *rapacity* of our enemies."[33] On a practical level, this also meant that it could be played in many more (and smaller) venues. The version for children's voices meant that the work had the potential to have greater reach and to be performed in venues beyond the professional concert series.[34]

Noël in Performance

Debussy performed *Noël* at a number of wartime charity concerts. He remarked that his three charity concerts were financially successful due to the popularity of *Noël*.[35] Below appears a selective list of wartime performances of *Noël*, including the fund-raising concerts in which the composer was involved:

> March 9, 1916: Casino Saint-Pierre, Geneva; Mme Rolland-Mauger[36]
> April 9, 1916: Concert des Amitiés franco-étrangères, Sorbonne; version for children's chorus, conducted by Jane Montjovet[37]

November 18, 1916: "Au profit de l'Ecole Professionnelle des Mutilés," Salle des concerts du conservatoire, Lyon; Paule de Lestang (soprano)[38]

December 21, 1916: Le Vêtement du prisonnier de guerre; Debussy (piano), Jane Bathori (soprano): *Noël des enfants qui n'ont plus de maison*, *Le Promenoir de deux amants*, *Chansons de Bilitis*

March 9, 1917: L'Aide affectueuse aux musiciens; Rose Féart (soprano): *Trois Ballades de François Villon*, *Fêtes galantes* (first series), *Noël des enfants qui n'ont plus de maison*

March 17, 1917: L'Aide affectueuse aux musiciens; Debussy (piano), Claire Croiza (soprano): *Le Promenoir des deux amants*, "De grève," "De soir" (*Proses lyriques*), *Noël des enfants qui n'ont plus de maison*

March 24, 1917: Le Vêtement du blessé; Debussy (piano), Claire Croiza (soprano): *Trois Ballades de François Villon*, *Fêtes galantes* (second series), *Noël des enfants qui n'ont plus de maison*; Debussy and Jacques Salmon: Sonata for cello and piano

May 5, 1917: Les Soldats aveugles; Debussy (piano), Gaston Poulet (violin): Sonata for violin and piano (première); Debussy (piano), Rose Féart (soprano): *Trois Ballades de François de Villon*, *Chansons de Bilitis*, *Noël des enfants qui n'ont plus de maison*[39]

December 9, 1917: Matinées nationales, L'Œuvre fraternelle des artistes; oration by l'abbé Wetterlé, literary texts by Edmond Rostand[40]

December 25, 1917: Concerts Bathori, Théâtre du Vieux-Colombier; Christmas-themed concert (discussed more extensively below)

February 19, 1918: Société musicale indépendente; Jeanne Montjovet (soprano), Gabriel Grovlez (piano)

The singers Debussy accompanied were among the most respected singers of French *mélodies* of their generation: Jane Bathori (1877–1970), Rose Féart (1881–1954), and Claire Croiza (1882–1946). Bathori and Croiza devoted themselves to contemporary music, and the latter was one of Debussy's favored singers from 1910 until his death. They were the most prominent female singers involved in the Société musicale indépendente and Société nationale concerts during the war.[41] Debussy dedicated *Noël* to Féart, although Bathori gave the first performance with the composer. Bathori considered Debussy to be the most significant composer of her generation and included his music in her numerous recitals, including her wartime concerts at the Vieux-Colombier.

One concert from Bathori's Théâtre du Vieux-Colombier series deserves particular attention. Jane Bathori was invited by Jacques Copeau, the director of the theater Vieux-Colombier, near Saint Sulpice in Paris, to take over its direction during his absence from the city between 1917 and 1919, when he and his company were based in New York. Bathori's concerts became famous for her efforts to promote the contemporary music of Ravel, Debussy, Satie, the future Les Six, and others, such as André Caplet and Reynaldo Hahn, many of whom were involved in some way in the war effort but came back when they could to participate in her concerts. She also put on productions of musical theater and opera, often in workshop fashion at the piano and with improvised staging. She mixed the new music with a repertoire that included early music that stretched back to Adam de la Halle's thirteenth-century forerunner to *opéra-comique* in an adaptation for voices and small ensemble by Julien Tiersot. Her programs reveal her desire to show the continuities between the past and present, between elite and more popular art.

Figure 3.1 shows the program of a performance Bathori gave of Debussy's *Noël* in a Christmas-themed program on Christmas Day 1917. She places the work in

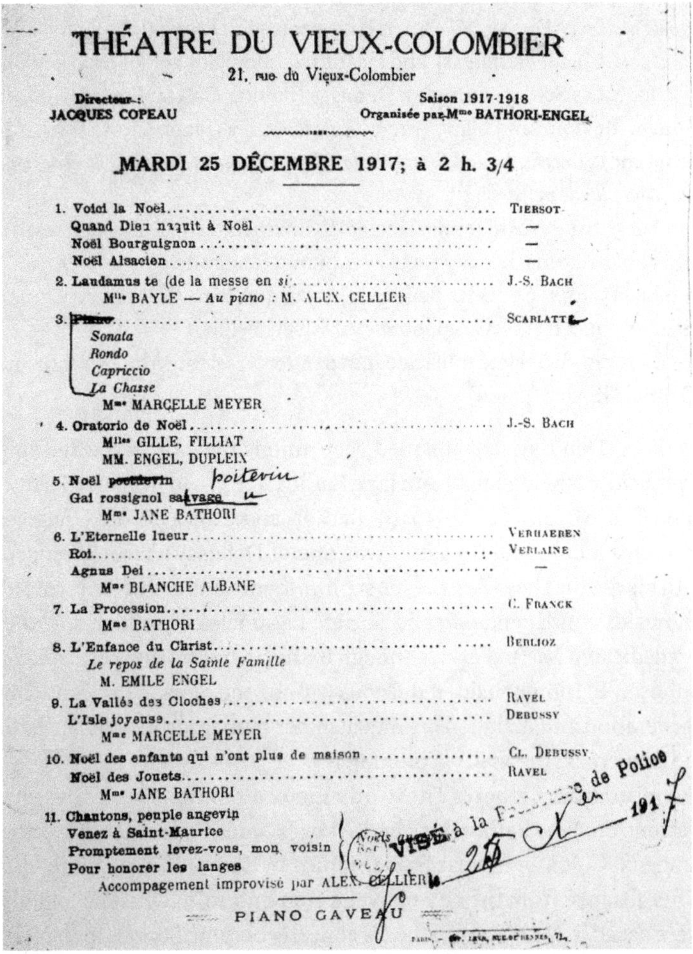

Figure 3.1. Concert program, December 25, 1917. Archives de Jane Bathori, Res Vm DOS—116. Reproduced with the permission of the Bibliothèque nationale de France.

THÉATRE DU VIEUX-COLOMBIER

21, rue du Vieux-Colombier

Directeur: Saison 1917-1918

JACQUES COPEAU   Organisée par Mme BATHORI-ENGEL

MARDI 25 DÉCEMBRE 1917; à 2 h. ¾

1.	Voici la Noël	TIERSOT
	Quand Dieu naquit à Noël	—
	Noël Bourguignon	—
	Noël Alsacien	—
2.	Laudamus te (de la messe en *si*)	J.-S. BACH
	Mlle BAYLE—*Au piano :* M. ALEX. CELLIER	
3.	*Sonata*	SCARLATTI
	Rondo	
	Capriccio	
	La Chasse	
	Mme MARCELLE MEYER	
4.	Oratorio de Noël	J.-S. BACH
	Mlles GILLE, FILLIAT	
	MM. ENGEL, DUPLEIX	
5.	Noël poitevin	
	Gai rossignol sauvage	
	Mme JANE BATHORI	
6.	L'Eternelle Lueur	VERHAEREN
	Roi	VERLAINE
	Agnus Dei	—
	Mme BLANCHE ALBANE	
7.	La Procession	C. FRANCK
	Mme BATHORI	
8.	L'Enfance du Christ	BERLIOZ
	Le repos de la Sainte Famille	
	M. EMILE ENGEL	
9.	La Vallée des Cloches	RAVEL
	L'Isle joyeuse	DEBUSSY
	M[me] MARCELLE MEYER	
10.	Noël des enfants qui n'ont plus de maison	CL. DEBUSSY
	Noël des Jouets	RAVEL
	M[me] JANE BATHORI	
11.	Chantons, peuple angevin	
	Venez à Saint-Maurice	
	Promptement levez-vous, mon voisin	
	Pour honorer les langes	
	Accompag[n]ement improviseé par ALEX. CELLIER	

PIANO GAVEAU

Transcription of Figure 3.1.

the context of repertoire that includes "classical" works by Bach, Scarlatti, Berlioz, Franck, Debussy, and Ravel but also includes Julien Tiersot's French regional folk-song settings. The latter included, for example, an arrangement of the well-known French carol "Quand dieux naquit à noël." Tiersot described the *Noël* as a distinct category of chanson, different from the "Chanson populaire" because it was written down and often had an attributed author. It was thus "semi-popular" because it was "designed to be sung among the people but written by the 'lettrés' and passed on by the book rather than by oral tradition."[42] For Tiersot, the text was the basis of the carol; the music, on the other hand, was generally borrowed from existing "airs" that would be familiar in towns and cities. Differentiating this urban music from rural or peasant chansons, he commented that "the Noël has something more alluring, more lively: it represents one of the most pleasant manifestations of the French spirit."[43] While Debussy's concerts, noted above, include *Noëls* in the context of his own vocal and chamber music, Bathori's act of programming Debussy's carol alongside Tiersot's arrangements of traditional French and regional carols (as well as classical and contemporary music) is illuminating; it throws light on the significance and success of Debussy's work. Bathori recognized that she needed to appeal to broader audiences during the war; Debussy, despite himself, seems to have achieved that too.

Bathori gave Debussy a special place in her concerts and in her own repertoire, including him in numerous programs. She wrote a book, *On the Interpretation of the Melodies of Claude Debussy*, in which she described in considerable detail how each song should be sung and interpreted.[44] Her instructions on singing *Noël* are revealing. Rather than regarding it as a work of lesser stature, she outlined its emotional power and sincerity: "There is nothing so simple, so spontaneous and heartfelt as this song of lament, which must be sung as it is written, without liaisons or vocal effects. Try to both think and express yourself as a child." She picks out certain lines of text for special treatment—for instance, proposing an accent on "Punissez-les" (Punish them!). She continues, "The beginning returns, then *Noel! Écoutez-nous*, as if you were saying it in secret, with an energized breath. Finally, the crescendo and a very strong ending. No one has written an appeal to mankind with such convincing force and simplicity."[45]

Noël showed that Debussy's esteem extended beyond elite circles and that even works of apparently slight musical value contributed to establishing his reputation as a French national symbol. Debussy's rare loss of restraint had had its effect. He had finally captured the public mood with something that was unambiguous in its message. The middle-aged avant-garde composer, who was fighting and losing a personal battle with cancer and was therefore precluded from action, had succeeded in speaking for the nation. The despair and pain he experienced on account of the extraordinary circumstances resonated with his compatriots. In a letter to Debussy two months before his death, his friend Robert Godet quoted the words of a young nurse who had heard his *Noël*: "How is it possible that the author seems to have sensed the war with more intensity than those whose flesh has been crushed or bruised, with more emotion than those of us who tend their wounds? . . . It was as if the common chord of all French hearts had been touched by the fingers of a magician endowed with superhuman powers."[46]

Noël as a Work of Its Time

If *Noël* made such an impression in its own time, what accounts for its relative obscurity today? According to the accounts above, the carol was performed to enraptured audiences. Yet indications of its success and presence are harder to find. In addition to Debussy's own performances and Bathori's Christmas concert, it was included at a concert of the Société musicale indépendente on February 19, 1918.[47] Paule de Lestang also sang it at a charity concert, "Au profit de l'Ecole Professionnelle des Mutilés," in Lyon on November 18, 1916, before Debussy's performances with Bathori, Féart, and Croiza. It was also programmed in one of Alfred Cortot's Matinées nationales concerts (December 9, 1917), where music and poetry served explicitly political and patriotic purposes.[48] Otherwise, traces of performances at classical or avant-garde concerts are not as numerous as contemporary accounts of its success might suggest. The task of finding performances is made more difficult by the fact that fewer journals and newspapers were in circulation during the war. However, it is possible that *Noël*'s success was relatively limited because, although it spoke for a nation at an intense but fleeting moment in time, it was arguably limited by its most powerful asset: its text. In sharp contrast to the evocative and timeless texts Debussy set in most of his *mélodies*, *Noël*'s context is inextricably tied to the atrocities of the Great War. Yet the song did not disappear entirely as memories of the war faded. It popped up in varied amateur, charity, educational, and professional contexts and was sometimes included in Christmas-themed concerts during the interwar period. Durand even marketed it in *La Revue musicale* as one of a collection of *Noëls*.[49]

Léon Vallas, one of Debussy's early biographers and an ardent nationalist, reflected on *Noël*'s timeliness and importance in his three biographies from 1926, 1932, and 1944. Unlike most commentators, he accorded more significance to the work as time passed, describing it in each book as a "chef d'oeuvre," simple and moving, in which the "breathless" vocal line "transcribes" the text.[50] In his third book, he claimed that the work was popular in Belgium between 1916 and 1918 and that it "took on the allure of a message from France, of a patriotic song, of a national protest against the German occupation." Motivated surely by the new global conflict of World War II and the new German occupation, he appreciated its resonance and currency, describing it as "too current" to perform now.[51] In his view, if it hadn't been so clearly tied to the 1914–1918 conflict, "[it] would seem to belong to French folklore and to be the work of an anonymous musician-poet from an indeterminate time."[52] While we may not share Vallas's view that *Noël* is the crowning achievement of a "master," we can concur with him that this little carol was remarkable for enabling Debussy to capture a "lively patriotic sentiment and more generally, a large sense of humanity."[53]

Noël is exceptional in several respects. It was rare for Debussy to set his own words to music; usually, he kept his creative work separate from his often frank public and private utterances. His decision to bring the two together reveals his palpable engagement with the tumultuous events of the Great War, despite his illness and incapacity to fight. Eschewing his usual tendency to suggest and evoke, there is no ambiguity possible in the carol's message. His decision to adopt the voice of a child only emphasized the powerlessness that he shared with many on the home front. While uncomfortable and a little surprised that he had captured the public mood, Debussy was surely also conscious of his position as arguably France's leading composer, whose voice could be heard above the melee to reflect the extraordinary time and place of Europe in 1915 to striking effect.

Notes

1. There are two autograph manuscripts of *Noël* at the Bibliothèque nationale de France (BnF). One is for solo voice and piano, and the other is a two-part arrangement for children's voices and piano with an English translation. See http://catalogue.bnf.fr/ark:/12148/cb44318247w and http://catalogue.bnf.fr/ark:/12148/cb44318508t. The score as published by Durand in 1916 is available online at http://catalogue.bnf.fr/ark:/12148/cb429394575. The title is also known as *Noël des enfants qui n'ont plus de maisons*; the manuscript versions and 1916 score use the plural spelling. However, Durand's contract also has *maison* in the singular. See Claude Debussy, *Correspondance, 1872–1918*, ed. François Lesure and Denis Herlin (Paris: Gallimard, 2005), 1958–59.

2. Glenn Watkins, *Proof through the Night: Music and the Great War* (Berkeley: University of California Press, 2003), 83–170; Marianne Wheeldon, *Debussy's Late Style* (Bloomington: Indiana University Press, 2009).

3. Hall Caine, ed., *King Albert's Book: A Tribute to the Belgian King and People from the Representative Men and Women throughout the World* (London: Hodder and Stoughton, 1914), 6.

4. This was first published by Theodore Presser (Bryn Mawr, PA) in 1933 as *Page d'album*. It was made available in 2014 as the digital Muzibook MCL1063, issued by Naxos Publishing Technologies (Vincennes). See http://www.muzibook.fr/produit/1241/3700681108466/.

5. Debussy also provided his own texts for his *Proses lyriques* (1892) and *Nuits blanches* (1898).

6. Similar themes emerge at roughly the same time for several English composers. See Christina Bashford's chapter in this volume.

7. Jane F. Fulcher, "Speaking the Truth to Power," in *Debussy and His World*, ed. Jane F. Fulcher (Princeton, NJ: Princeton University Press, 2001), 218–22.

8. Debussy, *Monsieur Croche et autres écrits* (1971; reprint, Paris: Gallimard, 1987); see, for example, 67, 141, 244, 280.

9. Ibid., 265–66.

10. Louis Laloy, "Ode à la France," *Musique* 1, no. 6 (1928): 245–49. Translation from *Louis Laloy (1874–1944) on Debussy, Ravel and Stravinsky*, trans. and ed. Deborah Priest (Aldershot, UK: Ashgate, 1999), 231–36; see 232.

11. Ibid., 233. The collaboration between Laloy and Debussy was incomplete at the time of Debussy's death in 1918. See Marianne Wheeldon, "Debussy's Legacy: The Controversy over the 'Ode à la France,'" *Journal of Musicology* 27, no. 3 (2010): 304–41.

12. Debussy, *En blanc et noir*, second movement (Paris: Durand, 1915), 15. Translation from Wheeldon, *Debussy's Late Style*, 44.

13. Jonathan Dunsby, "The Poetry of Debussy's *En blanc et noir*," in *Analytical Strategies and Musical Interpretation: Essays on Nineteenth- and Twentieth-Century Music*, ed. Craig Ayrey and Mark Everist (Cambridge: Cambridge University Press, 1996), 149–68.

14. See the title page of Debussy, Sonate pour violoncelle (Paris: Durand, 1915), Département de musique, BnF, VM BOB-16404.

15. See Debussy's letters to Durand, September 4 and 7, 1915, in *Correspondance*, 1929, 1932.

16. Fulcher, *Debussy and His World*, 223–24; Watkins, *Proof through the Night*, 101; Scott Messing, *Neoclassicism in Music* (Ann Arbor, MI: UMI Research Press, 1988), 45–49.

17. Wheeldon, *Debussy's Late Style*, 10.

18. Barbara L. Kelly, *Music and Ultra-Modernism in France: A Fragile Consensus, 1913–1939* (Woodbridge: Boydell, 2013), 139–47.

19. Watkins, *Proof through the Night*, 106.

20. See Wheeldon, *Debussy's Late Style*, 30.

21. Debussy, *Correspondance*, 1969. Here and below, translations are by the author unless otherwise noted.

22. "Believe me that war music is not made in times of war. Properly speaking, there is no such thing as war music." Debussy to Vuillermoz, January 25, 1916, in *Correspondance*, 1969.

23. Translation taken from the penultimate page of Debussy's manuscript, digitized copy available at http://catalogue.bnf.fr/ark:/12148/cb44318508t.

24. Wheeldon, *Debussy's Late Style*, 33–34.

25. "Tâchez de nous redonner le pain quotidian"; compare "Donne-nous aujourd'hui notre pain de ce jour" (Give us this day our daily bread).

26. Debussy to Robert Godet, May 7, 1917, in *Correspondance*, 2106.

27. Debussy to Jane Bathori, November 2, 1916, ibid., 2042.

28. Debussy to Godet, December 28, 1916, ibid., 2064.

29. Debussy to Paul Dukas, early April 1917, ibid., 2092.

30. Debussy to Godet, December 28, 1916, ibid., 2064. See also Debussy to Godet, May 7, 1917, ibid., 2106.

31. Laloy, "Ode à la France," in *Louis Laloy*, trans. and ed. Priest, 233.

32. Annette Becker, "Debussy en Grande Guerre," in *Regards sur Debussy*, ed. Myriam Chimènes and Alexandra Laederich (Paris: Fayard, 2013), 61–62.

33. Henri Busser to Debussy, October 1916, in *Correspondance*, 2040.

34. According to Léon Vallas, the version for children's chorus was "almost ignored." See Vallas, *Claude Debussy et son temps* (Paris: Librairie Félix Alcan, 1932), 368.

35. Debussy to Dukas, early April 1917, in *Correspondance*, 2093.

36. Roger Nichols asserts that "Mme Rollan-Mauger was to give the first performance ... on 9 March 1916 at the Casino Saint Pierre in Geneva." See François Lesure and Roger Nichols, eds., *Debussy Letters* (London: Faber, 1987), 312. François Lesure confirms that it took place. See Lesure, *Claude Debussy* (Paris: Klincksieck, 1994), 395.

37. Marcel Dietschy, *A Portrait of Claude Debussy*, trans. William Ashbrook and Margaret Cobb (New York: Oxford University Press, 1994), 180.

38. Program, Séances de musique de chambre, Bibliothèque Municipale de Lyon, Archives Léon Vallas, Ms Vallas 33, 1 (7).

39. See Wheeldon, *Debussy's Late Style*, 16, for a list of Debussy's wartime performances.

40. Rose Féart was due to perform *Noël*, but she canceled at the last moment; it is therefore unlikely that the song was actually performed. See François Anselmini, "Alfred Cortot et la création des Matinées nationales: L'Union sacrée mise en musique," *Revue de musicologie* 97, no. 1 (2011): 83. See also "Matinées Nationales," *Le courrier musical*, January 1, 1918, 16.

41. See Michel Duchesneau, *L'Avant-Garde musicale à Paris de 1871 à 1939* (Sprimont: Mardaga, 1997), 276–77, 310.

42. Julien Tiersot, ed., *Noëls français*, transcribed and harmonized by Julien Tiersot (Paris: Au Ménestrel, Heugel, 1901), i.

43. Ibid.

44. Jane Bathori, *On the Interpretation of the Mélodies of Claude Debussy*, trans. Linda Laurent (New York: Pendragon Press, 1998), 101. Originally published as *Sur l'interprétation des mélodies de Claude Debussy* (Paris: Les Éditions Ouvrières, 1953).

45. Bathori, *On the Interpretation of the "Mélodies,"* 101.

46. Godet to Debussy, January 23, 1918, in *Correspondance*, 2176–82.

47. According to Michel Duchesneau's listings, Jeanne Montjovet sang *Noël* accompanied by Gabriel Grovlez, but Bathori was singing in this concert too with Ricordo Vines, so it is possible that she performed the song. See Duchesneau, *L'Avant-Garde musicale à Paris*, 310.

48. See Anselmini, "Alfred Cortot et la création des Matinées nationales," 68–73.

49. See, for example, various unsigned articles: "Concert," *L'Avenir d'Arachon*, February 16, 1919, 2; "Une soirée de bienfaisance," *Le Ménestrel* (January 23, 1920): 38; "Station radio-téléphonique de l'Ecole supérieure des Postes et télégraphes," *L'Homme libre*, December 26, 1926; "Concert," Mme Leila Sedira, *L'Echo d'Alger*, December 12, 1931; and "Pour Noël," *La Revue musicale* 8 (December 1, 1926): 2.

50. Léon Vallas, *Debussy* (Paris: Librairie Plon, 1926), 175; Vallas, *Claude Debussy et son temps*, 368; Vallas, *Achille Claude Debussy* (Paris: Presses universitaires de France, 1944), 117.

51. Vallas, *Achille Claude Debussy*, 117.

52. Ibid.

53. Ibid., 118.

CHAPTER 4

Profitable Patriotism

John Philip Sousa and the Great War

PATRICK WARFIELD

In January 1918, a composer who had recently joined the US war effort wrote to D. S. Walker of Montreal. His letter concerned a poem that had first appeared in the London magazine *Punch* and from which the composer had created "the best song I have ever written." Hoping that "with the aid of a thoroughly competent dramatic singer" the work might find popular resonance, the composer hoped that Walker could assist in securing publication rights to the lyric. The poem was, of course, John McCrae's "In Flanders Fields," and the composer none other than John Philip Sousa, whose piano-vocal arrangement was published in late February and prominently featured the military ranks held by both composer and poet (see figure 4.1). Sousa completed an orchestral arrangement in March, and his band likely debuted the piece on June 26 in Poughkeepsie, New York. McCrae would never hear the song: the poet, stationed in France, died on January 28, 1918.[1]

This song's story gives some sense of the competing motivations behind Sousa's wartime activities. First, there is no doubt that the bandleader was a patriot who felt strongly about the Allied cause. He had grown up in the national capital, served his apprenticeship in the United States Marine Band, and made a name for himself with a repertoire that relied heavily on patriotic music. His setting may seem pedestrian to ears accustomed to the now more famous version by Charles Ives, but it was clearly a heartfelt response to the European slaughter.[2]

IN FLANDERS FIELDS
THE POPPIES GROW

Song with Piano Accompaniment
by
LIEUT. JOHN PHILIP SOUSA
Words by
LIEUT.-COL. JOHN McCRAE

Price, 30 cents, net
(No Discount)

New York · G. SCHIRMER · Boston

Figure 4.1. John Philip Sousa, "In Flanders Fields the Poppies Grow," cover, MBL.

Sousa, however, was as much businessman as patriot, and the financial aspects of his career had always relied on relevancy. Since 1892 he had led his own commercial band on annual tours across the United States. He played regularly to massive audiences, and his compositions were printed, advertised, and sold for the home market. He was, in other words, a popular musician whose commercial success relied on a deft understanding of a vast public's shifting taste. It is in the practical concerns of a popular musician that we can find Sousa's real motivation for writing to McCrae's agent in Montreal. His letters urge Walker to contact the poet in the field and secure "immediate consent to the use of the words." The song was ready to go, Sousa explained, and his publishers desired "to get it out immediately." He went on to suggest that "both of us will lose out if the song is not issued in a short time." For Sousa, transnational political events were turning to make the marketing of McCrae's text ever easier: "It won't be long before we, that is, your land and my land and the Frenchman's land and the Italian's land, will do up the Kaiser and his cohorts, and those that lie in Flanders Fields will be avenged."[3]

For Sousa, the timing of this conflict could not have been better. Since 1892 he had been a touring artist, performing hundreds of concerts per year. By the century's second decade, however, the March King was beginning to show his age. Starting in 1912, the band undertook only fall tours, parts of which consisted of extended stays at amusement parks and expositions. His programming, too, was beginning to falter. For two decades, Sousa had presented a repertoire that alternated the accessible with the sophisticated, the familiar with the novel. But modern novelties were becoming a bit too distant: the bandmaster embraced ragtime only with trepidation, and he had little use for the rebellion of contemporary art music. The currents of popular culture, in other words, threatened to leave him behind.

As Sousa would discover, war can be simultaneously tragic and fruitful. All military conflicts have noncombatant beneficiaries; the politicians who feed on jingoism and the industrialists who profit from destruction are only the most obvious. Songwriters, composers, performers, and cultural entrepreneurs can also capitalize on the fervor that accompanies national crisis. While Sousa's public statements between 1914 and 1918 can easily suggest a fickle waffling between indifference and aggression, it is better to read his gradual move from neutrality to preparedness, his carefully placed comments about youthfulness and uniformity, and his unseemly embrace of jingoism as intentional efforts to mirror the beliefs of a public he hoped to recapture. In short, the Sousa of 1914 sensed an opportunity, one that his skills as an entertainer would allow him to seize.

Neutrality

Throughout the fall of 1914, many Americans found the European war a distant conflict whose root causes were obscured behind a confusing web of past wrongs. It is hardly surprising that Sousa saw little value in commenting on the situation abroad. When interviews did veer toward the conflict, the bandmaster treated it with contempt for bringing European culture to a halt: "Music of course is at a standstill as far as production or continuance of further study is concerned." He even worried that the talents of particular musicians might be permanently lost: "There is Fritz Kreisler, fighting with the Austrian army—rumor even has him dead. Dr. Karl Muck, too, conductor of the Boston Symphony Orchestra, is somewhere in Germany, fighting or helping the fighters. The loss of these men would be a great blow to music." Sousa's public image had relied on the most pleasant of military trappings—glorious uniforms, parading troops, and marching bands—but a real war made clear that at least some of this pose was playacting. In September 1914, as if to admit the distinction, he proclaimed that war "never inspired great music. The destruction of man by man is not an inspiring thing." In another interview, he hoped that a conflict dominated by trench warfare, and thus deprived of frontline bands, would become "uninteresting, unromantic, and undesirable," thus making war itself "almost impossible."[4]

While the conflict in Europe may have been distant, its impact on American public discourse was substantial, especially in the debate between Wilsonian neutrality and the more aggressive stance advocated by the Roosevelt camp. As Wilson's policies of neutrality and a strong navy were cheaper than going to war and easier to swallow than universal military service, it is no surprise that they ruled public opinion in 1914. Sousa, for his part, happily fell into step: "I have not allowed my interest to be swayed to either side. . . . I think our president was right upon his neutrality proclamation, and I am trying to observe it." But Sousa's devotion to neutrality was not a simple parroting of Wilsonian policy; rather, it provided an opportunity to remind audiences of his international fame: "I am told the kaiser's favorite march is 'Semper Fidelis,' my march. I know the Turks play Liberty Belles [*sic*], and that England and French troops use my marches. They are my friends and it would be poor taste for me to even have an opinion."[5]

Sousa's past fame also echoed the American demographic realities that made it difficult for the United States to pick a side in the European conflict: "I have played in all the fighting countries excepting Serbia. I have been three times through Germany and five through England. Then, too, I am a member of the French academy, so I can give no expression as to the right or wrong of any nation, nor can I express the wish to see any one win." Neutrality thus had several benefits. It allowed Sousa to remain firmly in step with public opinion and political reality. More important, it enabled him to remind listeners of a fame that was rapidly fading. As the war continued, however, this popular entertainer—along with his listeners—would be forced to choose a side.[6]

Preparedness

The onset of war had only limited impact on Sousa's immediate financial concerns. He launched his 1915 tour in April and after traveling through the Midwest arrived in San Francisco for the Panama-Pacific Exposition. The political situation made a previously hoped for international tour ill-advised, and so Sousa found himself on the lookout for something to keep his ensemble in the public eye. An opportunity arose when Charles B. Dillingham offered the Sousa Band a featured role in his new extravaganza, *Hip Hip Hooray*, at the New York Hippodrome. A residency at the Hippodrome must have been appealing to the bandmaster; New York was the ensemble's official home, but it had not played an extended engagement there for a decade. *Hip Hip Hooray*'s long run in the city would provide a welcome homecoming as well as a vacation from touring. Even better, the 425 performances would be seen by some two million patrons; this extravaganza would provide just the sort of public arena Sousa needed.[7]

The band did not appear until *Hip Hip Hooray*'s second act, when it played a miniature concert that included a new march dedicated to Dillingham, "The New

York Hippodrome," and a grand patriotic ballet, "The March of the States." The show played twice per day, Monday through Saturday. On most Sundays, Sousa's ensemble was the anchor for an evening of superstar entertainment during which audiences were treated to operatic sopranos (Maggie Teyte, Nellie Melba), popular entertainers (Charlie Chaplin, Will Rogers), and composers playing their own work (Irving Berlin, Leo Ornstein). Of course, many of these performances engaged with the situation abroad. A number of Sundays were given over to fund-raising events (the French Soldiers' Fund, the German Relief Fund) or celebrations of performers associated with the war effort (Vernon Castle, the Tsing-tau Symphony Orchestra). On December 12, 1915, Emmy Destinn used a performance to announce her return to the Metropolitan stage. In the excitement, she spontaneously kissed the bandmaster, inaugurating a tradition in which "every good-natured prima donna would bestow a chaste salute on the blushing composer." Lest the doctrine of the day be forgotten, after Sousa received a peck from Tamaki Miura, one newspaper noted that the bandleader had been kissed by "a Bohemian and a Japanese prima donna," and thus "neutrality is vindicated."[8]

The voices calling for greater military preparedness had been growing in volume since early 1915, and the targeting of civilian and humanitarian vessels by German U-boats only aided their cause. For his part, Sousa was happy to endorse the awakening spirit of preparedness. His first comment on the issue, which came immediately after the April sinking of a British-flagged relief ship, reflected public fear for Americans abroad, while also reinforcing Wilson's preference for a defensive navy rather than an expanded army: "My travels around the world have convinced me that the United States ought to have a navy as large as any, and the most efficient in the world. Only then will we be safe."[9]

A concern that European powers might bring their war to the Eastern Seaboard had focused public attention on a defensive navy, but the May sinking of the British ocean liner *Lusitania*—which killed some 120 Americans in distant waters—provided new wind to the preparedness movement. After an initial response that proved too weak for the political climate, Wilson sought to articulate that neutrality did not mean inaction. In an October 11 address to the Daughters of the American Revolution, he reinforced the neutrality doctrine and asked "every man to declare himself, where he stands. Is it America first or is it not?" A few weeks later, the *Washington Post* declared that the president's speech "inspired John Philip Sousa, perhaps the world's greatest composer of march music, to go to work on another march, which he will christen 'America First.'"[10]

The meaning of the phrase *America First* had changed considerably by the time Sousa's march was given its dual premiere by the composer's ensemble at the Hippodrome and by the Marine Band at the Daughters of the American Revolution auditorium in the capital. The continued irritation of German attacks on merchant vessels forced even Wilson to embrace at least some level of military modernization. At the Washington performance, which occurred on George Washington's birthday and was attended by Wilson, State Department assistant solicitor Hampson Gary read a series of carefully curated statements from the first president that seemed to advocate for a strong national defense. In short, by the time of its premiere, the phrase *America First* was no longer just about keeping the country safe through neutrality, but about protecting the populace through readiness. Sousa even dedicated his march to Mrs. William Cumming Story, the president general of the Daughters of the American Revolution and herself a fierce advocate for military preparedness.[11]

With growing bipartisan support for a strong military, Sousa embraced preparedness quite publicly at the Hippodrome. On February 27, 1916, he introduced a new song by George Graff and Jack Glogau titled "Wake Up, America." The chorus was reprinted in a number of periodicals, and it advocated for readiness as a way to maintain neutrality (figure 4.2).

Sousa explained his new position at some length in articles about this very song. For him, as for many Americans, military buildup was meant not to prepare the United States for involvement in Europe's conflict but rather to ready the country for future wars that might arise out of Europe's ashes. "Let America keep out of this fight," Sousa explained. "There is no reason for us to get into it, but we want to be prepared so that at no future time will any nation or nations feel that they can attack us with impunity." He went on to stress, "I am for peace—and preparedness."

Figure 4.2. Jack Glogau, "Wake Up, America," chorus as it appeared in the *New York American* (March 5, 1916); MBL, HJ 43, p. 15.

As he had earlier, Sousa agreed with Wilson that a strong navy was the key to such peace: "With our enormous stretch of waterfront we need a navy large enough to patrol both coasts. We should at least have a navy as large as that of Great Britain. To my mind, an adequate navy is the best sermon for peace!" The sheet music cover, as printed by Leo Feist, underscored the conventional wisdom that naval strength was the key to American security: it was dominated by an oversize Uncle Sam placing battleships into New York Harbor (figure 4.3).[12]

Sousa's political positions were very much in line with those of many East Coast urbanites, who tended—for obvious reasons—to be concerned with the country's exposed Atlantic Seaboard. Midwestern farmers and organized labor, however, continued to resist a military buildup, and the issue was vigorously debated by Congress. If a compromise was to be found, it would rest largely on cost: the best chance of enticing rural representatives to preparedness was to find less expensive gestures that could take on the aura of defending the homeland. In interviews Sousa

Figure 4.3. Jack Glogau, "Wake Up, America," cover, MBL.

stressed how in tune he was with the American public: "Ninety-five percent of the people of this country want peace and not war. The people are waking up already, and they will demand that the politicians stop wrangling and appropriate sufficient money for defense." In such a political battle, musicians like Sousa could prove quite useful: "Men don't clutch their pocket-books so tightly when their hearts are touched, and that is another reason why such a song as 'Wake Up, America' will do much good. In fact, it might not be a bad idea to sing it to Congress!" Sousa had successfully straddled the issue: he was for both neutrality and a strong military. He had also positioned his art as a force in the ongoing debate.[13]

Sousa continued to be active as a composer in late 1915 and early 1916, but he tended to focus on the horrors of war rather than advocate for it. On Easter Sunday 1916, the Hippodrome presented a pair of elaborate benefits for the Permanent Blind Relief War Fund. It was probably at these concerts that Sousa premiered his setting of Rudyard Kipling's "Boots," a 1903 poem that expressed sympathy for British soldiers who had endured thousands of miles of forced marches during the Boer War. Kipling's sentiments found a renewed popularity with the European war, and Sousa would have had numerous opportunities to encounter the poem in reprintings, recitations, and musical settings. His own version uses an increasingly frantic piano part, coupled with an unforgivingly tedious melodic line, to reinforce Kipling's warning that monotony can be as dangerous as munitions (see figure 4.4). For the Hippodrome performance, Sousa chose orator Alfred E. Henderson, whose speech-song delivery must have driven the point home.

A New Uniform(ity)

Hip Hip Hooray closed in June 1916, but the Hippodrome engagement had been so successful that Dillingham decided to take the company on the road. On October 14, a scaled-down *Hip Hip Hooray* opened in Philadelphia and went on to play in Boston, Cincinnati, St. Louis, Kansas City, St. Paul, Chicago, and Cleveland, where it closed the following March. Sousa continued to give regular concerts along the way, and his programs betray little sense of the political climate.

When Wilson won reelection in November, it still seemed plausible that the United States might remain neutral. By the new year, however, the German threat on American trade, coupled with public knowledge of the Zimmermann Telegram (see Gayle Magee's chapter in this volume, 57n47), forced Wilson's hand; on February 3, the United States suspended diplomatic relations with Germany. The public call for war mounted, and on March 22 some twelve thousand demonstrators crowded into Madison Square Garden to demand that the president recognize the de facto state of war. Sousa's band, which provided patriotic music

Figure 4.4. Verse three of Sousa's "Boots," author's transcription from the 1916 T. B. Harms sheet music, MBL.

for the rally, "could not be heard for the roar of approval." On April 6, Congress agreed, and the United States officially entered the war in Europe.[14]

On April 12, the Hippodrome held its anniversary parade, and given the climate it is hardly surprising that the event quickly turned into a patriotic demonstration. "It was supposed to be the parade of the Sixth Avenue Association and the Hippodrome forces," one reporter explained, "but it turned into something more than that. . . . Sousa makes patriotism sing." Indeed, the March King seems to have recaptured his public significance, as the afternoon's biggest cheers came "when the pied piper of patriotism, John Philip Sousa, and his band marched through Times Square under waving flags and through long lines of people."[15]

Having earlier aligned himself with neutrality, Sousa quickly adopted a new stance, echoing the confrontational rhetoric of Theodore Roosevelt. The former president had been positioning himself to lead a brigade to France, and according to one press report, "John Philip Sousa, his whiskers fairly bristling with bellicose spirit, notified the doughty Colonel that he, too, desired to take a crack at the Germans, and that he would be glad to accompany the brigade in the capacity of bandmaster." A trip to the front was in the cards for neither Roosevelt nor Sousa, but both found in the war a way to recapture former glory.[16]

The pathway for Sousa came shortly after, when composer John Alden Carpenter visited the Great Lakes Naval Training Station outside of Chicago and noticed that the recruits were suffering from a lack of musical training. "'Where' Mr. Carpenter asked himself 'is there somebody who knows how to teach the boys, organize a band for them, and do it because he is both a patriot and musician?'" Answering his own question, Carpenter wrote to Sousa, who responded by telegram: "Will be with you Sunday. Letter follows." In mid-May Carpenter arranged a meeting between himself, Sousa, and the base commander, Captain William A. Moffett. Joining them was Lieutenant James M. Bower, a member of Moffett's staff who also happened to be Sousa's brother-in-law. On May 31, 1917, John Philip Sousa, now sixty-two years of age, took the remarkable step of accepting a commission as a lieutenant in the recently formed Naval Reserve Force at Great Lakes.[17]

The navy had several reasons for wanting to engage America's March King. Sousa, of course, remained the most famous entertainer whose reputation was linked directly to American patriotism. Given that the United States still had a relatively small military, the declaration of war would require all-out recruiting and fund-raising efforts, and Sousa was a natural figure to help stimulate the required public generosity. With the onslaught of recruitment events, the navy would need dozens of bands. Here, too, Sousa could help. Having already served as leader of the Marine Band and organizer of his own commercial ensemble, he was well positioned to provide structure and training for the hundreds of young men swarming into the musician corps.

The navy was not alone in benefiting from Sousa's enlistment; the bandleader, too, would find the association useful. While there should be no doubt that Sousa had a strong desire to serve his country, he also had tangible interests at stake. With many of his players called to service, the band's usual transcontinental tours would prove impractical, but the navy could provide Sousa with a replacement ensemble. More important, Sousa was now the government's chief musical spokesperson, a position from which he could remain reliably in the public eye even while his touring band was on hiatus. Indeed, while interest in Sousa may have been dwindling before the war, his every appearance and utterance—on topics large and small— would now be followed by an enthusiastic press.

Great Lakes

Given Sousa's fame, it is hardly surprising that there were unusual aspects to his agreement with the navy. First, the Sousa Band had already been booked for several engagements, and the bandmaster was able to secure special permission to fulfill his commercial obligations. Second, the complexity of establishing a large number of emergency agencies led the federal government to draw upon the expertise of many experienced executives. Most of these men were already fabulously wealthy (and many stood to gain a great deal from the war) and had no need for a government compensation. Federal law, however, prohibited the government from accepting the unpaid service of volunteers. These civilian experts thus drew nominal salaries and became collectively known as "dollar-a-year men." Sousa was just such a figure: a successful businessman whose expertise could be put to good use in the national struggle. He thus agreed to a token payment of just one dollar per month (see figure 4.5). Sousa's salary,

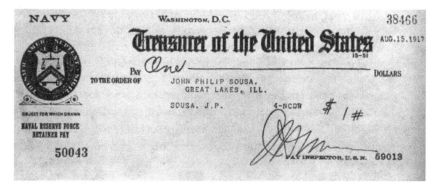

Figure 4.5. Sousa's military paycheck, August 15, 1917, MBL.

like his enlistment itself, attracted the press, and he happily fanned the flames with a widely distributed poem:

> I joined the Reserves on the last day of May,
> I gave up my band and a thousand a day,
> A dollar a month is my government pay,
> My God, how the money rolls in![18]

The bandmaster's first task was to organize the musicians at the Naval Training Station, which by the end of May 1917 amounted to 242 men. Sousa found his first view of these lightly trained players "a little disconcerting." The bandmaster's efforts to establish an organized network of military ensembles from this "unruly mob" attracted a great deal of attention. No small number of reporters explained how, as his pool of available players grew to a peak of some 1,500 men, Sousa arranged for a band battalion of 300 musicians as well as fourteen smaller bands to be assigned to the station's regiments. This ingenuity allowed for a large band that could appear at major fund-raising and recruitment events, along with a series of smaller ensembles such that whenever there was "a telegram from the Department asking us to send a band to some ship or another station," Sousa was "able to send an organized whole—a group of men who knew one another, possessed a common repertoire and understood how to play together." By the end of the war, a remarkable 3,056 musicians had passed through Sousa's training system.[19]

The principal reason for engaging Sousa, however, was not his administrative prowess but rather his celebrity. To finance the war effort, Secretary of the Treasury William Gibbs McAdoo settled on a combination of taxation and borrowing. Much of the latter would be done through the sale of war bonds, which the government issued in isolated blocks to allow for tightly focused drives. Regions of the country were given quotas and pitted against one and other to prove their patriotism in four wartime Liberty Loan campaigns, plus a post-Armistice Victory Loan.

The $2 billion First Liberty Loan drive, which took place in the summer of 1917, was aimed largely at financial institutions and involved limited effort to engage the public. Instead, Sousa and his band of recruits played mostly in and around Chicago, making short excursions to other midwestern cities as part of navy enlistment events. By the time of the second campaign, which took place in October 1917, there was a consensus that more had to be done to target the average American, and so patriotic rallies and recruitment drives began to double as occasions for the sale of war bonds. As Sousa's ensembles generally consisted of rather young and inexperienced instrumentalists, who could not be expected to present complete programs, these events should not be understood as concerts. Rather, the ensemble—and Sousa—acted as draws to rallies, where they presented patriotic selections and accompanied mass singing by the crowd. With the audience thus whipped into a patriotic fervor, well-known military and political speakers attempted to convert public enthusiasm into material support.[20]

Youth and Uniformity

In the interval between the second and third loan drives, Sousa found an ingenious way to keep his face—quite literally—in the newspapers. Sometime around November 18, 1917, he slipped quietly away between acts of an opera and shaved off his beard. This seemingly trivial gesture produced a truly staggering amount of press, much of it silly. The *Dallas Times* wondered if "fiddle strings made out of John Philip Sousa's beard would just naturally play themselves." The *Cleveland Plain Dealer* noted that "another famous landmark has fallen before the ruthlessness of war. John Philip Sousa has taken off his beard." The *New York Clipper* warned, "A war tax on unnecessary hair must be imminent. Sousa has shaved." Newspapers ran interviews, photo essays, and articles on the history of facial hair (see figure 4.6). A staff writer for the *Chicago Tribune,* Guy F. Lee, even penned a poem following the tune of "The Old Oaken Bucket":

How dear to this heart are the tunes of my boyhood,
    "The Washington Post" and "The Manhattan Beach";
"The S. S. Forever," a sermon in joyhood
    That love of the Union forever will preach;
"The Thunderer," too. And the trumpets that blew them
    Afar on the breezes in tones shrill and weird.
And e'en their inventor, whose job was to do them
    Up brown, with baton and with sharp-pointed beard:
The dignified Sousa, the hirsuted Sousa,
    The John Philip Sousa with sharp-pointed beard.

O Miracle Man of the drum and the cymbal
    O Samson of Sound, that Delilah beguiled?
O King Tintinabulate, pray, does a symbol
    Of weakness appear in your razoring wild?
Haste! tell us that Vandyke adieu is a trifle
    That shall not abate the boom-boom of your fin.
Say not that the loss of the whisker will stifle
    The rattlety-slam of your bing-bangy din.
Say you're the Big Noise yet, the star-shaking Noise yet,
    The John Philip Noise yet that once hid his chin![21]

Sousa's shave was hardly an empty gesture; rather, his action echoed Progressive Era desires for standardization and efficiency. In one interview, after noting

Sousa Sans Whiskers—"War to Be Won by Smooth-Faced Men," He Says

Photo by Underwood & Underwood

John Philip Sousa as the March King Looks To-day

The Beardless Sousa

For at least twenty-two years, John Philip Sousa's face has been familiar to all the world. During that time one of the distinguishing feature traits of the popular composer conductor was his luxuriant growth of sable chin.

SOUSA,
Sans beard, sans Sousa's Band, came all except a dollar a day from Uncle Sam and a lot of additional honor.

Figure 4.6. "Sousa sans Whiskers," *New York Tribune*, December 2, 1917, MBL, HJ 47, p. 114 (*left*); "The Beardless Sousa," *New York Currier*, November 29, 1917, MBL, HJ 47, p. 98 (*right*).

that only two of the twenty-seven thousand faces at Great Lakes carried beards, Sousa connected uniformity to the war effort: "The revolution was won by smooth-faced men. The Civil war was a war of bearded men. The men fighting today wear no beards. I am in this war." In another interview, Sousa tied his shave directly to efficiency: "I felt that the day of the beard was far past, and that modern efficiency called for as smooth a face as a man could present." Of course, if Sousa was a bit old-fashioned, connecting himself to youth had obvious benefits: "That is what I am striving for—youth. . . . I had it in my veins and I wanted it to shine from my face. The first time I held my baton over my Great Lakes Training Station Band of more than 600 pieces the sensation of youth came surging over me. The average age of the band is under 20 years. The boyishness of those boys comes forth from their instruments in a tide." Such themes of efficiency, uniformity, and youth would come to dominate a number of Sousa's activities during the war years. Together, they reminded listeners that—despite his age—Sousa remained active, virile, relevant, and in step with public sentiment.[22]

A Building Fire

As American involvement in Europe's war reached its climax in 1918, the home front saw ever-greater displays of patriotic sentiment embellished with darker outbursts of jingoism. Celebrity personalities found a host of opportunities to enter the public discourse within this environment, and as the tone veered increasingly toward an anti-Teutonic rhetoric, the door opened to the expression of rather appalling sentiments. During this period, Sousa continued his path away from neutrality and toward the uglier side of American nationalism.

Hoping to reinvigorate a funding system that had proved less than ideal, Secretary McAdoo approached a number of popular entertainers for the Third Liberty Loan drive, which would run between April 6 and May 4, 1918. On opening day, the anniversary of the war declaration, the capital was treated to open-air celebrations featuring Mary Pickford, Marie Dressler, Charlie Chaplin, and Douglas Fairbanks, while President Wilson appeared in Baltimore, Secretary McAdoo in Philadelphia, and Secretary of the Navy Josephus Daniels in Cleveland. Sousa and his battalion band marched with Vice President Thomas Marshall in St. Louis.

The Federal Reserve Act of 1913 had created twelve banking districts, and for the third campaign Moffett sent band detachments to five of them. The deployment of these ensembles demonstrates the complexity of Sousa's organization. A single band of sixty pieces was sent to the third district to tour eastern Pennsylvania and New Jersey. A fifty-four-piece detachment was sent to the fourth district and traveled through Ohio, western Pennsylvania, and West Virginia. The seventh district received six bands of twenty-five pieces each, plus a thirty-member fife and drum corps, which toured Illinois, Michigan, Indiana, Wisconsin, and Iowa. The eighth district played host to five bands of twenty-five pieces each, which worked independently through Missouri, Arkansas, northern Mississippi, western Tennessee, western Kentucky, and southern Illinois. Finally, a band of fifty pieces visited the tenth district to tour Kansas, Oklahoma, Nebraska, Colorado, Wyoming, and northern New Mexico.[23]

Sousa, meanwhile, took his larger battalion band to St. Louis, Lexington, Cincinnati, and Chicago. Audiences stormed to hear the ensemble wherever it appeared. At an outdoor event in St. Louis, the "crowd grew more vehement in its demands for encores and more officious in its effort to get near" the ensemble. Finally, Sousa struck up "Over There" to lead his players away, but he ended up taking "all the crowd along, and men and women and automobiles followed." In the end, Sousa "gave the crowd just what it wanted—what it appeared to need, and it ran after him for more."[24]

Such enthusiasm for the March King gave Sousa ever more opportunities to speak with the press, and his comments became ever more jingoistic. In this, of course, he was not alone: many musicians and performing ensembles discarded German repertoire, distanced themselves from German artists, and disparaged the German influence on American culture. In May 1918, the American Defense Society's Committee on the Suppression of All Things German publicly requested that Sousa compose a march suitable to replace those of Wagner and Mendelssohn at American weddings. Sousa was quick to agree: "My only word to the young men and women of America is that from a musical standpoint it is their duty to hesitate until proper music can be prepared for their great experience. In other words, don't propose until I compose."[25]

Sousa's "Wedding March," completed near the end of July 1918, was published with great fanfare and accompanied by a publicity campaign that unfolded with remarkable speed. According to the *Musical Leader*, the band arrangement was rushed to publication at the request of the Naval Publicity Bureau so that it could be played as part of the Liberty Loan drive, and announcements were made that the piece could be performed at weddings free of royalties: "This action was taken on patriotic grounds and is further evidence of that sterling Americanism for which the Lieutenant has always been noted." Despite hopes that the march would "live forever in history as a monument to this thorough and wholehearted idealistic American," it never caught fire. Nevertheless, dozens of newspapers published extramusical programs for the piece, praises of Sousa's fight against German *Kultur*, and in a few cases defenses of Mendelssohn and Wagner.[26]

As anti-German rhetoric found greater acceptance in the public arena, Sousa's embrace of it grew in the press. Theodore Roosevelt, while celebrating well-integrated Americans of German descent, declared it a moral treason to hold any sort of hyphenated loyalty. Sousa seems to have first weighed in on this subject in December 1917, when he wrote an editorial for the *Milwaukee Journal*. His subject had been provided by a fan who asked for the March King's opinion on teaching German in the public schools. After declaring that only English-language instruction was appropriate, Sousa echoed Roosevelt's sentiments: "We first must impress our national aims on all within our gates. . . . We can best start on the proper path by making the newly arrived immigrant less conversant day by day with the forms, laws and languages of his former home." Sousa hoped that the United States could "do away with our most pernicious system of grouping the foreigner." After all, he wrote, "We want the comer to our shores to imbibe Americanism and only Americanism. The quicker we make an American out of him the better for him and for ourselves."[27]

Such rhetoric had grown even stronger by mid-1918. In a Chicago editorial, Sousa argued that one might reasonably play German music "for art's sake," but that the German—believing himself "a superman"—would insist that his was "the only music fit to play." It was therefore the duty of every American to "leave German music to the Germans." After all, Sousa wrote:

> In this western world of ours it is an undisputed fact that we have not one German tradition; we dress our women as the French suggest; our laws are based on those of the English; our ideas of chivalry are Spanish; our standard of honor is British. If we speak of the greatest writer we speak of Shakespeare; if we wish to link a poet of our land with that of another, we couple a Tennyson with a Longfellow; of a humorist, a Thackeray with a Twain; when we enumerate our states we find some named for the Spanish; some for the French; some for the English; some for the Indian; but not one remotely named for the German.

Having once supported neutrality, Sousa turned his full voice to separating American listeners from German culture: "It is the duty of every American to suppress anything and everything that in any way brings comfort, profit or satisfaction to the Hun. He has forfeited every consideration from a fair-playing world and the only way to get it through the hide of his vanity, obtuseness and stolidness is to bludgeon him physically, mentally, morally, financially, and perpetually."[28]

There are many more examples of Sousa's efforts to retreat, at least rhetorically, into jingoism: he took part in a number of efforts to identify a new national anthem (one that would avoid "The Star-Spangled Banner's" connection to a foreign power); he advocated for the National Association of Shotgun Owners, an organization that sought to prepare American civilians against foreign enemies and domestic traitors; and he even offered aiming advice to soldiers in the field: "You want to see all the Huns you can when you've got a gun handy."[29]

As with Theodore Roosevelt, the public's turn toward unbridled patriotism allowed Sousa to rediscover a place in the popular imagination. A rumor even circulated that both men might recapture their former glory by leading troops into Berlin. Sousa happily fanned the flame: "I have had many triumphs in my life. I have done things of which I am proud, but the greatest ambition of my life is to lead a band down Wilhelmstrasse in Berlin playing 'The Star Spangled Banner.' I will be satisfied with my life work when that is done." Such comments circulated widely, and many papers reported that the March King might appear in the German capital. Poet Clyde B. Wilson even set the idea to a verse that fits a bit too suspiciously to Sousa's most famous march. By the spring of 1919, vaudevillian Sidney Phillips was reciting the poem to the melody of "The Stars and Stripes Forever":

> With a brassy blast of trumpets and a gatling rip of drums,
> And a crash of cracking trombones there's a thrilling vision comes;
> And my head reels with the rhythm as the rousing strains begin
> Of the "Stars and Stripes Forever," played by Sousa in Berlin.

Oh, the splendor of the vision makes the blood beat through my veins;
And my heart pounds like the drum thuds cannonading through the strains
Of that fight-inspired, Yankee-firing, Kaiser-killing din
Of the "Stars and Stripes Forever," played by Sousa in Berlin.

I can hear the tubas bellow bold derision at the Huns
As the rumbling notes go tumbling down those wild chromatic runs;
And I hear the cornets cackle at the Kaiser and his kin,
With the "Stars and Stripes Forever," played by Sousa in Berlin.

Can't you see them lined like flag stripes, tramping past the palace door?
Full two hundred tooting Jackies and a half a hundred more.
And they raise the mongrel bristles on the Kaiser's creeping skin,
With the "Stars and Stripes Forever," played by Sousa in Berlin.

See them strut with Yankee swagger; see their jaunty caps of snow,
And the buttons fairly bursting from their jackets as they blow.
For the tune that sounds our triumph and the dirge of Prussian sin
Is the "Stars and Stripes Forever," played by Sousa in Berlin.

I can see their metal flashing as they toot to beat the band,
And with blasts of mocking music raid the air of Kaiser land.
And they shoot like Yankee gunners, with a deadly Yankee grin,
Of the "Stars and Stripes Forever," played by Sousa in Berlin.

Then I see the waving symbol of this riot-raising march,
Flaunt its colors as it's carried through Wilhelm's Triumphal Arch.
And it's here my fancy flees before real armies marching in
To the "Stars and Stripes Forever," played by Sousa in Berlin.[30]

The War's End

Much of Sousa's most aggressive language was, of course, playacting: while he may have entertained ideas about replacing the national anthem, he also served on a Bureau of Education committee, alongside German-born conductor Walter Damrosch, to standardize "The Star-Spangled Banner"; he may have offered aiming advice to soldiers, but most of his own shooting was done safely on the amateur trapshooting circuit; he may have advocated for a policy of America First, but his interests had long been international. Perhaps it is not surprising, then, that Sousa, even at the height of his jingoism, did not limit his efforts to the United States. Transcontinental tours often took the Sousa ensemble to Canada, and the war years were no exception. In July 1917, his civilian band spent the better part of a month at Montreal's Dominion Park and Toronto's Hanlan's Point. They returned in the summer of 1918 and this time added benefit concerts at Montreal's Gray

Nun's Home and Khaki Club (where they played Sousa's new setting of a Canadian poem, "In Flanders Fields").[31]

Indeed, Sousa was in Canada when the Armistice was signed; his band of navy boys had arrived in Toronto on November 10 to take part in a Victory Loan campaign. At 2:00 p.m., they paraded to Queen's Park, where they joined the Toronto Choral Society for a Sunday-afternoon concert of hymns in front of what was described as the largest crowd ever assembled in the city. News of the Armistice arrived early the next morning, and "pandemonium reigned supreme." The Victory Loan committee had already planned a parade for November 11, which now became a massive celebration. Sousa's battalion band appeared alongside Canadian veterans and civilians, and the conductor noted that "never before had he heard such roaring multitudes."[32]

After this celebration, the band returned to Great Lakes. While the ensemble was spared influenza, the bandmaster was not so lucky.[33] Ill with a badly abscessed ear, Sousa was granted permission to return to his home in Sands Point, New York. John Philip Sousa was officially relieved from duty in January 1919. Now on inactive status, he was promoted to the rank of lieutenant commander, and he would wear this uniform for much of the rest of his career.

At the war's start, Sousa had faced two problems. The conflict in Europe and the mobilization at home made his usual transcontinental and international tours at best impractical and at worst impossible. This challenge, thankfully, would prove temporary, and after the war Sousa's band could resume its touring schedule. Of greater concern was that the March King—the public persona Sousa had created for himself over a quarter century of touring—was becoming less and less relevant to American audiences. As popular culture turned away from the social dances that had so successfully accompanied his marches and from the operettas that had inspired his melodies, Sousa found himself, for the first time, out of step with the public. As one reporter put it, "The limelight passed on," and Sousa "was not the 'march king' any more."[34]

The war and his enlistment provided Sousa solutions to both of these problems. Through the navy, he could create a temporary replacement band, and while it may not have contained the caliber of players to which he was accustomed, it did allow him to remain on tour for much of the conflict. More important, from his perch as America's most visible military entertainer, Sousa was able to reclaim his former relevance, a relevance that mapped easily onto the desires and concerns of his audience. So long as the war remained distant, he could use the international crisis to remind readers of his former fame, and when the nation shifted from observant to participant, Sousa could ride public sentiment and allow his own rhetoric to mirror the growing anti-German discourse.

Just how successful an enterprise this was is difficult to assess. The same reporter who had earlier noted the passing of the limelight, declared that with the war, "Sousa's marches are springing back into popularity" and that Sousa was now "doing an army work as important as that of Pershing himself." In short, "John Philip Sousa has come back!" The band's touring schedule after the war seems to confirm that the March King had indeed returned. The year 1919 saw more than four hundred concerts in seven months, and the ensemble kept up a similar schedule through the 1925–26 tour. Nevertheless, many of his most famous players had moved on to other work during the war, and his reconstituted band never had the same following or the same loyalty to their conductor (a fact made abundantly clear by an embarrassing strike in 1920).[35]

Despite the continued activity—Sousa would conduct up to the day of his death in 1932—it is clear that the war years were the last time the March King was truly relevant. For two decades, he had straddled the emerging line between art and popular music, but as these endeavors retreated into their own corners after the war, Sousa was left standing alone, no longer timely or transcendent. As professional concert bands gave way to school ensembles in the 1920s, Sousa became a precursor rather than a contemporary. This process was well under way before the war, but an international conflict allowed for a moment where once again a military bandleader could serve as national hero, political barometer, and reflection of shifting trends in American politics and popular opinion.

Notes

1. Sousa's letter can be found as Sousa to Walker, January 23, 1918, Sousa Family Papers, United States Marine Band Library and Archives, Washington, DC (hereafter MBL). Information on the premiere is from "Sousa Draws Big Crowd," clipping labeled *Poughkeepsie (NY) News*, June 26, 1918, HJ 49, p. 53. MBL houses more than eighty press books—cataloged by HJ number—that contain newspaper accounts related to Sousa and his ensemble. These are now available online through the Marine Band's website: https://www.marineband .marines.mil/About/Library-and-Archives/Sousa-Band-Press-Books/. Sousa later claimed to have encountered McCrae's text in July 1917 when the poet, through Walker, asked for a musical setting. See John Philip Sousa, *Marching Along: Recollections of Men, Women and Music* (Boston: Hale, Cushman, and Flint, 1928; reprinted and ed. Paul E. Bierley, Westerville, OH: Integrity Press, 1994), 321 (page citations are to the reprint edition). It is clear through Sousa's correspondence that he believed Walker either controlled or could secure final permission for the use of the text. See, for example, Sousa to Walker, January 14, 1918, Sousa Family Papers, MBL. Subsequently, the poet's brother addressed textual inconsistencies, including the blow-grow discrepancy, in McCrae to Sousa, February 13, 1918, MBL.

2. On Sousa's early career, see Patrick Warfield, *Making the March King: John Philip Sousa's Washington Years, 1854–1893* (Urbana: University of Illinois Press, 2013). Sousa's song may have been more powerful in performance than it seems from the sheet music: for the first performance, he chose the British opera singer Ruby Helder, billed as the "woman with the man's voice." For details on the many settings of McCrae's poem, see Jennifer A. Ward,

"American Musical Settings of 'In Flanders Fields' and the Great War," *Journal of Musicological Research* 33 (2014): 96–129. See also the chapters in this volume by Gayle Magee and Brian C. Thompson.

3. Sousa to Walker, January 14, 1918, MBL.

4. "Music of course" is from "Sousa Talks of the War," *Elwood (IN) Call Leader*, October 21, 1914, HJ 39, p. 16. Sousa's concern about Kreisler and Muck is from "Sousa Deplores War's Effects upon Music," clipping labeled *Pittsburgh Sun*, September 17, 1914, HJ 39, p. 1. Both men would survive the war, the former wounded and the latter banished. Kreisler told his own story in *Fritz Kreisler: Four Weeks in the Trenches* (Boston: Houghton Mifflin, 1915). Muck's wartime difficulties have been assessed by many, including Joseph Horowitz, *Moral Fire: Musical Portraits from America's Fin de Siècle* (Berkeley: University of California Press, 2012), 62–71; and Matthew Mugmon, "Patriotism, Art, and 'The Star-Spangled Banner' in World War I: A New Look at the Karl Muck Episode," *Journal of Musicological Research* 33 (2014): 4–26. "Uninteresting" is from "Sousa Discusses Elimination of Music in Warfare," clipping labeled *Musical Leader* (Chicago), August 29, 1915, HJ 41, p. 105.

5. "I have not" is from "Sousa Talks of the War." "I am told" is from "Sousa Glad There Is No Frontier in Music," clipping labeled *Pittsburgh Sun*, September 15, 1914, HJ 39, front cover.

6. "I have played" is from "War, without Music, Passe," clipping labeled *Sioux City (IA) Journal*, May 6, [1915], HJ 41, p. 17.

7. For a detailing of performances at the Hippodrome during this period, see Milton Epstein, "The New York Hippodrome: Spectacle on Sixth Avenue from 'A Yankee Circus on Mars' to 'Better Times,' a Complete Chronology of Performances, 1905–1939" (Ph.D. diss., New York University, 1993).

8. "Every good-natured" is from Sousa, *Marching Along*, 306. "A Bohemian" is from "Sousa Is Kissed Again," clipping labeled *Baltimore Evening News*, January 10, 1916, HJ 42, p. 83.

9. The quotation is from "Sousa Says U.S. Needs Best Navy," clipping labeled *Columbus (OH) Citizen*, April 17, 1915, HJ 41, p. 8. The standard source detailing the impact of German military policy on American public opinion is Ernest R. May, *The World War and American Isolation, 1914–1917* (Cambridge, MA: Harvard University Press, 1959).

10. Wilson's comment appears in his address to the Daughters of the American Revolution, October 11, 1915. The announcement of Sousa's march was made in "Wilson Inspires Sousa," *Washington Post*, October 16, 1915.

11. "Celebration of Washington's Birthday at Washington Memorial Hall," *American Revolution Magazine* 48, no. 4 (1916): 255–58. For a study focusing on the internal struggles of federal policy makers in the wake of German attacks, see John Patrick Finnegan, *Against the Specter of a Dragon: The Campaign for American Military Preparedness, 1914–1917* (Westport, CT: Greenwood Press, 1974), 57–72.

12. "John Philip Sousa Praises 'Wake Up, America,' New Preparedness Song Introduced at Hippodrome," clipping labeled *American*, March 5, 1916, HJ 43, p. 15.

13. Ibid. The political fight over preparedness is discussed in Finnegan, *Against the Specter of a Dragon*, 128–29.

14. "'War Is Here, Hit Now, Hit Hard,' Is Shout of 15,000," clipping labeled [New York] *Evening World*, March 23, 1917, HJ 45, p. 20.

15. "Patriotism Fired by Sousa's Music," clipping labeled [New York] *Sun,* April 13, 1917, HJ 45, p. 24.

16. The quotation is from "Sousa Would Join Roosevelt," clipping labeled [New York] *Telegraph,* April 13, 1917, HJ 45, p. 20. For details on Roosevelt's remarkable efforts to secure a military unit, see J. Lee Thompson, *Never Call Retreat: Theodore Roosevelt and the Great War* (New York: Palgrave Macmillan, 2013), 171–75.

17. The quotation is from "Sousa Coming to Teach Music at Great Lakes," *Chicago Tribune,* May 23, 1917. Carpenter's wartime efforts are briefly discussed in Howard Pollack, *Skyscraper Lullaby: The Life and Music of John Alden Carpenter* (Washington, DC: Smithsonian Institution Press, 1995), 157–63. Details on Sousa's service can be found in Jill M. Sullivan, "John Philip Sousa as Music Educator and Fundraiser during World War I," *Journal of Historical Research in Music Education* (2017): 1–27.

18. The poem can be found in Sousa, *Marching Along,* 311. Surprisingly little has been written about these "dollar-a-year" men, many of whom—like Sousa—actually received a dollar per month. For a profile of another such patriot, see Robert D. Cuff, "A 'Dollar-a-Year Man' in Government: George N. Peek and the War Industries Board," *Business History Review* 41 (Winter 1967): 404–20. Peek was an agricultural economist and equipment executive.

19. "A little" is from Edward C. Moore, "Run the Scale, Sousa's Edict," clipping labeled *Chicago Evening Journal,* May 31, 1917, HJ 45, p. 88. "Unruly mob" and "a telegram" are from Sousa, *Marching Along,* 311–12. For details on Sousa's training system, see Michael D. Besch, *A Navy Second to None: The History of U.S. Naval Training in World War I* (Westport, CT: Greenwood Press, 2002), 87.

20. For an example, see "M'Adoo Sees Victory with Liberty Loan," *Chicago Daily Tribune,* October 3, 1917. For an overview of the economic side of war bonds, see Sung Won Kang and Hugh Rockoff, "Capitalizing Patriotism: The Liberty Loans of World War I," National Bureau of Economic Research, Working Paper 11919 (2006), http://www.nber.org/papers/w11919. For another composer who supported the bond movement, taking a very different path, see Gayle Magee's discussion of Charles Ives and the insurance industry in chapter 2 of this volume.

21. "Fiddle strings" is from a clipping labeled *Dallas Times,* November 20, 1917, HJ 47, p. 115. "Another famous" is from a clipping labeled *Cleveland Plain Dealer,* November 24, 1917, HJ 47, p. 109. "A war" is from "New Tax Imminent," *New York Clipper,* December 5, 1917, HJ 47, p. 118. The poem first appeared in "A Line o' Type or Two," *Chicago Daily Tribune,* November 24, 1917, and was widely reprinted. Sousa would later set another lyric by Lee as the song "Pushing On." It appeared in the *Tribune* on September 29, 1918.

22. "The revolution" and "that is" are from "Average Age of Sousa's Band 20," clipping labeled *Indianapolis Times,* April 13, 1918, HJ 48, p. 45. "I felt" is from "Lonely Minus Whiskers," clipping labeled *Chicago News,* November 19, 1917, HJ 47, p. 95. Another composer, Irving Berlin, reinvented himself to some extent after entering military service; see Jeffrey Magee's account in chapter 5 of this volume.

23. For a pictorial history of the band's involvement in the third campaign, see C. R. Ketridge, "Great Lakes Band the Liberty Band," *Great Lakes Recruit* 4, no. 6 (1918): 6–19, 98. The ensemble was also involved in the smaller fourth campaign, held between September

28 and October 19, 1918. It was for this fourth campaign that Sousa wrote the march "Flags of Freedom," using national airs from Allied countries. He was only tangentially involved in the postwar Victory Loan campaign.

24. "Throng Hears Sousa's Band in Street Concert," *St. Louis Post-Dispatch*, April 7, 1918.

25. The request was reported in "Ban Hun Wedding Marches, Seek Substitute by Mr. Sousa," *New York Herald*, May 28, 1918, HJ 49, p. 17. The quotation is from "'Don't Propose until I Compose,' Sousa Warning," *New York Herald*, May 30, 1918, HJ 49, p. 13. For a useful overview of the anti-German discourse in American music, see Jessica C. E. Gienow-Hecht, *Sound Diplomacy: Music and Emotions in Transatlantic Relations, 1850–1920* (Chicago: University of Chicago Press, 2012), 177–209.

26. The quotation is from "Sousa's Wedding March Featured," clipping labeled *Musical Leader* (Chicago), October 12, 1918, HJ 49, p. 142. For a hypothetical program, see "Go to the Hitching Post to the Tune of a Yankee March," clipping labeled *Detroit News Tribune*, July 18, 1918, HJ 49, p. 112. For thoughtful commentary on the subject of *Kultur*, see "On Wedding Marches," clipping labeled *Musical American*, June 13, 1918, HJ 49, p. 91; and "Wedding Marches and Loyalty," clipping labeled *Minneapolis Tribune*, June 30, 1918, HJ 49, p. 88. A useful examination of anti-German rhetoric in one American city is Barbara T. Tischler, "One Hundred Percent Americanism and Music in Boston during World War I," *American Music* 4 (Summer 1986): 164–76. Sousa continued his compositional activity during 1917 with the marches "Liberty Loan," "U.S. Field Artillery," and "Naval Reserve," the last of which was adapted from Sousa's song "Blue Ridge, I'm Coming Back to You." The year 1918 saw the songs "We Are Coming," "Pushing On," and "When the Boys Come Sailing Home" and the marches "The Volunteers," "Chantyman's March," "USAAC," "Solid Men to the Front," "Sabre and Spurs," "Anchor and Star," and "Bullets and Bayonets."

27. The quotation is from "Wean Immigrant from Alienism, Says Sousa," clipping labeled *Milwaukee Journal*, December 12, 1917, HJ 47, p. 120. Sousa had endorsed the idea of "pure" Americans somewhat earlier, but seemed to suggest that "the hyphenated American is disappearing" by natural means. See "Sousa Says Pure American Is Needed," clipping labeled *Pittsburgh Post*, September 23, [1915], HJ 41, p. 65. Roosevelt articulated his position in a 1915 speech to the Knights of Columbus. For details, see Thompson, *Never Call Retreat*, 49, 94–95, 141–42. On the backlash toward immigrants and its role in national politics, see Louis L. Gerson, *The Hyphenate in Recent American Politics and Diplomacy* (Lawrence: University Press of Kansas, 1964), 47–95.

28. Sousa, "Leave German Music to Germans," clipping labeled *Musical Leader* (Chicago), October 10, 1918, HJ 49, p. 143. A far more subtle response to the dominance of German culture was expressed by Claude Debussy, who was in far closer proximity to the war; see Barbara L. Kelly's account in chapter 3 of this volume.

29. Sousa, quoted in "Sousa Says Shoot with Eyes Open," clipping labeled *New York Telegraph*, July 7, 1918, HJ 49, p. 105.

30. The quotation is from "Sousa Would Lead Band in Berlin," clipping labeled *Montreal Star*, June 22, 1918, HJ 49, p. 78. The poem seems to have first appeared in the *Indianapolis Star* on December 23, 1917. It was widely reprinted. On Phillips's performance, see *Variety*, March 7, 1919, 32, and March 21, 1919, 20.

31. For details on Sousa's touring career, see Paul Edmund Bierley, *The Incredible Band of John Philip Sousa* (Urbana: University of Illinois Press, 2006), 143–94. For information on Sousa's efforts regarding "The Star-Spangled Banner," see Patrick Warfield, "Educators in Search of an Anthem: Standardizing 'The Star-Spangled Banner' during the First World War," *Journal of the Society for American Music* 12 (August 2018): 268–316.

32. "Band Battalion Makes Big Hit in Toronto," *Great Lakes Bulletin* 2, no. 115 (1918): 2.

33. Sousa survived the flu but many did not; see Deniz Ertan's chapter in this volume.

34. Franchon Carson, "War Makes a 'Come-Backer' of Lieut-Sousa," clipping labeled *Chicago Post*, June 29, 1917, HJ 45, p. 90.

35. The quotation is from Carson. For Sousa's later career, see Bierley, *Incredible Band*, 31–40.

CHAPTER 5

From the Great War to *White Christmas*

The Long Reach of Irving Berlin's *Yip Yip Yaphank*

JEFFREY MAGEE

In November 1943, an American all-soldier musical revue by Irving Berlin entitled *This Is the Army* opened at the London Palladium. One scene in act 2 included two songs that connected past and present, America and Britain. In tones reminiscent of a radio broadcast, an announcer introduced the first number with a nostalgic tinge: "And now we take you back twenty-five years to another war and another soldier show. We take you back to *Yip Yip Yaphank*, our soldier show of the last war—singing the song he wrote and sang then, Mr. Irving Berlin."[1]

The curtain opened to reveal Berlin in his vintage World War I uniform, sitting on a cot in a tent, wrapping a puttee around his ankle. When the orchestra began playing, Berlin stood and stepped toward the footlights as the curtain closed behind him.[2] Everyone in the house knew what was coming next: the whimsical soldier's lament "Oh! How I Hate to Get Up in the Morning." One of the most popular American songs of the Great War, it had remained well known on both sides of the Atlantic and stood among Berlin's most enduring standards for decades.[3]

Sixteen men joined Berlin onstage for the second chorus. When they finished, the packed 2,286-seat Palladium rose en masse for a standing ovation. Berlin stepped forward, quieted the crowd, and, according to the script, spoke directly to the audience: "And now I'd like you to hear a song I wrote since I've been here." Backed by the same chorus of sixteen men, he then sang a song written just days earlier: "My British Buddy."[4] According to the show's stage manager, Alan Ander-son, Berlin then invited the audience to join in for one more chorus, creating "an emotional moment . . . with applause and 'bravos' — and tears."[5] A bond of transat-lantic citizenship, established toward the end of World War I, had been reinforced by words, music, and ritual participation "in what turned out to be the best per-formance of the show we'd ever given," according to Anderson. "What made this show in particular a triumph was the dazzling audience to go with the dazzle of the show—added to which was the response of sophisticated, theatre-wise Londoners and the genuinely warm, loving friendship of the British for the American soldier."[6] That friendship yielded real results, for all profits from the show's performances in the British Isles went to the British Services Charities Committee, a gesture acknowledged by Lady Mountbatten in a precurtain speech.[7] Berlin had declared in the London *Daily Mail*, "I hope the song will be a big hit, not only because of the money it will bring into the British services, but because it means something more to me. I want it to bring about a still closer relationship between our two countries."[8]

For Irving Berlin, songwriting was transactional, and the transaction remained incomplete until the song reached an audience that responded with warmth, applause, singing, or investment in the products and by-products of songwriting: sheet music, theater tickets, and sound recordings. Business savvy and exceptional craftsmanship went together. But above all, the songwriter sought a human con-nection that enriched the social bond with his audience. And no Irving Berlin show so meaningfully engaged a bigger and more appreciative audience in its initial run and tour than *This Is the Army*: 1,264 performances for more than 2.5 million mili-tary and civilian spectators between 1942 and 1945. The success of the show's 1943 British tour had convinced General Dwight Eisenhower that Berlin should take the company to other war zones, including Italy, North Africa, the Middle East, and the South Pacific. More than that, a feature film based on the show, made in Hol-lywood before the company embarked for England and starring future politicians George Murphy and Ronald Reagan, would become the Warner Brothers' biggest grossing movie to date, second only to MGM's *Gone with the Wind* in that era.[9] For all of these reasons, Berlin, maker of hit songs and shows across more than half a century, would go on to call *This Is the Army* "the best thing I've ever been connected with."[10]

So important was *T.I.T.A.*, as the company often called it, that Berlin and his staff kept notes and records of all activities during the show's overseas tour in preparation for a book about it. Berlin himself began to write that book but never came close to finishing it. In the short time he spent on it, his mind went back to the Great War. "No story of *T.I.T.A.* would be complete without beginning at the beginning," he wrote, "and the beginning is *Yip Yip Yaphank*."[11]

"A Military Mess"

Beginning is an apt term in more ways than one: it applies to Berlin's legal status as an American. Berlin became a US citizen on February 6, 1918, and he was drafted into the army soon thereafter, just shy of his thirtieth birthday. By this time, Berlin had already achieved international renown as the writer of "Alexander's Ragtime Band" (1911) and several other hit songs since his breakout year of 1909. He had also made his mark on Broadway with several numbers for the *Ziegfeld Follies* and his first show, *Watch Your Step* (1914), an on-the-town escapade featuring the latest dance crazes modeled by Vernon and Irene Castle and a crowd-pleasing opera spoof. Now, as a celebrity soldier, he was stationed at Camp Upton in Yaphank, Long Island. As he reported later, he hated many aspects of army life, especially reveille. But as Berlin had done before, he turned privation into opportunity and convinced his commanding officer that he could best realize his patriotic duty by writing a camp show featuring the soldiers around him. For that he was given the rank of sergeant—and the right to sleep as late as he wished.[12]

Yip Yip Yaphank,[13] conceived and developed at Camp Upton in the summer of 1918, established the style and structure of a show that he would create for the Second World War, and his catalyst was the challenge of fusing army content with show-business conventions. Hatched in the heyday of the revue, the World War I show reflected the revue's impulse to adopt and parody aspects of current music and theater, while being unified around a central topical theme: the US Army and the common soldier's experience. In this show, Berlin discovered the musical theater in army life—a discovery that would continue to resonate in his work for decades, not just in *T.I.T.A.* but in the films *Alexander's Ragtime Band* (1938) and *White Christmas* (1954) as well.

Billed as "A Military 'Mess' Cooked Up by the Boys of Camp Upton (in Aid of the Fund to Establish a Community House at Camp Upton for the Wives, Mothers, and Sweethearts Who Visit Their Boys at Camp),"[14] *Yip Yip Yaphank* ran for just thirty-two performances at two different Manhattan theaters: the Century (August 19–31, 1918) and the Lexington (September 2–14, 1918). Although the run was brief by Broadway standards, it actually had to be extended from the limited eight-performance run that had been planned.[15] This was a remarkable achievement for a show in the Century Theatre, a massive house with more than twenty-three hundred seats. The show succeeded beyond expectation—earning a reported $50,000 from its packed houses by September 1—and had to be moved because the Century was scheduled to host a very popular Al Jolson vehicle called *Sinbad* that had moved there from the Winter Garden.[16] Sime Silverman, founder and lead writer of the premier entertainment publication *Variety*, witnessed opening night and the "admiration" of the "over-seasoned Broadwayites" in the theater and predicted that the show could run for "a couple of months."[17] The *New York Times* likewise mused, after reflecting on the opening-week crowds, that the show "probably could go ahead for seven or eight more [weeks] if the members of its cast were not required to become soldiers again."[18]

The show had come together quickly. Berlin's inscription on the bound manuscript piano-vocal score indicates that it was written in August 1918, and most of the copyrights of the show's numbers share that date.[19] The cast and crew moved to Manhattan during dress rehearsals. Every day they marched in formation from their quarters to the theater.[20] The march itself drummed up interest in the show and, like a minstrel parade, served as a harbinger of a show-business tradition that would shape the show within the theater. When the show opened, guards stood near the entrance to impart the aura of an official military function; as *Variety* reported, however, the guards made a point of smiling. The spectacle on the street, then, broadcast the show's savvy synthesis of military protocol and musical theater.

Military camp shows were nothing new. Indeed, thousands of soldiers created and performed in ad hoc minstrel shows, vaudevilles, revues, and musical comedies in both wars.[21] But for the most part, such shows never went beyond their home camps. The notion of staging a soldier show *on Broadway* required an imaginative leap, for it would be inevitably compared with the genre's paradigms. Indeed, an all-soldier revue might have seemed a contradiction in terms in the genre's heyday. Unlike most revues, most notably the *Ziegfeld Follies*, about which the show features an entire number, *Yaphank* could not depend on stars or feminine display. The *New York Times* viewed the largely amateur cast as an "immeasurable advantage over the commercial musical show, for the fact that it is being played by men in service can never be lost sight of."[22] Moreover, two shows staged earlier in 1918 had paved the way for Berlin's undertaking: a musical comedy called *Good-Bye, Bill*, created and performed by the US Army Ambulance Corps, and *Biff-Bang!*, a revue staged by the Pelham (NY) Naval Training Camp.[23] Both shows received strong reviews, and the *Times* even went so far as to claim in the spring of 1918—in a report that might well have spurred Berlin's vision—that "these 'service' shows . . . are the high spot in the past year of musical entertainment."[24] Still, most of Berlin's cast members were amateurs. Sime Silverman noted with awe that "of all these 350 boys not over 20 ever appeared on the professional stage before. . . . It's only show people who can fully appreciate what that means."

The *Yaphank* cast members were amateurs in more than theater. They were young recruits and had never seen combat. The servicemen were thus performing multiple roles at once: civilians acting as soldiers and soldiers acting like many other people. Indeed, much of the show's impact and humor depended on masquerade. With its all-male, all-white (with a notable exception), and mostly amateur cast, Berlin's show opened up opportunities for the performers to act like anyone but who they were: white women, black men, black women, black children, and celebrities, both male and female. Some of the privates impersonated officers, and Berlin—a real celebrity who had been made an officer—got to portray a lowly private in one of the scenes that audiences found most humorous and memorable.

That minstrelsy fueled the style, spirit, and structure of the masquerade deserves comment. In the long view, Berlin's musical theater represents a synthesis of all that was available on the American musical theater scene, from opera to vaudeville, but minstrelsy formed its foundation, for it was a flexible, abundant source from which to construct his vision of a distinctively American musical theater. Berlin had engaged with minstrelsy since his career began, and it is no wonder since it continued to thrive into the first decades of the twentieth century, in prominent companies such as those of George Primrose and Lou Dockstader and in the troupe led by George M. Cohan and Sam H. Harris (the Cohan and Harris Minstrels)— the latter two being, respectively, Berlin's idol and future partner. Minstrelsy did not appeal simply for its racial masquerade, however. The so-called minstrel first part, with the full troupe seated on risers onstage, and with the formal interlocutor smoothly directing the traffic of solo and group performances of skits and songs, meanwhile exchanging riddles and jokes with the end men who often mocked him: all of this required masterful timing, a sense of pace and seamless flow among varied acts, which fired Berlin's imagination. (The closest modern equivalent to reach the American mainstream was Garrison Keillor and *Prairie Home Companion*.)

In that spirit, the first several scenes and musical numbers featured nearly three hundred soldiers seated on steep risers in conventional fashion. A sergeant played the role of interlocutor, the master of ceremonies who moves the show along, announces individual performances, and banters with the end men, here played by the wise-cracking privates seated on the stage at either end of the risers. (Only the end men appeared in blackface; the rest of the soldiers were "in the conventional khaki.")[25] In the beginning, the Sergeant-Interlocutor calls the troops/troupe to attention. A captain enters and delivers a rousing speech, telling the soldier-actors that their "enemies" were in front "and to show them no quarter," according to Silverman, who wrote an unusually detailed account of the show that helps to clarify what happened onstage.[26] Silverman failed to note that, by equating the audience with the "enemy," the show played off of the theatrical slang that a successful performance is one that "kills."

Silverman reported a typical comic exchange that bridged military and theatrical impulses. Comedian Bobby Higgins had been trying to tell a joke, wrote Silverman, "but could not secure permission. When finally allowed, it was: 'Why are the legitimate theatres losing business to the picture houses?' 'Because,' said Mr. Higgins, 'it is easier to fil-um.' For that he was ordered before a court martial.

When told he would be shot at four in the morning, Higgins replied he did not get up that early. And again, for that one, he was ordered executed immediately." Higgins won a reprieve, apparently, because he then sang a song. The scene encapsulated an ingenious merger of minstrel-show repartee and military regimentation.

The musical numbers also took off from minstrel conventions. A "Tambourine Drill" exhibited some fancy work with one of minstrelsy's stock instruments instead of rifles, demonstrating the company's collective choreographic precision. For it, Berlin wrote a vigorous, syncopated march tune that he would strategically place twice more in the show—the last time with words for the stirring grand finale. As in a typical minstrel-show first part, a quartet sang a sentimental old favorite in four-part harmony, with Berlin changing the words to suit the occasion, like many minstrel lyricists before him. The song was the nineteenth-century parlor ballad "Silver Threads among the Gold," about growing old and gray in an enduring romance. Berlin wrote:

> Darling I am not too old;
> I am only twenty-three.
> There's no silver 'mongst the gold,
> And the draft is after me."

The number went over so well with the opening-night audience that the quartet repeated it several times, according to Silverman.

A courtship number ("Mandy [Sterling Silver Moon]") and a wedding number ("Ding Dong") also made predictable appearances, allowing for the minstrel show's double masquerade of blackfaced white men in drag.[27] Comedian Danny Healy played Mandy as a dozen other men portrayed "girls" and "boys" in the chorus. The "girls" are described in the program as "pickaninnies," theatrical lingo for little black girls often sporting stiff, Topsy-style braids sticking out from the head in all directions.[28] In the wedding scene, Bobby Higgins—having avoided execution in the previous scene—sang "Ding Dong" with a chorus, while "real colored picks" (not blacked-up men in drag), as Silverman put it, held up the bride's train. (The bride was played by Private Howard Friend—who won claim to fame as the soldier who earned the dedication of "Oh! How I Hate to Get Up in the Morning" because he occupied the cot next to Berlin's at Camp Upton.)[29] The appearance of "real" African Americans—three boys and one girl—must have come as a surprise to the audience led to expect an all-white-male show.[30] More than that, two critics singled out the little girl for special praise. Silverman noted that she won "a riot of applause with her mannerisms and sense of rhythm." And *Theatre Magazine* made the racially pointed observation that "the only real lady in the cast [was] a colored baby-vampire, who acted as flower-girl, and fairly stopped proceedings with a pair of eyes that would be worth a million dollars in the movies if they were topped with Pickford curls instead of Topsy pigtails."[31] The final section of the song, featuring the wedding vows, forms a three-way musical dialogue among the minister, the bride, and the groom, with the groom in a hurry to get to the end, where he sings, "And now I'll kiss the bride." It remains unclear whether the two men then proceeded to kiss, but that was clearly the line's comic implication. Either way, "Ding Dong" struck Silverman as one of the three from the show that "will be popular hits." (That it actually enjoyed only modest success beyond the show only serves to suggest its effectiveness onstage.)

Other numbers put military spins on song and stage conventions. In "The Ragtime Razor Brigade," Berlin tapped into a well of late-nineteenth of imagery connected with so-called coon songs—a stage stereotype of the aggressive razor-wielding black bully—while updating it for a time when African American troops had seen combat in modern war. The song avoids the stage dialect spellings common to such songs, perhaps because the refrain is presented as the words of an officer giving the orders, but its pairing of the terms *ragtime* and *razor* in the context of a minstrel-show sequence leaves no doubt about its racial implications.

The minstrel sequence also offered two topical songs that link soldier and civilian interests. In "What a Difference a Uniform Will Make," a soldier relates how an army uniform has increased his romantic possibilities in an early exemplar of a Berlin song in which clothes make the man. Another topical number, "Bevo," focused on the closest thing to alcohol that a soldier could drink during wartime. Here is a perfect example of Berlin's knack for zeroing in on a current topic that both soldiers and civilians could laugh about. Bevo was a nonalcoholic malt beverage introduced by Anheuser-Busch after the US armed forces prohibited alcoholic beverages in 1916. It was probably the most widely known of many such drinks called "cereal beverages" and "near beer" that were on the market in the wartime period, as breweries came to grips with the inevitability of Prohibition.[32] "Bevo" represents a rare early example of product placement.[33] With Prohibition on the horizon, Anheuser-Busch surely understood that any publicity was good publicity, and the company reportedly offered Berlin $10,000 for this particular "advertisement." Berlin donated the money to help build Camp Upton's Community House.[34]

The minstrel sequence excited the opening-night crowd. While noting lapses of memory and nerve among the performers, Silverman raved about it and its impact on the audience. "In the opening scene, a minstrel first part, 277 were on stage at the finale—and not a miss. . . . The unison . . . was near perfection. 'Bones' and 'banjos' always in accord without a blemish. There were 32 'bones' in the front line and the 'banjos' extended high up into the flies almost." Every individual act within the minstrel show earned his praise. The audience, which included "army and navy dignitaries" as well as celebrities such as Al Jolson, Irene Castle, and George M. Cohan, was also demonstrative.[35] During the minstrel sequence, Silverman perceived a shift in the audience's collective attitude, from benevolent tolerance to true enjoyment: "The first part woke up the house. Their early attitude of forebearance [*sic*] because 'it's for the Service' gave way to pleasure, then admiration, and as the show progressed the house realized it was watching one of the best and most novel entertainments Broadway has ever witnessed."

That Silverman could claim that a revue with a prominent and extended minstrel-show component could be one of the "most novel" Broadway shows may seem hyperbolic. But it is more understandable if we consider the fundamental creative insight, a fundamentally American one, embodied in the show's opening scene: the realization that the army and the minstrel show shared several qualities. Both were all-male preserves, and both required their members to be highly trained and operate with precision as a collective body. Both, moreover, depended on a rigid hierarchy that featured a single man in charge of concerted action; the minstrel show's interlocutor is an officer leading the men through a show. The end men and other comedians drawn from the ensemble are the common soldiers who make jokes within a system in which they must perform their jobs on orders.

The act 1 finale, "Send a Lot of Jazz Bands over There," merged the country's newly exportable musical style and its army's mission—with a nod to George M. Cohan's recent hit, "Over There." The past year of 1917–18 had seen Tin Pan Alley's eager embrace of all things jazz not long after the Original Dixieland Jazz Band's appearances at Reisenweber's restaurant on West Fifty-Eighth Street, in early 1917. Berlin, as usual, had been among the first songwriters to embrace the jazz fad, with his summer 1917 publication of "Mr. Jazz Himself."[36]

It seems quite possible that Berlin's act 1 finale was an extended number that may have included a medley of other songs—as suggested in a line of his refrain: "Make 'em play a lot of snappy airs." Certainly, the scene's spectacle invited a much longer musical exhibition than the song's verse and chorus indicate. Silverman reported that "it finished off with the drops going up showing a dozen or more pianos and players perched up on a high platform, and made a striking spectacle."

The rhetoric of the song's music and lyrics deserves scrutiny, for in them Berlin deploys the words and sounds of *ragtime* and *jazz* as synonyms referring to a distinctive American style that Berlin himself developed. To signal that fusion, and Berlin's role in it, he launches the verse with phrases that are clearly modeled on the analogous passage in "Alexander's Ragtime Band."

The chorus cements the conflation of jazz and ragtime as agents of morale building—specifically the Berlin brand of ragtime embodied in his most famous song to date:

Send a lot of jazz bands over there
To make the boys feel glad.
Send a troupe of Alexanders
With a ragtime band to Flanders.

It would be easy to claim that this lyric simply reflects the period's widespread confusion about the difference between ragtime and jazz.[37] Yet given the verbal exactitude that was the hallmark of Berlin's writing, it might be more accurate to suggest that the lyric aims to *capitalize* on that confusion and to offer clarity by implicating his own work in the discourse—as if to claim "Alexander's Ragtime Band" (a metonym for all of Berlin's other "ragtime" songs) as the wellspring of jazz. That theme, implied here, would become explicit two decades later in the 1938 film *Alexander's Ragtime Band*—where the violinist-bandleader (played by Tyrone Power) who established ragtime with the title song becomes the featured performer in the climactic "jazz" concert at Carnegie Hall.[38]

Act 2 reset the scene in Camp Upton to set up the show's hit number. In the midst of a show in which so many musical numbers spoofed and echoed musical theater conventions and trends, one song stood out as entirely grown from the army camp experience. The story of "Oh! How I Hate to Get Up in the Morning" has been told many times, by Berlin himself and his many biographers. "There were a lot of things about army life I didn't like," Berlin later recalled in an oft-quoted statement.

> And the thing I didn't like most of all was reveille. I hated it. I hated it so much that I used to lie awake nights thinking about how much I hated it. To make things worse I had this assignment that kept me working late into the evening, so I didn't get too much sleep. But I wanted to be a good soldier. So every morning when the bugle blew I'd jump right out of bed just as if I liked getting up early. The other soldiers thought I was a little too eager about it and they hated me. That's why I finally wrote a song about it.[39]

If, as Charles Hamm has claimed, many of Berlin's early songs may be heard as "biographical documents,"[40] then we could well extend that claim to Berlin's musical complaint about reveille. His comically hyperbolic plans for vengeance may be the easiest to trace directly to his experience. Berlin wrote the song on June 18, 1918, and published it before the show opened.[41] Thus, from the beginning, it had a life apart from the show. One of his biographers, Edward Jablonski, notes that soon after Berlin wrote it, "the song spread through his barracks and then around the rest of his camp, raising his status in the eyes of his fellow draftees. This was subversive stuff, considering the tenor of the patriotic Tin Pan Alley outpouring typified by Cohan's 'Over There.'"[42]

If not quite "subversive," the song nevertheless had the effect of cutting closer to the truth of army camp life than other popular songs depicting soldiers as rugged, manly, and proudly patriotic. Reviews of opening night reveal that the song actually had spread well beyond camp before the show opened. Silverman referred to it as "already popular among war songs," and the *New York Times* even called it a "classic bugler lyric" and an "old" number that was the "most appreciated" by the opening-night audience.[43]

Part of the number's appeal lay in Berlin's inspired choice to set the lyrics in the style of a quickstep march. That is, instead of the heavy two-beat tread of earnest march tunes like Cohan's "Over There" (or Cohan's earlier hit, "Yankee Doodle Boy"), Berlin opted for a skipping triplet pattern known from Sousa marches such as "The Washington Post." The verse quickly sets up a lightly ironic tone, claiming that army life "is simply wonderful," the "food is great," and it's all "very lovely." Pivoting on an emphatic "but," Berlin then launches the refrain, including its catchy wake-up line, "You've got to get up, You've got to get up, / You've got to get up this morning!" set to a paraphrase of "Reveille" in that lilting 6/8 meter. What really lends the song its humor, however, is its hyperbolic plans for revenge on the bugler, including the line "amputate his *reveille* / And step upon it *heavily*," with its unique three-syllable rhyme, and the second refrain's double-rhyming claim that he'll then "get that oth*er pup* / The one who wakes the bugl*er up*."[44]

The number also demonstrated keen theatrical sense by marking the first appearance of the show's creator and star—a gifted and proven vaudevillian headliner. Up to this point, Berlin himself had not been seen onstage, so when an officer came to Berlin's tent calling for him to get up, the show created a great deal of anticipation that its creator was about to emerge—not quite yet in full uniform, as it turned out. As *Theatre Magazine* reported, "Of course, there was a welcome that rocked the theatre, but to his credit as a good actor, there he stood, while his friends waited for a nod of recognition, staring dreamily ahead, and buttoning up his coat."[45]

The act continued with impersonations of *Ziegfeld Follies* performers (whose show competed for audiences across town at the New Amsterdam Theatre); another appearance by Berlin as a lowly private on "kitchen patrol," in a song called "Kitchen Police (Poor Little Me)"; and a scene set in the YMCA featuring a soldier writing a comforting letter home to his mother, in song: "(I Can Always Find a Little Sunshine in) The Y.M.C.A." Twenty-five years later, during the Second World War, a reviewer would remember it fondly as a "touching little ballad."[46] At some point, toward the end of, or just after, the YMCA sequence, "the boys were alerted that they were going overseas," Berlin recalled.[47]

Then came the coup de théâtre. The ensuing finale trumped all that preceded it by slicing through the show's layers of theatrical reflexivity and conjuring the reality of war. The vigorous syncopated music that had accompanied the well-synchronized "drill dances" in both acts now reappeared with lyrics as the men marched down ramps and into the aisles singing the stirring march-style refrain "We're on Our Way to France."

In some accounts, the final performance introduced a novel twist of making it appear that the soldiers were actually going straight from the theater to a boat that would take them to France. As biographer Edward Jablonski put it, "For that last night . . . [a]s the cast, in full uniform, with rifles and other military regalia, sang 'We're on Our Way to France,' Berlin led them not into the wings but offstage, down the aisle, and out of the theater. The audience, in midcheer, was stunned: clearly, the men were literally demonstrating the lyric of the song. According to reports, there were gasps, muffled outcries, sobs—the soldiers were, it seemed, bound for a troopship, the trenches, possibly death."[48]

Yet *Variety*, and Berlin himself, indicated that the notion of marching down the aisles had been part of the show's original conception. *Variety's* review of *opening* night noted that "many troopers marched down the aisle and onto the boat in full equipment." And Berlin himself remembered, "They marched through the Theater, went out to the street and backstage where they boarded a transport, and as the lights lowered, the transport, on wheel, slowly moved offstage. It was a very touching and emotional scene." This was not just a description of the last performance, for Berlin goes on to suggest that he had "that finale in mind" before the show even opened.[49]

Jablonski's source for his description of the audience's reaction to the number—with "gasps, muffled outcries, sobs"—remains unclear (he refers to unspecified "reports"), but it does match a later re-creation of the scene in the film *Alexander's Ragtime Band*. This is where the line between film legend and theatrical fact blurs, but that may be appropriate for a scene in which Berlin strove to break down the theater's "fourth wall" and bring the ensemble into the audience for a moment in which they appeared transformed from actors to soldiers. A show that had at once sustained and parodied theater's conventions through masquerade and reflexivity now appeared to strip away all artifice and remind the audience of the dangers in the larger world.

One thing that we know did *not* happen in the finale of *Yip Yip Yaphank*: the musical number originally intended for the scene was not used. Berlin had written "God Bless America" as the number the men would sing while striding down the aisles, but, as he recalled, "having that finale in mind, it seemed painting the lily to have solders sing 'God Bless America' in that situation, so I didn't use it."[50] Yet he seems to have come close to using it. In a letter to Harry Ruby, who was his musical secretary at Camp Upton, Berlin noted that "I did let the boys hear it and decided that 350 soldiers in overseas outfits marching down the aisle of the Century Theater going off to war, sing 'God Bless America,' was wrong."[51] Ruby himself believed that he might have been "partly responsible" for the song's omission from the show. "There were so many patriotic songs coming out everywhere at that time . . . when he brought in 'God Bless America,' I took it down for him, and I said, 'Geez, another one?' And I guess Irving took me seriously. He put it away."[52] Whether Ruby influenced Berlin's choice or not, the accounts of its deletion from the show indicate a finely tuned sense of theater. "We're on Our Way to France" was more tightly focused on the immediate situation, whereas "God Bless America" was deliberately timeless, abstract, and hymnlike—a style that held less weight in a revue striving for immediate appeal to the "mob" that Berlin strove to engage all his life.

Yaphank, Revised and Memorialized

Despite its short run, *Yip Yip Yaphank* had long resonance. *This Is the Army* took its tone, structure, and some musical numbers from its predecessor. Like *Yaphank*, the show succeeded not through flag waving and sentiment but by focusing instead on the ordinary experiences of the common soldier to which civilians could relate: getting wrenched out of bed too early, having to clean the kitchen, finding solace in a safe haven for R&R, facing rigid rules with nimble wit, and dreaming of the girl left behind. Striving to reflect the shared preoccupations of soldiers and civilians, Berlin's new army show again steered clear of war's violence and chaos, tragedy and loss. It did not need to remind its audience of life's brutality, as Berlin knew from long experience. Since his days as a barroom busker on the Lower East Side, where he once got stabbed, Berlin's entertainment impulse arose from a fervent effort to create a space for levity and pathos in a dangerous, unstable world. As a result, he helped to normalize the American experience of an abnormal event: a world at war.

Although *Yip Yip Yaphank* served as his template, Berlin grasped that the new war required a new kind of show. In an interview, he made a pointed contrast between the two wars: "Today we're fighting a war all over the globe. There is no longer an 'Over There.' . . . It's 'Over Here' too. . . . Our feelings have changed about war. It's become more personal to all of us and less sentimental."[53] Likewise, he told a reporter visiting Camp Upton that "the boys are different from those who served in 1918. . . . They are more serious and grim. They know what they are up against. There is only one thing about them that is old-fashioned—one thing they have in common with the boys in the other war—that's their patriotism."[54] The war and feelings about it may have been different, but Berlin's compass, as ever, remained pointed at the American everyman. He would walk around Camp Upton, talking to the soldiers, overhearing conversations, longings, and complaints: he wanted to grow the show from deep engagement with the soldiers' ordinary feelings in an extraordinary situation.

T.I.T.A., like its model, melded military themes and theatrical conventions. Thus, the new show opened with soldiers in minstrel formation on risers and a sequence of numbers and humorous skits that follow *Yaphank*'s routines. Three numbers reappeared intact from the Great War show: "Mandy," the wedding number from the opening minstrel sequence; "Ladies of the Chorus," a cross-dressing number inspired by the turn-of-the-century hit "Tell Me, Pretty Maid," from *Florodora*; and, of course, "Oh! How I Hate to Get Up in the Morning."

In addition to serving as the template for the World War II stage show *This Is the Army, Yip Yip Yaphank* was twice memorialized on film over the next quarter century. Its portrayals tell us much about its place in Berlin's imagination, for he had a strong voice in the shaping of films using his songs—especially the "cavalcade" films whose plots take shape around Berlin's song catalog. For example, *Alexander's Ragtime Band* (1938) portrays the Great War—and *Yip Yip Yaphank* itself—as a pivotal moment for the protagonist. It tells the story of a respected classical violinist, San Francisco aristocrat Roger Grant (Tyrone Power), who turns his musical talent toward popular music and changes his name to Alexander in the 1910s. The title song serves as the vehicle with which "Alex" develops jazz and ultimately forges a substantive connection between jazz and classical music, as portrayed in the Carnegie Hall concert that forms the film's culminating scene. (The film's problematic whitewashing of history, while synchronized with Benny Goodman's historic Carnegie Hall concert the same year, deserves an entire chapter of its own.)

The Great War interrupts Alex's career, and the plot develops along the general outlines of Berlin's personal experience as a soldier and showman at Camp Upton, Long Island. The film sets the wartime atmosphere with Berlin's rousing "For Your Country and My Country" sung as a US Army recruiting song from a moving truck on a busy Manhattan street. Alex appears next as a raw recruit with friend and former sideman Davey (Jack Haley, who would appear as the Tin Man in the following year's *Wizard of Oz*) stumbling through army camp drills. In his distaste for army regimens, Alex convinces the camp's commanding officer to allow him to put on an army show by pointing to a navy precedent. The next scene portrays the show's development in rehearsal as Alex conducts a barbershop quartet singing the poignant epistolary ballad "(I Can Always Find a Little Sunshine in) The Y.M.C.A." Soon, we see the drill sergeant forcing Davey out of bed in the barracks, and as the camera pans back we see that he is actually on a stage. He begins singing, and Alex is shown conducting the orchestra in "Oh! How I Hate to Get Up in the Morning" in a packed theater. Afterward, an air of military urgency creates backstage commotion, and Alex calls the entire cast together to announce a new staging of the finale, "We're on Our Way to France," for which the soldier-performers will march down the aisles, out of the theater, and onto a transport waiting on the street, where they'll be taken to a ship to France. The stirring scene brings the audience to its feet, with some cheering and some others, mostly wives and mothers, gasping, weeping, and trying to get the attention of their "boys" as they march by. The film cuts to the battle front and features a war montage culminating in a triumphal march through the streets of New York. The entire war sequence is presented as a critical step toward Alex's realization of his merger of jazz and concert music.

The *Yaphank* sequence in *Alexander's Ragtime Band* clearly served as the template for a similar sequence in the film version of *This Is the Army*, released five years later, in 1943. The film overlaid a sentimental and patriotic plot, starring George Murphy as showman Jerry Jones and Ronald Reagan as his son Johnny Jones (both B-movie actors and future Republican politicians), onto the original revue so that the film is more about the making of *T.I.T.A.* and the offstage romances of its creators and performers than it is a presentation of the show itself. In that context, *Yip Yip Yaphank* becomes essential to the storytelling, and, per Berlin's prescription that "no story of *T.I.T.A.* would be complete without beginning at the beginning," the movie starts in 1917 and shows the development of Berlin's Great War show within the first ten minutes.

The *T.I.T.A.* film's depiction of *Yaphank*'s development and performance derives its trajectory from *Alexander Ragtime Band*: a scene establishing the period with a street performance of Berlin's "For Your Country and My Country" as a wartime recruitment song; a comic scene featuring the protagonist (as Berlin's avatar) as a raw recruit in marching drills; the commanding officer's decision to allow that protagonist to put on a show; rehearsals for the show, including a barbershop-style ballad (here "Kitchen Police [Poor Little Me]"); the performance culminating in the stirring finale, "We're on Our Way to France," with its shocking march down the aisle and off to war; and the montage of battle scenes in France.

The differences are also telling and reflect the needs of the plot and events since 1938. Most notably, "God Bless America"—absent from *Alexander's Ragtime Band* because it was unknown when that film was released—makes an appearance in the rehearsal sequence of *T.I.T.A.* as one of the notable cuts from the show, setting up its return in Kate Smith's stirring performance as the film shows America gearing up for World War II. The film captures something of the situation's reality: as Berlin had noted, he "did let the boys hear it" and only then determined it was "wrong."

What was right was using "We're on Our Way to France" instead. Indeed, viewed together, the films suggest that no scene in Berlin's films is so iconic for the *songwriter* than the finale in which the soldiers march off the stage, singing, ostensibly to go straight to the battlefield. Only Bing Crosby's performances of "White Christmas" in *Holiday Inn* and *White Christmas* can rival the core value of *Yip Yip Yaphank*'s finale, and its audience's reaction, as a movie scene. For there, Berlin not only "broke the fourth wall" but found a way to depict the way the theater of war impinges on the theater itself. The opening sequence of *White Christmas* extends that impulse by depicting Crosby (as Bob Wallace) performing and speaking on a makeshift stage near the European battlefront in World War II, only to be interrupted by an air attack. Here, as in *Yaphank* and its memorialization in the movies, theater serves as a refuge from war, and war interrupts theatrical performance—which the *Yaphank* finale, "We're on Our Way to France," and its cinematic depictions paradoxically reveal to be a theatrical coup de grâce. Berlin's wartime shows give rich meaning to the phrase *theater of war*.

Adding to the resonance of *Yip Yip Yaphank* in the film *White Christmas* are several songs that hark back to the army show of thirty-six years earlier: the whimsical quickstep tunes "We'll Follow the Old Man" and "Gee, I Wish I Was Back in the Army," both with sprightly 6/8 meter and jokes about army life à la "Oh! How I Hate to Get Up in the Morning." Finally, *White Christmas* stages "Mandy"—a revision of the wedding song "Sterling Silver Moon" from *Yaphank*, which, revised as "Mandy," first appeared in the *Ziegfeld Follies of 1919*—as a minstrel rehearsal with all the trappings of the old-fashioned minstrel show but without the blackface.

White Christmas, saturated in the experience and legacy of war, linking wartime brotherhood with postwar entertainment, and resonating with the humor arising from army privations, remains one of the most potent legacies of Berlin's Great War show. That it remains a staple of the American holiday experience and one of Berlin's best-known works, internationally, confirms that *Yip Yip Yaphank*'s reach was long indeed.

Notes

Portions of this chapter have been adapted from *Irving Berlin's American Musical Theater* by Jeffrey Magee and have been reproduced by permission of Oxford University Press: https://global.oup.com/academic/product/irving-berlins-american-musical-theater-9780199381012?cc=gb&lang=en&. For permission to reuse this material, please visit http://global.oup.com/academic/rights.

1. *This Is the Army*, typescript of British version, Library of Congress, Music Division, Irving Berlin Collection (hereafter LC-IBC), box 204, folder 2.

2. Stage directions ibid.

3. Berlin had written new verses for the song, but it is unknown whether he sang them in the British production. The verses do not appear in Robert Kimball and Linda Emmet, eds., *The Complete Lyrics of Irving Berlin* (New York: Alfred A. Knopf, 2001). One gives the flavor of a typical Berlin update to match an occasion: "A quarter of a century has passed and now we see / A very different Army just as different as can be / The guns, the drills, the uniforms have changed to fit the game / It's all so very different but the bugler's just the same" (typescript in LC-IBC, box 190, folder 3).

4. Accounts of the song's creation and preshow development appear in Kimball and Emmet, *Complete Lyrics*, 365; and Alan Anderson, *The Songwriter Goes to War* (Pompton Plains, NJ: Limelight, 2004), 151–52.

5. Anderson, *Songwriter Goes to War*, 154.

6. Ibid., 153.

7. Ibid., 154.

8. Quoted in Kimball and Emmet, *Complete Lyrics*, 365.

9. Jeffrey Magee, *Irving Berlin's American Musical Theater* (New York: Oxford University Press, 2012), 204.

10. Mary Ellin Barrett, *Irving Berlin: A Daughter's Memoir* (New York: Simon and Schuster, 1994), 205.

11. Irving Berlin, notes on *This Is the Army* in LC-IBC, box 269, folder 11, reprinted in Kimball and Emmet, *Complete Lyrics*, 169.

12. John Philip Sousa managed a similarly canny and opportunistic response to enlistment; see the chapter by Patrick Warfield in this volume.

13. The show title's punctuation differs widely from source to source, as will be clear in the source citations throughout this chapter. The title *without punctuation*, used here, reflects the title as printed in the opening-night program (as reprinted in Richard C. Norton, *A Chronology of American Musical Theater* [New York: Oxford University Press, 2002], 2:155), in Berlin's typescript about the show, and in the review printed in *Variety* after opening night. Kimball and Emmet, *Complete Lyrics*, 165, and David Leopold's *Irving Berlin's Show Business*, 49, both completed in close association with the Irving Berlin Music Company, use commas between the words *Yip, Yip, Yaphank*, as does a review in *Theatre Magazine* (October 1918): 222. A piece of sheet music reprinted in Leopold's book (49) indicates dashes, as in "*Yip-Yip-Yaphank*." *New York Times* articles about the show regularly inserted exclamation points after each word: "Yip! Yip! Yaphank!" (articles of August 25, August 30 [two articles], and September 1, 1918); yet *New York Times* articles of July 27 and September 11, 1918, used commas instead. Three recent biographies (Laurence Bergreen, *As Thousands Cheer: The Life of Irving Berlin* [New York: Penguin, 1990]; Edward Jablonski, *Irving Berlin: American Troubadour* [New York: Henry Holt, 1999]; and Philip Furia, *Irving Berlin: A Life in Song* [New York: Schirmer, 1998]) print the title as *Yip! Yip! Yaphank*, without an exclamation point at the end. The manuscript score (not in Berlin's hand but autographed by him and dated "Feb. 3, 1920") does not indicate a title (LC-IBC, box 213, folder 7).

14. Quoted in Kimball and Emmet, *Complete Lyrics*, 165.

15. "'Yip, Yip, Yaphank' Coming," *New York Times*, July 27, 1918, 7; "'Yip! Yip! Yaphank!' Goes On," *New York Times*, August 25, 1918, 32.

16. "'Yip! Yip' to Move to Lexington," *New York Times*, August 30, 1918, 9; "What News on the Rialto?," *New York Times*, September 1, 1918, 36.

17. Sime [Silverman], "Yip Yip Yaphank," *Variety*, August 23, 1918, 8.

18. "'Yip! Yip! Yaphank!' Goes On."

19. *Yip Yip Yaphank* manuscript score, LC-IBC, box 213, folder 7; Kimball and Emmet, *Complete Lyrics*, 165–72. There are at least three exceptions that point to a longer development: The opening number ("We Live at Upton . . .") was written "on or just before May 10, 1918." The show's big hit, "Oh! How I Hate to Get Up in the Morning," bears a copyright date of July 23, 1918. And "Kitchen Police (Poor Little Me)" was introduced in the *Ziegfeld Follies*, which had opened in June.

20. "Yaphank Actors Here," *New York Times*, August 6, 1918, 24.

21. Charles M. Steele, "Say, Let's Have a Show," *Theatre Magazine* (November 1918): 284; "The Theatre and the Armed Forces," *Theater Arts* (March 1943). For related soldiers'

performances in England, see Michelle Meinhart's account in this volume of the entertainments put on at Longleat.

22. "'Yip! Yip! Yaphank!' Makes Rousing Hit," *New York Times*, August 30, 1918, 7.

23. See Norton, *Chronology of American Musical Theater*, 2:146–48; "Soldiers Give a Play: 'Good-Bye, Bill' Written and Acted by Army Men," *New York Times*, March 11, 1918, 9; and "Pelham Navy Boys Play in 'Biff-Bang!,'" *New York Times*, May 31, 1918, 15.

24. "Pelham Navy Boys Play in 'Biff-Bang!'"

25. "New York Cheers 'Yip, Yip, Yaphank,'" *Theatre Magazine* (October 1918): 222.

26. [Silverman], "Yip Yip Yaphank." All further quotations of Silverman come from this review.

27. See William J. Mahar, *Behind the Burnt Cork Mask* (Urbana: University of Illinois Press, 1999), 13. Mahar reprints twenty-five representative minstrel-show playbills of the 1843–59 period, five of which feature "wedding" numbers.

28. Norton, *Chronology of American Musical Theater*, 2:155.

29. Kimball and Emmet, *Complete Lyrics*, 169.

30. A photograph of the scene, with four black children and the "bride," appears in *Theatre Magazine* (October 1918): 223.

31. "New York Cheers 'Yip, Yip, Yaphank,'" 222. The description seems to have caused some understandable confusion among Berlin's biographers, two of whom interpreted the "real lady" line to indicate either Mandy or the bride (see Bergreen, *As Thousands Cheer*, 160; and Furia, *Irving Berlin*, 83). But the program clearly indicates that white men played those roles (Private Healy played Mandy, and Private Friend the bride), and the "real colored picks" appeared as the bridesmaids and flower girl only in the "Ding Dong" number. For the cast-member identifications based on the opening-night program, see Norton, *Chronology of American Musical Theater*, 2:155; and Kimball and Emmet, *Complete Lyrics*, 167.

32. Information on Bevo comes from http://www.houblon.net, http://www.beerbottle collector.com, and http://en.wikipedia.org/wiki/bevo. The article at houblon.net is credited to Max Rubin and *American Heritage* and dated July 7, 2002.

33. There was a precedent, however, in the first edition of the *Follies* (1907), which had featured a song called "Budweiser's a Friend of Mine." Ann Ommen Van der Merwe, *The Ziegfeld Follies: A History in Song* (Lanham, MD: Scarecrow, 2009), 3.

34. "New York Cheers 'Yip, Yip, Yaphank,'" 222.

35. Audience members were identified in "New York Cheers 'Yip, Yip, Yaphank,'" 222.

36. Kimball and Emmet, *Complete Lyrics*, 155. The song was copyrighted on August 27, 1917.

37. See Jeffrey Magee, "Ragtime and Early Jazz," in *The Cambridge History of American Music*, ed. David Nicholls (Cambridge: Cambridge University Press, 1998), 407.

38. For a critical analysis of the film's mythmaking, see George F. Custen, "I Hear Music and . . . Darryl and Irving Write History with *Alexander's Ragtime Band*," in *Authorship and Film*, ed. David A. Gerstner and Janet Staiger, AFI Film Readers (New York: Routledge, 2003), 77–95.

39. Kimball and Emmet, *Complete Lyrics*, 169.

114 • JEFFREY MAGEE

40. Charles Hamm, "Irving Berlin's Early Songs as Biographical Documents," *Musical Quarterly* 7, no. 1 (1993): 10–34.

41. Kimball and Emmet, *Complete Lyrics*, 169.

42. Jablonski, *Irving Berlin*, 77.

43. "'Yip! Yip! Yaphank!' Makes Rousing Hit."

44. In 1919 Arthur Fields made what has been described as a "number-one selling recording" of the song (Kimball and Emmet, *Complete Lyrics*, 169) that includes the following words (here italicized) at the end of the second chorus—another comical overreaction to the bugler's playing—that appear neither in the song's original sheet music publication nor in Kimball and Emmet, *Complete Lyrics*: "*I'll sneak into his room some night*, / *And fill his horn with dynamite*, / And spend the rest of my life in bed."

45. "New York Cheers 'Yip, Yip, Yaphank,'" 222.

46. Marion Spitzer, "Two Wars and Two Shows," *New York Times*, July 12, 1942.

47. Berlin letter to Abel Green, July 19, 1954, quoted in Kimball and Emmet, *Complete Lyrics*, 321–22.

48. Jablonski, *Irving Berlin*, 81.

49. Berlin, letter to Abel Green, July 19, 1954, quoted in Kimball and Emmet, *Complete Lyrics*, 321–22.

50. Ibid.

51. Berlin to Harry Ruby, October 26, 1971, quoted ibid., 322.

52. Ruby quoted in Max Wilk, *They're Playing Our Song: Conversations with America's Classic Songwriters* (1991; reprint, New York: Da Capo, 1997), 275.

53. Albert D. Hughes, *Christian Science Monitor* (n.d., but probably September 1942), clipping in LC-IBC Scrapbooks, Microfilm 92-20013, Reel 3.

54. S. J. Woolf, "Sergeant Berlin Re-enlists," *New York Times*, May 17, 1942, clipping in LC-IBC Berlin Scrapbooks, Microfilm 92-20013, Reel 3.

Interlude: The Middle

WILLIAM BROOKS, CHRISTINA BASHFORD, AND GAYLE MAGEE

The five composers discussed in part 1 lived and worked in musical communities, some of which were very small and others far-reaching. Charles Ives's circle consisted of only his family and a very small number of friends, Frank Bridge had a modest reputation in London, Irving Berlin was a pervasive force in entertainment internationally, and Debussy and Sousa were iconic figures. But this is always the case: music is created for and within communities of practitioners and listeners. World War I, however, created new communities where none had existed, and it radically reshaped others that were of long standing.

The essays in part 2 discuss five such reshaped or newly created musical communities. The range of these expands gradually from the very local community formed at Longleat, England, to the wholly transnational population affected by the influenza epidemic. The intervening chapters discuss communities formed by musical practices, by nationality, and by shared experience.

Under the impact of the war, Britain's industries and social structures were compelled to change. Right from the start, the government had taken control of its citizens' lives, mobilizing a mass male army, initially through volunteers (a campaign in which women were central, as discussed earlier) and from March 1916 by conscription. Alongside came a reconfiguration of Britain's industrial economy, as women took jobs in factories or worked with munitions, communications, farming, nursing, and other war-effort duties—encouraged by national advertising and the temporary dissolving of gender stereotypes, including as regards clothing. One poster, promoting the Women's Land Army, depicted a woman tilling a field with a horse-drawn plow and proclaimed, "God speed the plough and the woman who drives it."[1] In the musical world, some of the empty chairs in professional orchestras (particularly their string sections) and cinema bands, created as men went to war, were temporarily taken over by women, who had long been denied such opportunities in the workplace.[2]

Women—especially those from the wealthier strata of the British class system—also played a significant role in fund-raising for the war effort and in related voluntary initiatives at home, and music featured in many such undertakings. In chapter 6, Michelle Meinhart explores how, with the cooperation of aristocratic families, some British stately homes were turned into military hospitals, and she spotlights the efforts of Lady Bath and her daughters at Longleat House in Wiltshire, where a transnational mix of British, Belgian, Canadian, Australian, and New Zealander soldiers were treated. Using the hospital's commercially available magazine (the *Longleat Lyre* [1916–18]) as her lens, she shows how the Baths worked to encourage musical entertainments that served to promote a sense of united community beyond the walls of Longleat and to transform a once socially exclusive space into one that cut across divides of class and nation.

In the more public realm were concerts, often involving high-profile artists, that aimed to raise money for wartime charities, to distribute both at home and abroad (for example, through the British Red Cross or the British Society for the Relief of Belgian Wounded Soldiers). Considerable debate, however, ensued in the music profession about the assumption that musicians should give their services free, especially those rank-and-file players whose livings were hard won. Two organizations, the Music in War-Time Committee and War Emergency Entertainments, had some success in addressing these issues, making a further contribution to Britain's wider Allied effort, which aimed to keep members of the civilian workforce functioning as normal, while also encouraging national unity and positive morale.[3]

Additional sources of employment for British musicians included performances for soldiers. Concert parties, often featuring well-known music hall personalities (such as the singer Harry Lauder), were sent off to Flanders, to keep up soldiers' spirits, and they gave many performances, though well behind the lines. Especially notable in the development of troop entertainments was Lena Ashwell, a successful Shakespearean actor and a supporter of women's rights who campaigned vigorously during the early months of the war for the creation of touring programs abroad in aid of the British war effort. She proceeded both to raise considerable sums of money to fund them and to get the YMCA involved, albeit by promoting an "improving" diet of accessible numbers from classical music, alongside recitations of poems and group singing.

Meanwhile, music infiltrated the lives of Britain's soldiers behind the line in other ways, helping to avert boredom, strengthen mental health, and encourage camaraderie. Many soldiers made their own music with instruments brought from home or commandeered locally (especially pianos) and using sheet music that British publishers had mailed overseas. Group singing was inevitably popular and extended to parodies of popular songs, some of which were funny: "It's a Long Way to Tipperary" famously became "It's the Wrong Way to Tickle Mary," for instance—though others were darker. Indeed, something of the psychological reality of being on active service is revealed by the book *Tommy's Tunes*, an anthology from 1917, with lyrics ranging from the explicit "I Don't Want to Be a Soldier" and "I Want to Go Home" to others glossed with sarcasm or biting satire.[4] Church of England hymns are among the targets for parody: an apt means of attacking the establishment credo that wartime sacrifice was all for God, king, and country. To Arthur Sullivan's tune of "Onward, Christian Soldiers," the book presents a stanza that begins:

Onward! Queen Victorias,
Guarding the railway line.
Is this "foreign service"?
Ain't it jolly fine?[5]

Many classically trained musicians were among the men on active service, and some of them were young composers on the brink of significant careers, such as George Butterworth, Cecil Coles, Arthur Bliss, and Ivor Gurney (the first two died in Flanders). The older Ralph Vaughan Williams volunteered for the medical corps. All were deeply disturbed by the experience and found outlets in their music, though most of this corpus of work was composed after the conflict ended or at least away from the action.[6] (Writing music in the trenches was particularly challenging in practical terms, requiring special paper and a certain amount of silence, if not a piano within reach.) Exceptions include Coles's orchestral suite *Behind the Lines*, in progress when he died, and a small group of songs by Gurney; the latter evince the composer's yearnings for his native Gloucestershire countryside, but they also contain traces of his anger and revulsion at what was happening around him, as in his powerful setting of John Masefield's "By a Bierside," written in a "disused Trench Mortar emplacement" in August 1916, in a spell away from frontline duty.[7]

After the sinking of the *Lusitania* in 1915, President Wilson moved very carefully, squeezed as he was between militants like Theodore Roosevelt, on the one hand, and advocates of neutrality, on the other. His solution was "preparedness": the nation would get ready for war but seek to avoid it. This campaign also had musical results; in 1916 alone, copyright was registered for at least ninety songs containing some version of "prepare" in the title. But a more important consequence was that Wilson managed to squeak through the 1916 election by promoting himself as the man who kept the country out of war. In 1917, however, things quickly turned ugly. At the beginning of February, Germany announced it was resuming unrestricted submarine warfare, and in March the so-called Zimmermann Telegram was made public in which Germany proposed an alliance with Mexico, suggesting another border war to keep the United States busy at home. American sentiment shifted overwhelmingly to the Allies, and on April 6, 1917, the United States officially entered the war.

There followed a great upswell of patriotism, manifested musically in George M. Cohan's "Over There," allegedly written in a couple of hours the day after the US entry. "Over There" was a harbinger of times to come, in that it was popularized as much by recordings as by sheet music. The most remarkable was made by legendary tenor Enrico Caruso, who recorded two verses, in two languages.[8] This disc, of a song written by an Irish American and recorded in America by an Italian singing in English and French, was hugely successful in the United States, Britain, Canada, France, and Australia. There is no better musical instance of the alliance that had been formed.

Cohan's song quickly became a musical icon representing commitment and engagement. It was quoted in hundreds of songs that followed, and the title was appropriated on the home front for campaigns of every possible description. But other icons more truly represented America's international alliance. "Joan of Arc, They Are Calling You," wrote Alfred Bryan in a late megahit, and indeed, Joan of Arc, the fleurs-de-lis (and, more generally, lilies), and the Statue of Liberty appeared in various guises in literally thousands of lyrics and sheet music covers.[9]

As in Britain, American industry and society changed radically, once the country was truly engaged. Wartime production increased demands on industry, and as many workers entered the military, new populations were hired and trained on the home front. Like Francophones in Canada and the Irish in Britain, African Americans faced significant challenges while serving in the military. Although initially Wilson's administration avoided recruiting African Americans, and although African American regiments never served under white American officers, their troops fought with the French and compiled a remarkable record of service and valor. For many, the opportunity to serve overseas offered unprecedented freedom from racial segregation and Jim Crow laws while providing possible leverage for meaningful reform, perhaps even equality, back at home.[10] Sarah-Jane Mathieu explains, "Black intellectuals and veterans believed that, having proven their mettle by putting their lives on the line for democracy, white Americans would surely recognize the race's merit. Bestowing full civil rights to African American men would then be the rational next step."[11]

However, the reality was different. Black soldiers faced discrimination and segregation within the military; many were assigned to menial work as dreary as digging latrines and as horrific as collecting body parts from the battlefield.[12] A large number labored under backbreaking conditions as stevedores, enduring inadequate housing, food, and rest. Even the small number of commissioned African American officers "had few opportunities for upward advancement and coped with unrelenting hostility from their white counterparts and superiors," according to historian Chad L. Williams.[13]

Despite these conditions, the impact of African American music and musicians during and immediately after the Great War cannot be overstated. James Reese Europe and others assembled exceptional bands that played a strikingly new kind of music when they were not fighting at the western front; Europe's "Hellfighter" band caused a sensation when it appeared in France on New Year's Day, 1918. The stylistic innovations that he and other African Americans produced would transform popular music in the postwar decade, in America as well as France. Gone would be ragtime; in its place, jazz. Gone would be mournful ballads; in their place, the blues. Even more important, gone would be coon songs and the most despicable of racial stereotypes; in their place arose the beginnings of dignity and honor for people of color. Though the gains were short-lived and seemingly erased by the reactionary politics of the 1920s, the service of African Americans in the Great War laid the foundations for the Harlem Renaissance of the interwar period and, eventually, the civil rights movement of the midcentury.[14]

Women, too, advanced their political agenda: the drives for Prohibition and women's suffrage both reached their climax during the war, and the relevant constitutional amendments came into force in 1920. During the war itself, women—of necessity and by choice—filled many roles that had previously been occupied by men, in industry, law, and education. The music industry was equally affected; in chapter 7, Kendra Preston Leonard traces some of the steps that women took before and during the war to establish themselves as professional musicians in theaters and movie houses. In a series of case studies, she demonstrates specific ways in which women's contributions not only eroded gender stereotypes but also advanced stylistic, compositional, and technological practices, significantly affecting the future course of film and improvised music.

 An estimated 360 Canadians, or more than a quarter of the total casualties, were lost in the sinking of the *Lusitania*, although the precise number is difficult to know since Canadians traveled under British passports. Many were wives and children of British-born enlistees taking the transatlantic journey to join soldiers near training bases in England and looking forward to reconnecting with family in Britain. Other Canadian-based victims were impatient to join the war effort through the Canadian Expeditionary Force (CEF) and were traveling to enlist in the British army. Immediately, the *Lusitania* became a rallying cry for the Canadian war effort.

In fact, at the moment of the *Lusitania*'s sinking, Canadian troops were fighting their first major battle of the war. Between April 22 and May 25, 1915, the CEF's First Division fought alongside French and British troops at the Second Battle of Ypres, and, as was reported in the British and Canadian press, the untested but tenacious Canadians performed valiantly. Despite the division having more British veterans than Canadian-born soldiers, the victory became part of national lore almost immediately, with accolades by British leadership praising "the grand colonial type of manhood that we now recognize as the cream of the race."[15]

Of course, only white English-speaking soldiers merited such praise. Indeed, contemporary and later representations of Canadian soldiers in the war tend to privilege white Anglophones over all other groups, while the presence of First Nations, African Canadian, and other nonwhite soldiers remained all but invisible until very recently. It is estimated that nearly four thousand First Nations and Métis soldiers contributed to the war effort, comprising around a third of the country's total indigenous population.[16] Although Canadians of African, Chinese, and Japanese descent were initially banned from enlisting, the need for more troops eventually removed even these barriers as well.[17] Like their African American counterparts, all faced varying levels of discrimination and found that their sacrifices did not equate to recognition or equality after the war.

Instead, sanctioned narratives throughout the war and afterward emphasized the emergence of British Canadian national pride and the widespread belief of Canada's newfound autonomy on the world stage, through heroic victories such as the Second Battle of Ypres. As Brian C. Thompson notes in chapter 8, performances, publications, and programming in the cosmopolitan city of Montreal through the war reflect the complex intersections between Canada's musical past and present, the growing tensions between Anglophone and Francophone populations, and the musical counterpoints that accompanied its transition from colony to emerging nation.

Behind a public relations campaign that emphasized glory and sacrifice, the CEF suffered terrible losses at Ypres. Around a third of the division's 18,000 men were killed, wounded, or missing, with many casualties resulting from the war's first use of chlorine gas. For all its horror, though, the battle inspired one of the most important creative acts of the war, when Boer War veteran and Canadian physician Lieutenant Colonel John McCrae wrote the poem "In Flanders Fields" near the grave site of a young friend who had died from a German shell the day before. The date was May 3, 1915—two days after the *Lusitania* left New York Harbor and four days before it sank.

The last year of the war saw the introduction of conscription in Canada, which resulted in violent, deadly riots within Quebec as French Canadian citizens took to the streets. The postwar era witnessed a new low in English-French relations that would fuel separatist sentiments for the rest of the century. Monuments to the 60,000 Canadian soldiers who died in the conflict, and the more than 130,000 who were injured, were erected throughout Europe as symbols of Canada's dedication and sacrifice.

Still, Canada's most enduring legacy from the war may be McCrae's poem, which became famous throughout the world, especially after McCrae's death in January 1918, in Wimereux, France. After appearing in the British publication *Punch* on December 8, 1915, the poem would be reprinted in English-language newspapers around the world. Of the nearly seventy musical settings made between 1917 and 1922, one by Charles Ives was performed at an insurance executives' luncheon in Manhattan on April 15, 1917, and would be published in the composer's seminal collection *114 Songs* in 1922.[18] By comparison, John Philip Sousa's setting (discussed by Patrick Warfield in chapter 4) was probably heard most frequently, simply because his band played it on tour.

The central imagery of McCrae's poem became so ubiquitous that poppies are now synonymous with the First World War, along with other common symbols of shared grief and military sacrifice. In chapter 9, "On Stars, Soldiers, Mothers, and Mourning," William Brooks details the path from patriotism to remembrance between the US entry into the war and the conflict's aftermath, through music associated with now standard American service flags and "gold star" traditions. As Brooks notes, the US war effort engaged an increasingly diverse complement of publishers, song styles, songwriters, and lyricists, including women who contributed primarily as a creative outlet for their patriotic sentiments. Following the war's end and the passage of the Nineteenth Amendment in 1920, a new generation of women in the Jazz Age would find their opportunities expand significantly beyond roles of motherhood, and the narratives of sacrifice and service for all Americans would recede—at least temporarily.

On November 11, 1918, news of the end of hostilities spread rapidly across an exhausted Britain. But even on a day of wide jubilation and relief, death still hovered. The influenza epidemic, which was to wipe out vast numbers of the population worldwide, had already taken hold in the spring of 1918. It soon intensified, bringing more anxiety and grief to British families in the months to come as people succumbed in the thousands, the disease often carried home from the trenches by returning Tommies touching their loved ones. Such personal tragedies were replicated in the Allied nations. In chapter 10, Deniz

Ertan captures the mood of despair that took hold in America in the wake of the flu's ravages, arguing that the pandemic created a significant rupture with the old order and signaling a new era of fear, helplessness, and danger, all set against the otherwise optimistic advances of modernity. She shows how the impact was especially hard in America, in terms of both numbers of fatalities and how its musical life responded—often through silence (venues were closed in the interests of public health), but also through the writing of music, noting an absence of expressions of grief from composers and exploring the consequences that flowed from such denial. In a wide-ranging discussion, she further links the rupturing force of the pandemic to the development in the 1920s of American individualism and to a new, quintessentially American music, placing both in the context of a reconfigured transnationalism.

Notes

1. The artist was Henry George Gawthorn (1879–1941); a digitized copy of the poster can be seen at https://www.loc.gov/item/2003675370/.

2. See Cyril Ehrlich, *The Music Profession in Britain since the Eighteenth Century: A Social History* (Oxford: Clarendon Press, 1985), 161; and Laraine Porter, "The 'Missing Muscle': Attitudes to Women Working in Cinema and Music, 1910–1930," *Popular Music & Society* 40, no. 5 (2017): 502–8.

3. As argued by Jane Angell in her "Music and Charity on the British Home Front during the First World War," *Journal of Musicological Research* 33 (2014): 184–205.

4. F[rederick]. T[homas]. Nettleingham, comp., *Tommy's Tunes: A Comprehensive Collection of Soldiers' Songs, Marching Melodies, Rude Rhymes, and Popular Parodies, Composed, Collected, and Arranged on Active Service with the B.E.F.* (London: Erskine MacDonald, 1917), digitized copy available at https://hdl.handle.net/2027/inu.39000003409450.

5. Ibid., 59.

6. On British wartime composition, see Kate Kennedy and Trudi Tate, "Literature and Music of the First World War," *First World War Studies* 2, no. 1 (2011): 1–6; and Kate Kennedy, "Silence Recalled in Sound: British Classical Music and the Armistice," in *The Silent Morning: Culture and Memory after the Armistice*, ed. Trudi Tate and Kate Kennedy (Manchester: Manchester University Press, 2013), 211–34.

7. Gurney was both poet and composer and mostly wrote poetry in France. His experiences of war unraveled through injuries into serious mental collapse, and he would write most of his war-induced art songs in an asylum back in postwar Britain. On Gurney as songwriter, see Kate Kennedy, "'But Still He Died Nobly': Reinterpretation of the Pastoral Elegy before and during the Asylum Years," *Ivor Gurney Society Journal* 15 (2009): 117–54; and her "Ambivalent Englishness: Ivor Gurney's Song Cycle *Ludlow and Teme*," *First World War Studies* 2, no.1 (2011): 41–64.

8. Cohan's "Over There" was issued first by the William Jerome Publishing Company (New York), copyright June 1, 1917, but it was popularized by Nora Bayes even earlier. See

"Cohan's Patriotic Song," *New York Clipper*, May 23, 1917, 15. Bayes recorded it on July 13 on Victor 45130 (mx B-20335, take 2), but she was anticipated by the American Quartet on Victor 18333 (mx B-20306, take 2), recorded on June 28. Caruso did not make his recording until November 7, 1918, released on Victor 87294 and Gramophone 5-2593 in Britain (mx B-22125, take 4). Leo Feist purchased the copyright in 1917 and early in 1918 released an edition that included a French translation (copyrighted December 12), with an iconic cover by Norman Rockwell; a digitized copy can be seen at https://www.loc.gov/item/ihas.100010517/.

9. Jack Wells (music) and Alfred Bryan and Willie Weston (words), "Joan of Arc, They Are Calling You" (New York: Waterson, Berlin, and Snyder, 1917), copyrighted May 15, digitized copy available at https://www.loc.gov/item/2014564885/.

10. See Adriane Danette Lentz-Smith, *Freedom Struggles: African Americans and World War I* (Cambridge, MA: Harvard University Press, 2009).

11. Sarah-Jane Mathieu, "Great Expectations: African Americans and the Great War Era," review of *Torchbearers of Democracy: African American Soldiers in the World War I Era*, by Chad L. Williams et al., *American Quarterly*, 63, no. 2 (2011): 411.

12. For a harrowing account of the brutal, often violent treatment of African American recruits by white soldiers and officers, see Williams et al., *Torchbearers of Democracy* (Chapel Hill: University of North Carolina Press, 2010), 109–11.

13. Ibid., 6. For a discussion of the terrible working conditions of black stevedores as well as the openly racist, minstrelized atmosphere that surrounded this work, see ibid., 111–12.

14. See Mathieu, "Great Expectations," 410, 414; and Mark Whalan, *The Great War and the Culture of the New Negro* (Gainesville: University Press of Florida, 2008), which explores the legacy of African American soldiers on the writings of the Harlem Renaissance.

15. Cited in Jonathan F. Vance, *Maple Leaf Empire* (New York: Oxford University Press), 64.

16. Some indigenous Canadians enlisted as early as 1914, despite an official ban from the British government that was lifted in late 1915. See Timothy Charles Winegard, *For King and Kanata: Canadian Indians and the First World War* (Winnipeg: University of Manitoba Press, 2012), 54–87; and Alison Norman, "'In Defense of the Empire': The Six Nations of the Grand River and the Great War," in *A Sisterhood of Suffering and Service: Women and Girls of Canada and Newfoundland during the First World War*, ed. Sarah Glassford and Amy Shaw (Vancouver: University of British Columbia Press, 2012), 34–36.

17. James W. St. G. Walker, "Visible Minorities in the Canadian Expeditionary Force," *Canadian Historical Review* 70, no. 1 (1989): 1–26.

18. Alan Houtchins and Janis P. Stout, "'Scarce Heard amidst the Guns Below': Intertextuality and Meaning in Charles Ives's War Songs," *Journal of Musicology* 15, no. 1 (1997): 66–97.

PART 2

Communities

Tommy Critics, an Unlikely Musical Community, and the *Longleat Lyre* during World War I

MICHELLE MEINHART

BBC One's documentary series *All Change at Longleat* (2015) followed the present Marquess of Bath, his heir and family, and the diverse characters who today make Longleat—an Elizabethan stately home, grounds, and safari park in rural Wiltshire—thrive as an international tourist destination.[1] But the Thynne family of Longleat first opened its gates to another disparate and unlikely crew one hundred years ago. During World War I, Lord and Lady Bath volunteered their home as an auxiliary military hospital, treating British, Canadian, Australian, New Zealander, and Belgian soldiers and employing scores of civilians as staff and clergy.[2] This community fostered numerous musical entertainments involving the entire array of the house's inhabitants. Moreover, like its 2015 counterpart, this 1915 Longleat assemblage publicized these activities to local, national, and international audiences through an important media outlet of its time: the hospital's commercially available magazine, the *Longleat Lyre*. At the forefront of producing the *Lyre*'s content were the convalescing soldiers. Writing witty, comical, often self-deprecating reviews, these Tommy critics chronicled the rich musical life at their hospital, including the music performed, performers, and reception.[3] Typically, wounded men at both municipal and country-house hospitals during the war performed British music hall and American Tin Pan Alley hits, as well as other musical entertainments, often under the direction of ladies of the families.[4] But the frequency and detail of musical content in the *Lyre* demonstrates a musical life at Longleat that was exceptionally active, engaging performers and listeners from an array of social and national backgrounds.[5]

The following account in the *Lyre* of a musical entertainment on February 7, 1918, is typical of the magazine's many reviews in its chronicling of repertoire, performers, audience response, and overall tone of the entertainment:

> Those who found their way into the Coliseum on the 7th February were rewarded with a most delightful evening. The programme was admirably arranged by the Chaplain, and the accompanist was Mrs. Cocks, who fulfilled this difficult part in the splendid way so characteristic of herself. All the turns were good: L-Corpl. Getty sang the "Song That Reached My Heart," and as he looked in a certain direction from time to time, there was some heart *he* desired to reach. Pte. Cheatham gave us "The One Man Band," quite in approved style and costume. Lady Kathleen, always delightful, was especially so in her rendering of "Poor Butterfly." Pte. Linton sang "When the Ebb Tide Flows," and he ebbed and flowed accordingly. Pte. Russ was good in "The Sands of the Desert," in fact we could see the camels all the time. There was a full house. This song has a well-known chorus and all heartily joined in. Pte. Graff was a "nib"; his song, "The Beauty of the Guards" quite caught on, but Sister Mc'Rory was on the warpath. His guards' uniform did not harmonise with a draughty pair of hospital trousers, and his encore "Nothing to Wear" so touched her heart, that she refitted him the next morning with an entire new suit—all anxiety as to his catching cold is not at an end. Gnr McNally recited "Gungadene" ["Gunga Din"], a faithful rendering of a faithful story, and his encore "Jim Blookstone" was well received. Sister Mason and Pte. Linton then filled the bill with a duet, "Watchman, What of the Night?" and we could imagine our watchman going her rounds with the everlasting candle—a light that never fails. This was loudly applauded, and then Sister Mason, a typical "Red Rose of England" herself, sang it, and once again charmed us. The Chaplain turned our thoughts to our brothers at sea, by "The Boys of the Ocean Blue," and modestly declined his encore.
>   What can be said of the concerted item? "A Yorkshire Lad in London," by Pte. Landon, M. M., and Pte. Graff? It brought the house down. Pte. Landon's imitation fits ought to procure him his ticket, and his song "Parley Vous [Hinky Dinky Parley Vous]" created much amusement.[6]

Lady Kathleen, Reverend Cocks, Private Russ, and Sister Mason; "Poor Butterfly," "Song That Reached My Heart," "Watchmen, What of the Night?" and "Hinky Dinky Parley Vous": these are just some of the characters and selections that constituted Longleat's wartime musical life and community—a community solidified, idealized, and promoted by the *Lyre*.

This review serves as a launching point into my discussion of Longleat's musical life and its representation in the *Lyre*. After first placing the *Lyre* in the context of Longleat hospital, other hospital magazines, and the larger soldiers' press, I will detail the hospital's performers and repertoire and address the social and political functions of these musical events as chronicled in the *Lyre*. Not only did they entertain wounded soldiers, but the musical community they fostered and reinforced—composed of amateur musicians, listeners, and affiliated *Lyre* readers— transformed this once socially exclusive space into a center of social and cultural exchange that cut across traditional class and national boundaries. Ultimately, the magazine presented Longleat and its inhabitants as unified in their support for imperial Britain and adaptable to wartime changes.[7]

Longleat Hospital and the *Lyre* in Context

During the First World War, many stately homes were voluntarily converted to military hospitals. Peter Mandler has argued that, despite their opening to the public in the 1850s and '60s as a form of tourism, country houses and the elite culture they represented were under fire from the mass public by the late nineteenth century.[8] By the early twentieth century, owners of the houses had largely withdrawn from the public sphere. The First World War, then, as both Mandler and David Cannadine contend, enabled owners to "right" themselves with the general public. In once again opening their houses, the landed elite appeared to promote national heritage and improve class relations, combating claims that the upper classes were not doing their bit for the war effort.[9] Soon after the war started and the first wounded began to arrive back in Britain, society magazines such as the *Lady* and the *Tatler* featured articles on stately homes that had become hospitals, encouraging others to follow suit.[10] Financial and logistical support for these Voluntary Aid Detachment (VAD) hospitals fell almost exclusively to the houses' owners and medical volunteers, as the War Office offered little aid. These homes treated unranked British and white dominion soldiers, usually Canadians, Australians, New Zealanders, South Africans, and Irishmen.[11]

Initially, Lord and Lady Bath offered their home as a hospital for officers, only to have the War Office quickly respond that the more pressing need was for soldiers from other ranks. So, as Lady Bath relates, with the transformation of rooms into wards, the posting of three trained nurses to the house, and the arrival three days later (November 7, 1914) of thirty-one wounded soldiers, her stately home was speedily transformed into a hospital. Her account of this transition in the July 1916 issue of the *Lyre* captures the excitement of preparations but also initial surprise in seeing these patients approach the house. They were "a motley crew . . . [with] all sorts of colours, all sorts of headgear; little tiny caps, some blue, some blue and yellow, with little tassels hanging down in front—no Englishmen would surely wear such caps! No, they were not English, they were Belgians."[12] Fortunately, this disappointment soon wore off, and the members of this "motley crew" were gradually incorporated into the wartime Longleat community, in spite of differences in dress, language, and religion. For example, regarding the last difference—that of the soldiers' Catholic faith—Lady Bath brought in a Catholic priest from the nearby town of Frome to hold services in the Longleat chapel.[13] Although the patients who followed these initial Belgians were from the British Isles, Canada, Australia, and New Zealand, the same kinds of community-building efforts were undertaken, of which musical entertainments and the publication of the *Lyre* were central components. Within the first year of the hospital's opening, a surgical unit was established and additional rooms were emptied to make way for more beds—increasing from thirty to ninety beds by the fall of 1915 and to one hundred beds by the fall of 1916; by 1919 the hospital had treated 2,044 soldiers. More medical staff were also added, including another trained nurse and a host of VAD nurses. At times, they were so stretched to capacity in terms of space, food, and beds, especially in light of rationing, that by February 1917, in order to continue sustaining 150 soldiers, staff, and family members, former flower gardens were being used to grow vegetables.

While this music making in wartime country houses was often documented in personal correspondence and diaries (and, sometimes, participants' music collections), soldiers at Longleat took on more direct and official roles in chronicling the house's musical life.[14] Published monthly between April 1916 and December 1918, the *Lyre* featured a variety of writings, of which reports on music formed one substantial part. Its longevity and success were undoubtedly due to the efforts of Corporal E. Humphrey, who served as editor from the magazine's inception until December 1917.[15] It is not clear whether all contributions were published, but the editor seems to have received numerous submissions.[16] The magazine regularly featured columns by the hospital matron relaying hospital-related news (such as changes in nursing staff) and by the aforementioned hospital chaplain, the Reverend W. Cocks, which included everything from contemplative devotions to reminders about upcoming services. Periodically, Thynne family members also contributed, writing articles on the histories of the house, its artwork, and its hospital. But soldiers were the main contributors to the *Lyre*, penning short stories, humorous anecdotes, and poetry about a variety of subjects, such as their time at the front lines and experiences at Longleat. Soldiers and staff could also propose anonymous questions for the recurring gossip column, "Things We Want to Know," but most extensive were soldiers' reports on entertainments. These events included beauty shows (in which the men dressed up as women), competitions of various sorts (such as whistling, trivia, and song parodies), and musical and dramatic performances. Of these diverse entertainments, musical ones are reported the most often. Indeed, that the magazine's name includes the word *lyre* is telling, broadcasting at the outset both its avid interest in music and the rich musical life at Longleat. While most reviews in the magazine are anonymous, a Private A. G. Barrett, a reporter before the war, wrote much of the music-related material beginning in March 1918, which the editor gratefully acknowledged.[17]

That Longleat Hospital published an ongoing magazine is not out of the ordinary. Many hospitals on the British home front had such publications, which not only eased boredom and boosted morale but also played an integral part in soldiers' convalescence. After the founding in April 1915 of the first hospital magazine, the *First Eastern General Hospital Gazette*, at the First Eastern General Hospital in Cambridge, such magazines grew in popularity so quickly that, as Jeffrey Reznick observes, "by the end of the first year of the war, nearly every general military hospital in the country had initiated a similar literary project."[18] But most of the home-front hospitals that produced magazines were not of the country-house sort; rather, these magazines were assembled by bigger hospitals set up in municipal buildings in urban areas.[19] Thus, Longleat and the *Lyre* are special in this regard.[20]

Hospital magazines can be particularly useful to historians, for they "open a window on to the soldier's multifaceted experience of recovery."[21] Like music and handicrafts, the reading and writing these publications promoted were considered valuable curatives, both physically and emotionally. Such was certainly the goal of the *Lyre*, as implied by magazine's motto, printed prominently on the title page of the first issue: "Keep your face to the sun. The shadows will fall behind." Anna Carden-Coyne contends that such magazines offer the men's perspective on their healing experiences and, by extension, insight into the politics of these institutions and what she terms the "sociality" of the hospitals' inhabitants—the array of relationships (both positive and negative) among wounded men, male and female medical staff, and hospital volunteers and visitors.[22] And, as I argue below, musical content in the *Lyre* reifies this culture of sociality.

Hospital magazines were part of a larger soldiers' press that also included periodicals produced in trenches, detainee and training camps, and supply depots at the western, Ottoman, and Russian fronts.[23] As Graham Seal has shown, such publications varied in quality and professionalism, ranging from just a few handwritten pages produced in a trench to professionally printed monthly journals of upwards of twenty-five pages, which lasted the duration of the war and were supported by advertisers. The distribution of these periodicals varied; smaller ones had minimal circulation outside of the unit, while the more professional ones were available by mail subscription and for purchase at newsstands throughout the country. International circulation was also common, since many soldiers sent copies to families and friends, even in dominion countries.[24]

In terms of length, degree of professional quality, and distribution, the *Lyre* lies in the middle of this spectrum. Although its first issue (April 1916) featured a handful of typed articles bound in brown card tied with purple ribbon, from May

1916 through the rest of its run, it averaged around sixteen pages; was profession-ally printed by Messrs. Barrell, Ltd.; and included advertisements by businesses in nearby towns, such as Boots Pharmacy in Frome and W. S. Everett, a grocery shop in Warminster. There were 6 copies of the prototype issues made and 150 of the first printed issues, rising to 500 by December 1916.[25] (See figure 6.1 for the cover of the November 1917 issue.)

The *Lyre* could be purchased in a variety of local shops, including, as Corporal Humphrey stated in the December 1917 issue, "Messrs. W. H. Smith & Son, of Frome, Messrs. Coates & Parker, of Warminster, and Mr. Hulbert, of Horningsham, . . . all of them foregoing any commission on the sale."[26] Postal subscriptions were also available. In November 1917, the cost of the magazine was two pence, but by March 1918 the price had been raised to three.[27]

The content and tone of the *Lyre* resemble those of other British and dominion soldiers' press, including hospital magazines. Typically, these periodicals include serialized fiction writing, poetry, dramatic sketches, drawings, anecdotes about the hospital or trench, and rumor and gossip columns—many of which were titled "Things We'd Like to Know," just as in the *Lyre*; there were also editorials, anecdotes or short memoirs of a personal but humorous nature, and articles chronicling

Figure 6.1. "The Longleat Lyre," *Longleat Lyre* (November 1, 1917): 1.

the history of the publication's location (such as Lady Bath's "History of Long-leat Hospital"). Within these genres, topics often favored unofficial news, gossip, weaponry, the enemy, the Allies, and what life might be like after the war.[28] As with most soldiers' press, the tone of the writing in the *Lyre* is almost always cheerful, communal, and humorous and rarely personal or negative. Moreover, like soldier contributors to other magazines and newspapers, those in the *Lyre* (with the exception of the editor) often did not identify themselves. Seal shows that in most cases, the writers came from the lower ranks and therefore were usually working class.[29] Such we know was certainly the case with the *Lyre*, for not only did the hospital house lower ranks (nonofficers) only, but also, in instances where authors are identified, a rank abbreviation usually precedes identifying name initials. For example, unlike later issues, the first issue of the *Lyre* lists the authors on the front cover; the soldiers represented here are privates, bombardiers, and gunners—all from "other ranks," as was the higher-ranking Corporal Humphrey.[30] While many of the more professional publications were overseen by commanding officers or managed through other official channels, I have not found direct evidence that the *Lyre* was supervised by anyone except the editors. They do on occasion thank Lord and Lady Bath for their support, delicately acknowledging their financial assistance in producing the *Lyre*, part of their ongoing and hefty financial contribution to the survival of the hospital.[31]

What distinguishes the *Lyre* from other hospital magazines and the overall soldiers' press is the amount of attention it gives to music. In the thirty-two volumes of the *Lyre*, there are 164 references to performances of specific songs; additionally, there are countless other references to music being performed—usually a song—in which titles are not given.[32] Usually, these performances took place in the Coliseum, a section of the Stable Yard that Lord Bath had converted for concerts, or sometimes in the Great Hall and Soldiers' and Nurses' Dining Rooms.[33] In some cases, programs were printed and distributed. Reports of the musical events occur in sections of the magazine called "Entertainments" and, after early 1918, also in "Pierrot Entertainments." The amount of musical discussion in the *Lyre* indicates the passion for music and entertainments among the house's inhabitants, whether actual or perceived by the *Lyre*. As the next section will show, many of these inhabitants—from the family to nurses and from clergy to soldiers—were directly involved in creating and maintaining this lively musical life.

Performers at Longleat

In addition to the soldiers, many others were active in Longleat's musical life. As was typical of country-house entertainments for soldiers during the war, the ladies of the family were involved in the organization and performance of music, all of which the *Lyre* frequently reported on. Lady Bath often played the mandolin for soldiers, while her daughters, the Ladies Kathleen and Mary, sang and played the piano for concerts, variety entertainments, and other special celebrations, such as on the night of Armistice Day.[34] Described by the *Lyre* as "the hospital's most energetic friend," Lady Kathleen seems to have been the most active of the Thynne women.[35] The *Lyre* reports regularly and favorably on her musical offerings, such as her performances of "Poor Butterfly" (based on Puccini's *Madam Butterfly*) during the February 7, 1918, entertainment in the Coliseum and Samuel Coleridge-Taylor's "Life and Death" on April 13, 1918.[36] Lady Bath organized and directed skits that starred soldiers and included music as, for example, "Ici on parle français," a "highly popular and successful farce," performed on October 18 and 20, 1917, the second performance of which was attended by visitors from the nearby village of Horningsham. Nurses also participated in music at Longleat, often leading entertainments, such as "a very enjoyable Concert" directed by Sister Brayley in October 23, 1917, and singing solos.[37] The most frequent nurse performer reported on by the *Lyre* was Miss Mason; it recorded six performances by her and listed the songs' titles, including "Love's Garden of Roses," "Bird of Love Divine," and "God Send You Back to Me."[38] The last song was a favorite at Longleat; it had been sung by Nurse Ellis on April 19, 1917, and Lady Kathleen on May 26, 1917.[39]

Just as central to the musical life of wartime Longleat as the Thynne ladies and nurses was the hospital's chaplain, the Reverend W. Cocks. Although he offered two to three worship services per week and worked tirelessly to offer spiritual guidance to the community in various forms—including writing articles for the *Lyre*—he also frequently organized programs of music.[40] In fact, the *Lyre* often referred to him as the hospital's "Musical Director."[41] Additionally, he sang solos, such as "Sergeant of the Line" at an entertainment on October 23, 1917, while his wife regularly accompanied solos, duets, and group singing on the piano and sometimes played solos herself, as described in performances from October 23 and 26, 1917.[42] The efforts of all involved created a musical life at Longleat that was regular and jovial for its patients.

But as the review of the February 7, 1918, entertainment demonstrates, soldiers were not just the recipients of Longleat's music; they were also performers. Certain soldiers were known for their singing, becoming regulars on the stage during their time at the hospital. One example is Private Roma, whom the *Lyre* recorded singing ten times between January and October 1918—more than any other soldier at Longleat. But others performed just as frequently within a much shorter period of time, such as Longleat's "ragtime specialist" and "old friend" Private Russ.[43] According to the *Lyre,* he sang six times between December 1917 and February 1918, rousing Longleat with "the ragtime favourite" "Down Home in Tennessee" on January 23 and "Auntie Skinner's Chicken Dinner" and "Naughty

Melody" on February 2 (the latter two reprised two weeks later).[44] As this suggests, sometimes the men were known for their singing of certain numbers that in turn became audience favorites, such as Lance Corporal Getty's memorable renditions of "The Song That Reached My Heart," offered twice in February 1918.[45] The *Lyre* also noted new talent, as in its account of a Boxing Day 1917 entertainment. In addition to performances by "old favourites Corpl. Standbridge, Pte. Moore, Miss Mason, and the Chaplain," the concert featured the "new singers Bombr. Cox and Rlfln Linton." Their songs, "Echo" and "Neptune," respectively, proved they were "singer[s] of no mean distinction."[46]

While the regular concerts reported on by the *Lyre* varied in terms of organizers and performers, there was one standing entertainment group put together in late 1917: the Longleat Pierrot Troupe. Led by Cocks, it comprised many of the same nurses and soldiers who performed at the other entertainments. Like Longleat's other musical entertainments, the Pierrot Troupe featured solo singing, choruses (designed for audience participation), recitations, solo piano music, and humorous skits. For example, the troupe's February 18, 1918, performance had, according to Barrett, "opening choruses screwed out of the piano by Mrs. Cocks," followed by many new songs and "encores [of] all the old favourites." Rev. W. Cocks sang "Long Live the King" and his original song "Jack Briton," and Private Russ sang "Santa Fe" and "There Was No One to Harmonise."[47] The two men also performed a duet, "The Twins," which "did not mean they were twins"; Miss Mason, the VAD nurse, performed "Gretna Green" and "Until"; and Private Graff reprised "The Beauty of the Guards" from a February 7 entertainment,[48] followed by another favorite from that same event: Privates Graff and Landon's sketch, "A Yorkshire Lad in London." The men "were right on the spot . . . and some new features were introduced, in fact they were better looking than ever. . . . Their duet, 'Done We Harold? Yes, Reggie, we do!' was much applauded. Private Englemann appeared in the sketch as Madame Melba, and her song was profitable to Private Landon; it produced many fits. He showed us how to juggle with biscuits."[49] The evening closed with a chorus of "In the Old Plantation," which "was nicely sung, and the jokes and side-play created merriment."[50]

But this "most enjoyable evening" that yielded "feelings of pleasurable anticipation" beforehand, the *Lyre* commented, was also bittersweet, as it prompted "feelings of regret, because it was in some respects a farewell gathering" for some of the regulars. One who would be particularly missed was Private Landon. Despite having a cold and knowing this night "was his last attempt to *swing it*" before departing the next day, he still "kept [the audience] amused with tales grown in his fertile brain." But during the choruses, "he showed visible signs of uneasiness. Was it the music which upset him, or thoughts of his last joy ride on the *swings*?"[51] He and three other soon-to-depart performers were recognized at the end of the evening: "Three bumping cheers were given for Ptes. Landon, Graff, and Russ, who, as pointed out by the Chaplain, were leaving us on the following day. Special reference was made to Pte. Landon, without whom no programme would be complete, and Pte. Graff, as he said, had been his right hand man; Pte. Russ, too, had a warm corner in his heart, and this was his second time on earth. All three made suitable replies."[52] This send-off of the three privates demonstrates these entertainments were gatherings central to fostering and maintaining the Longleat community. Moreover, this account of the Pierrot Troupe performance, in addition to chronicling the range of performers and specifics of repertoire, illustrates how reviews often referenced previous reviews and performances, creating an ongoing discussion about certain performers, songs for which they were known, and humorous incidents at the performances. The musical events promoted community, but the *Lyre*'s reporting reinforced those ties.

This musical community was not just composed of people staying and working at Longleat. The *Lyre* proudly reported on musical visitors, giving special attention to those from abroad, such as the Australian "Perham Artistes," who first appeared at Longleat on October 29, 1917. Boasting a "long and varied programme," the entertainment included "that rousing song 'Up from Somerset' and as an encore, 'Because,'" sung by "Pte Quigley, who possessed a rich baritone voice"; "Holiday, in the Summertime," sung by Private Nicholls; monologues by Sergeant Runsdale; a skit; character impersonations by Private Cunningham; and a ventriloquial sketch by Private Pering. The Marquess of Bath attended and approved, the *Lyre* also emphasized.[53] After this resounding success, the Perham Artistes returned in January and February 1918, playing to audiences that included Longleat's residents and staff alongside members from the local community. So popular was this troupe, the *Lyre* reported, that after their February concert at Longleat, they still had thirty more engagements to fulfill. Barrett described it as "a real 'bumper'" of an evening in his *Lyre* review; in addition to citing the music performed (some of which was original), he emphasized the transnational experience of the event, casting it as a community-building showcase. It brought many together—even those who did not normally attend the entertainments, such as some of the Longleat nurses (much to the dismay of the *Lyre* writers) and Australian officers. Even the Americans were there in spirit, Barrett stated, for the "chairs on the platform [were] covered with Stars and Stripes in generous tribute to our American Allies."[54] But the Americans were there in spirit in others ways as well: in particular, through the repertoire.

Repertoire, Transnationalism, and Class Connotations

In addition to detailing the performers at Longleat's musical entertainments, the *Lyre* also recorded the musical programs. Much of the repertoire consisted of British music hall and American Tin Pan Alley songs, particularly those addressing war-time sweethearts and "home"—whether real homes of Tipperary or Yorkshire or fictional, idealized ones of Tennessee or Texas.[55] That American repertoire and styles found their way to rural Wiltshire attests to the growing global prowess of the American sheet music industry as well as the transnational wartime circulation of music. That the *Lyre* deems a singing soldier "our ragtime specialist" and comments on Mrs. Cocks's "efforts to *swing* it" at the piano indicates America's musical presence at these entertainments even before the United States entered the war, making the content of Longleat's programs as transnational as their performers.[56]

While popular selections certainly dominated the Longleat programs, classical music was occasionally mentioned in the reviews. For example, a concert in January 1918 included performances by violinist Lance Corporal Dallady of Elgar's "Salut d'amour" and an unnamed Cavatina that, according to the *Lyre*, demonstrated he "really knew how to play." This same entertainment also had renditions of "Roses of Picardy" by Lady Kathleen in "her usual good style," the raucous ragtime favorite "Just Try to Picture Me: Down Home in Tennessee" by Private Russ, and "spirited choruses" led by Mrs. Cocks.[57] Additionally, these entertainments often included patriotic music, such as "Boys of the Ocean Blue" or "God Save the King," most typically sung or led by Reverend Cocks at the conclusion of the evening, as in the entertainment of October 26, 1917.[58]

By and large, these musical entertainments were modeled after those from the front, which in turn were modeled after music hall variety shows. Even performance spaces where entertainments took place were named after big music halls, such as "Empire," "Hippodrome," and, as in the case of Longleat, "Coliseum." J. G. Fuller recognizes parallels in tone, writing that "just as music hall tended 'to laugh at misfortune rather than give it the bitter articulation of the broadsides,' so the concert party troupes presented the soldier's plight in comic fashion."[59] Such fashioning of wartime entertainments, Fuller argues, brought vestiges of the home front to the trenches, providing the soldiers not only amusement but also "a more general application of value systems deriving from civilian life, which brought subtle benefits for morale." Indeed, the popularity of music hall among the working classes prior to the war ensured it was familiar to the mass of noncommissioned soldiers from the British Isles and the dominions.[60] Moreover, on the home front, imitating these war-front concert parties created an idealized version of war events for the people at home, while also creating the illusion of shared experience—a point to which I will return.

Additionally, these different repertoires carried class connotations highlighting the social differences among Longleat's residents. First and foremost, music hall was associated with the working classes throughout the Victorian and Edwardian periods.[61] Families in country houses prior to the war would not have not attended such entertainments, nor did they play such music in their homes (as their sheet music collections indicate). Furthermore, as indicated in the reviews cited above, these entertainments always included group singing—specifically, during the choruses of music hall songs, a key audience participatory activity associated with the genre.[62] Such was certainly the case at Longleat. For example, Private Barrett implies in a "fictional" interview with Lady Kathleen that her participation in such choruses is a lowering of herself, leading to disastrous consequences, such as "sing[ing] them [the music hall choruses] instead of the responses at [church] choir practice, [which] Mr. Cocks never forgives."[63]

Indeed, the social and political connotations of the repertory were on the minds of many at Longleat, arising even in *Lyre* columns not specifically about musical entertainments. For example, the February 1918 issue reported on recent debates on pressing issues of the day, such as whether conscription should end after the war, whether bachelors should be taxed, the appropriateness of women's labor after the war, and whether the war would end sooner if America entered it.[64] But another pressing matter, led by Private Iverson, considered whether the programming of German music should be abolished during the war. The *Lyre* reported, "He gave his views as an observer, and contended that no programme was complete without such words as those of Wagner, Bach, etc. Some highly interesting speeches were made, notably one by Miss Farr, who proved her grip of the subject and opposed the motion. The house finally decided by nineteen votes to eleven 'that German music should NOT be abolished.'"[65] Even in rural Wiltshire and within a small amateur magazine, the national debate first raised during the early months of the war in classical music circles about "enemy music" was acknowledged and extended.[66]

Music and Community at Longleat and Beyond

The *Lyre* chronicled Longleat's wartime musical life generally, and the diverse mix of performers and transnational repertoires new to the country house in particular. Besides promoting healing, musical entertainments were believed to boost morale and promote discipline among the men, keeping them out of trouble.[67] Such was certainly the case at Longleat, where soldiers deemed well enough were allowed to leave the hospital premises on occasion. In a letter to her father, Lady Kathleen proudly boasted of keeping the men out of mischief on Armistice Day by leading them in the singing and dancing in the "Long Ward" until midnight. She wrote that during this music, "they were absolutely good" in "let[ting] their steam off" this way, rather than "break[ing] everything" and celebrating according to their original plan of going to the Canadian Wet Canteen to drink alcohol.[68] But while healing and discipline were certainly important functions of this music, I wish to highlight a third function: community building, the formation of which the *Lyre*'s music reviews clearly document.

Longleat during the war was transformed into not only a space of healing but also a "contact zone"—to borrow Stephen Greenblatt's term from mobility studies—where transclass and transnational social and artistic exchange took place that was new to the English country house and to Britain.[69] Prior to the war, these groups of people at Longleat—upper-class ladies, clergy, nurses, and working-class men from Britain, Canada, and Australia—spending time together, let alone making music together, would have been highly unlikely, especially in the formerly elite space of the stately home. Moreover, these vast social and national differences were magnified by other social barriers. While the *Lyre*'s reviews (and the musical events they chronicle) evoke a seemingly communal and harmonious atmosphere, the reality of hospital life on the English home front during the war was quite different. Private writings by soldiers in hospitals reveal feelings of alienation, discontent, and resentment toward civilians. As Reznick writes, "The soldier patient saw his surrounding ward environment, like his bed, as a site of substantial discipline where nurses and doctors upheld a range of rules and regulations to ensure institutional efficiency, economy, and social order."[70] Some soldiers actually disliked the barrage of (sometimes insensitive) visitors and the enforced music making.[71] Moreover, soldiers who found themselves in home-front hospitals were separated from their unit comrades with whom they had bonded and fought alongside. Their wounds separated them not only from their units but also from the civilians that made up the hospital community. Although I have not seen direct evidence of soldiers' discontent with hospital life, including music, at Longleat, it can be assumed it existed, given the degree to which it was expressed at other institutions.

It is within Longleat's environment of social difference that we can fully recognize music's role in creating a sense of community. Kay Kaufman Shelemay argues that music can be a key ritual in creating a collective identity among disparate peoples. "Musical transmission and performance" are important "not just as expressions or symbols of a given social grouping, but as an integral part of processes . . . [that] can at different moments help generate, shape, and sustain new collectivities."[72] In such "shared identities," whether "grounded in historical fact, . . . newly invented, or emerg[ing] from some combination of historical circumstance and creative transformation, . . . music helps generate and sustain the collective, while at the same time, it contributes to establishing social boundaries within the group and with those outside it."[73] At Longleat music was certainly central to the social life of the people who lived there—its regular entertainments and the repetition of repertoire and performers ensured that music became a common "symbol" of the Longleat "social grouping." Many of these symbols (such as the repertoire discussed above) originated from different class strata and places, reflecting the differences of the people involved. But over time, such entertainments and the *Lyre*'s recounting of them also "generate[d], shape[d], and sustain[d]" a "new collectivity"—the community of the house.

The collective identity formed and nurtured at musical events affected other aspects of life in the house. For example, the chaplain's leadership of music fostered friendly relationships between him and the soldiers, which in turn made them more likely to attend chapel services, as the *Lyre* suggested in a report from March 1918 on a recent Ash Wednesday service. ("May we appeal to all new patients to attend the Services in the Chapel on Sundays. The Chaplain is very good to us, and takes part in all our shows during the week, and is unsparing in his efforts to help us. It is only fair we should support him, and we shall certainly gain much 'food for thought' from his fearless preaching.")[74] Whether soldiers came to worship services on their own accord or out of friendly obligation to the chaplain, the Reverend W. Cocks's involvement with musical entertainments helped to build this diverse and lively community, not only through music but also, most likely, through faith.

The *Lyre* in turn reified this illusion of solidarity built largely around the social process of music making. It acknowledged and even parodied the "social boundaries" (between soldiers and civilians, men and women, working class and upper class, and British and dominion), while simultaneously "sustaining the collective" necessary to promote not only the recovery of soldiers but support for the war as well. While a goal of all soldiers' press was to promote comradeship, the task was even greater for hospital magazines, which had to foster community among men who did not know each other and were from vastly different backgrounds. Reznick argues that hospital magazines promoted and solidified a "soldiers' comradeship of wartime healing, an *esprit de corps* that combined with the comradeship of the trenches to underscore a collective sense of being a class apart from noncombatants in British society."[75] They created a sense of shared experience with people in similar circumstances—men "whose common endurance of institutional discipline and routines reinforced their shared front-line experiences," experiences that hospital workers and the family could not understand.[76] But the magazine also had to unify the larger hospital community. As the editor of the *Gazette of the Third London General Hospital* stated, the hospital magazine should encourage "friendly cooperation and mutual comradeship" within this "complex world of patients, sisters, nurses, officers, orderlies and miscellaneous staff," to make the institution a "place where there is no atmosphere of institutionalism."[77] Reznick contends that such a harmonious community could "work toward the official goals of efficiency, economy and social harmony," promoting "loyalty" and the "spirit of willing service."[78] Indeed, the *Lyre* reinforced and sustained the hospital community by reporting on entertainments in ways that often parodied the tensions (the "social boundaries") between nurses and soldiers, as, for example, in the musical skit "Topsey-Turvey," performed at Longleat on February 4, 1918.[79]

Equally important was the *Lyre*'s presentation of this united community to the larger public. In 1915 the magazine *Hospital* stressed the necessity of publicizing the harmonious environment and desired efficiency of wartime healing spaces, stating that the hospital's "affairs should be known to everybody . . . and its atmosphere should be everywhere appreciated."[80] In so doing, hospital magazines could "create a vision of the institution as a relatively relaxed and harmonious environment apart from the horrors of war."[81] In the *Lyre*, accounts of musical entertainments, more than any other kind of content, repeatedly envisioned and publicized these "harmonious environments" where different groups of people congregated and participated, eliding differences and tensions and temporarily forgetting the horrors of war. Nurses, soldiers (whether British, Canadian, Australian, New Zealander, or Belgian), family members, and the larger Wiltshire community were brought together by the musical entertainments, in which all sang together, laughed, and left in good cheer. When individuals did not attend the entertainments or left early, it was noticed, as recorded in the February and March 1918 "Things We Want to Know" columns.[82] Longleat's musical events were meant to bring everyone together; people were expected to participate, and the *Lyre* continually reinforced this sense of community.

The *Lyre*'s distribution range extended this musical network beyond the walls of Longleat. As cited earlier, the magazine listed a number of advertisers who supported the magazine and local businesses who sold it, showing it circulated in Warminster and Frome. But it is likely the *Lyre* found its way outside of Wiltshire and Somerset, for readers could also subscribe by mail. Reznick notes that many magazines' offering of postal subscriptions, as one editor put it, to "all interested in the Hospital, whether directly connected with it or not," indicates a widespread interest, even more than for trench journals.[83] Moreover, these magazines were sold in other hospitals and often read by patients and staff there.[84] National and international distribution was also likely, since soldiers often sent their publications to their families throughout Britain, Canada, and Australia. The *Lyre* seems to have been aware of this larger network and strove to maintain it. It commented when former Longleat residents and *Lyre* supporters sent news back to Longleat, such as in the March 1918 issue, when the editor wrote that Humphrey, the magazine's former editor, had sent a letter. The *Lyre* also regularly reported on those who had left Longleat, and it emphasized its role in maintaining ties with them.[85] Overall, such harmony and efficiency among soldiers and civilians in these convalescent spaces, as portrayed in hospital magazines and especially by the *Lyre*'s coverage of musical entertainments, were intended to ensure that soldiers would recover to return to the war fronts, that home-front and dominion countries would continue to support the war, and that ultimately the war could be won. In this sense, the hospital magazine is a form of propaganda.

Conclusion

The *Lyre* offers a plethora of detail about musical life at a country-house VAD hospital, opening a new window onto the rich musical life in Britain during the First World War that has not been addressed by musicologists or historians. It furthers our understanding of the role of music in the healing process for soldiers during the war and offers plentiful evidence of music boosting morale. But aside from specifics of performers and repertoire, the magazine also bears witness to the unprecedented mixing of and music making by upper-class landowners, middle-class nurses and clergy, and working-class British and dominion soldiers—people who would not have made music together before the war. Through music, as both a symbol and a ritualistic process, Longleat's inhabitants established and sustained a transnational and transclass wartime community—a diverse community that the *Lyre* in turn solidified and publicized, presenting the community to the British and dominion publics as international but united behind Britain. This country-house support of the war and its adaptability to necessary social change—change bolstered by its boisterous, egalitarian musical community—were certainly, for an uneasy, war-weary British public, "things they wanted to know."

Notes

1. The series consisted of three episodes; they aired on September 14, 21, and 30, 2015.

2. Longleat is the seat of the Marquesses of Bath. It was established in 1541; the present Elizabethan-style structure was completed in the 1570s. At the time of World War I, Sir Thomas Thynne, 5th Marquess of Bath (1862–1946), and his wife, Violet Caroline Mordaunt (1865–1928), occupied the house. Their younger son, Henry Thynne (1905–92), inherited the title and estate upon his father's death in 1946. Attempting to ensure the financial survival of Longleat, he opened the house to the public in 1949 and the safari park on the estate grounds in 1966. The family continues to reside in part of the house today.

3. "Tommy" was short for "Tommy Atkins" and since the eighteenth century had been slang for an unranked British soldier. It became most commonly used in World War I.

4. I deal with this subject in my monograph in progress, "Music, Healing, and Memory in the English Country House, 1914–1919."

5. An abbreviated version of this essay was read at the seventh Biennial Conference of the North American British Music Studies Association at Syracuse University, Syracuse, NY, August 4–6, 2016, and as a longer talk in the Music Research Forum series in the Department of Music at Durham University on November 29, 2016. The US-UK Fulbright Commission and grants from the National Endowment for the Humanities and the *Music and Letters* Trust supported archival research for this project. I would like to thank Kate Harris (curator of

Longleat Historic Collections), Emma Challinor (assistant archivist and records manager at Longleat), and staff at the British Library for their research assistance. I would also like to thank Christina Bashford, Eric Saylor, Harris, and Challinor for their helpful comments on earlier drafts of this essay.

6. A. G. Barrett, "Entertainments," *Longleat Lyre* (hereafter cited as *LL*) (March 1, 1918): 15. Publication information for songs performed at this entertainment, in order of performance, is as follows: "Song That Reached My Heart," composed by Jules Jordan (New York: Edward B. Marks, 1887); "Poor Butterfly," by Raymond Hubbell and John L. Golden (New York: Francis, Day, and Hunter, 1916); "When the Ebb Tide Flows," by Clifton Bingham and Stanley Gordon (New York: Joseph W. Stern, 1906); "Till the Sands of the Desert," by George Graff Jr. and Ernest R. Ball (New York: M. Whitmark and Sons, 1911); "The Beauty of the Guards," by Frank Leo and George Bastow (no publication information, other than it was performed by Bastow in music halls, 1912); "Nothing to Wear," by Dave Stamper and Gene Buck (New York: T. B. Harms and Francis, Day, and Hunter, 1914); "Watchman, What of the Night?," by James Sarjeant (London: Boosey, 1905); "Red Rose of England," by Ed. Teschemacher and Herbert Oliver (London: J. H. Larway, 1912); "The Boys of the Ocean Blue," composer and original publication unknown, but it was included in the *Royal Navy War-Song Album* (London: George Newnes, ca. 1914–18); and "Hinky Dinky Parley Vous" (also known as "Mademoiselle from Armentières"), by Harry Carlton (although that is disputed), ca. 1915. Nonmusical items performed at this entertainment were the poem "Gunga Din" (1892), by Rudyard Kipling, and the two skits "One Man Band" and "Yorkshire Lad in London," about both of which I have not been able to find information.

7. The majority of information on Longleat that I have gathered comes from the incomplete set of *LL,* digitized on the Adam Matthew database "Trench Journals and Hospital Magazines of the First World War," which I accessed at the British Library; exhibits displayed in the main archives exhibition (running between August 2014 and November 2015) and room interpretation boards (August 2014–November 2018) devised for the First World War centenary commemoration at Longleat House; and "Songs Performed at Longleat during World War I," an unpublished, fully referenced survey of the entire repertoire of songs, plays, poems, and instrumental music performed at Longleat as reported in the *LL*, compiled by Longleat House archivists. This survey was assembled both for Longleat's own commemorative event and for the opening event for the county's centenary commemoration in 2014 ("A Letter Home," World War One Centenary Concert at the Wiltshire Music Centre, Bradford on Avon, October 11, 2014) and to support the development of education projects both at Longleat and in association with the Wiltshire Music center in a program for composition students.

8. Peter Mandler, *The Fall and Rise of the Stately Home* (New Haven, CT: Yale University Press, 1997), 4, 109–10, 212–17.

9. Ibid., 109; David Cannadine, *The Decline and Fall of the British Aristocracy* (1990; reprint, New York: Vintage, 1999), 73–84.

10. For example, the first issue of the *Lady* after the outbreak of the war reports on a number of high-profile estates already being offered up, such as the king's lending of Balmoral Castle, Dunrobin Castle (Duke of Sutherland), Cardiff Castle (Lord Bute), and Clandon

Park (Lord Onslow). The article lists a number of other ways in which the upper classes were already helping as well. See "The *Lady* in Society," August 13, 1914, 270.

11. Soldiers of color from dominion countries were housed and treated separately. For example, the Royal Pavilion in Brighton was converted into a hospital for Indian soldiers during the war.

12. Lady Bath, "The History of Longleat Relief Hospital," *LL* (July 1, 1916): 6.

13. Ibid., 7.

14. The papers of Lady Alda Hoare of Stourhead, including her diaries, annotated music collection, and soldiers' letters to her, offer excellent and vivid depictions of wartime music making in a country house with soldiers. My monograph in progress deals with these sources extensively, as does my article "Memory, Music, and Private Mourning in an English Country House during the First World War: Lady Alda Hoare's Musical Shrine to a Lost Son," *Journal of Musicological Research* 31, nos. 1–3 (2014): 39–95.

15. Originally from Hackbridge in Greater London, Humphrey received a bullet wound in his leg in Ypres, from which he recovered at Longleat from February 1916 until January 1917. I have not yet been able to identify the editor who took over from Humphrey in January 1918; he did not include his name or initials in the *Lyre* issues.

16. For example, in his editorial in the July 1916 issue, a (frustrated) Humphrey urged those who wished to contribute not to procrastinate, implying that going through the plethora of submissions at the last minute was stressful for him. Corporal E. Humphrey, editorial, *LL* (July 1, 1916): 14.

17. "Editor's Notes," *LL* (March 1, 1918): 8.

18. Jeffrey Reznick, *Healing the Nation: Soldiers and the Culture of Caregiving in Britain during the Great War*, Cultural History of Modern War (Manchester: Manchester University Press, 2004), 66.

19. Examples of the latter are the *First Eastern General Hospital Gazette* (Cambridge), *Hydra: The Journal of the Craiglockhart War Hospital* (Edinburgh), and *Ration: The Magazine of the Reading War Hospitals*.

20. Of the 151 hospital magazines on the "Trench Journals" database, only five (including the *LL*) are from country-house hospitals. The other four are the *Chronicles of Cliveden*; *Fragments: The Wounded Soldier's Magazine of Heywood Auxiliary Hospital, Red Cross and Order of St. John*; *Gallowhill Auxiliary Hospital, Paisley. No. 20 Renfrew V.A.D.—a Collection of Verses*; and the *Worsley Wail: Being the Unofficial Chronicle of the Worsley Red Cross Hospital, Lancashire* (Manchester).

21. Reznick, *Healing the Nation*, 65.

22. Anna Carden-Coyne, *The Politics of Wounds: Military Patients and Medical Power in the First World War* (Oxford: Oxford University Press, 2014), 3–5, 191–274. Graham Seal, in *The Soldiers' Press: Trench Journals in the First World War* (New York: Palgrave Macmillan, 2013), also deals with hospital magazines, but only tangentially, as part of the larger soldiers' press. Neither book, nor Reznick's, addresses the musical content of these magazines in any depth, nor does the *Longleat Lyre* receive attention.

23. While not exhaustive of all British and dominion soldiers' press, the "Trench Journals" database, with its digitization of soldiers' press holdings from the Imperial War Museum, British Library, Staatsbibliothek zu Berlin, and the Library of Congress, does represent a

large sampling of such sources, as well as periodicals for French, German, and American soldiers.

24. Amanda Laugesen, "Australian Soldiers and the World of Print," in *Publishing in the First World War: Essays in Book History*, ed. Mary Hammond and Shafquat Towheed (London: Palgrave Macmillan, 2007), 106; Seal, *Soldiers' Press*, 22.

25. I thank the Longleat House archivists for sharing this information with me.

26. Corporal E. Humphrey, "Editor's Notes," *LL* (December 1, 1917): 11.

27. For comparison, the *Times*, in January 1917, cost one and a half pence. The *Worsley Wail* (the hospital magazine of the VAD Red Cross Hospital at Worsley Hall in Lancashire) cost six pence.

28. Seal, *Soldiers' Press*, 42.

29. Ibid., 23, 42. While lower ranks were almost always working-class men, officers, especially in the first half of the war, were public school educated and from the upper classes.

30. In addition to Corporal Humphrey, the other soldier contributors listed on the title page of this issue are "Bdr. [Bombardier] Morris," "Pte. [Private] Moore," "Gnr. [Gunner] Harvey," and "L/Cpl [Lance Corporal] Macaskill." The titles of bombardier and gunner were at the level of private. See the front cover of *LL* (April 1, 1916): 1. This issue is not in the "Trench Journals" database; rather, I viewed it at the "Longleat Relief Hospital in the First World War" exhibit at Longleat in August 2014.

31. I thank the Longleat House archivists for pointing this out to me.

32. To my knowledge, Longleat House Archives is the only location where all thirty-two volumes are still held. Just eight of these are digitized on the "Trench Journals" database cited above.

33. With the installation of electricity at Longleat in 1928–29, the Coliseum was converted into an engine and battery room. The Nurses' and Soldiers' Dining Rooms were formerly the Lower Dining Room and the Upper East Corridor, respectively. Today the latter is identified as the Robes Corridor.

34. The Thynne daughters were also involved in war-related work outside of Longleat, as reported in a feature page on the three women in the high-society magazine the *Tatler*. See "The Daughters of the Marquis of Bath," *Tatler* (September 11, 1915): 287. Lady Alice Kathleen Violet Thynne (1891–1977) worked as secretary for both Longleat Hospital and the Wiltshire Land Army and served as vice president of the Red Cross hospital in Frome. From September to December 1916, she worked for the YMCA at a canteen in Abbeville, France. Lady Emma Margery (1893–1980), not mentioned in the *Lyre* in relation to any musical activities, worked in munitions factories in London and Kent during the war. Lady Mary Beatrice Thynne's (1903–74) war work is not specified in the *Tatler* article, but given her young age during the war, it is likely her efforts were focused mainly in the home. The daughters were not the only children of the house to contribute to the war effort. John Alexander Thynne (1895–1916), 9th Viscount of Weymouth and son and heir of the Lord and Lady Bath, joined the British Expeditionary Force shortly after the war began. Second Lieutenant in the Royal Scots Greys, he was killed near Loos, France, in February 1916. The youngest brother of the 5th Marquess of Bath, Lieutenant Colonel Lord Alexander Thynne D. S. O., was also killed in action, in 1918.

35. "The Christmas Festivities at Longleat," *LL* (January 1, 1918): 6.

36. Barrett, "Entertainments," *LL* (March 1, 1918): 15; "Entertainments, Amusements, & c." (May 1, 1918): 5.

37. "Entertainments," *LL* (November 1, 1917): 7.

38. Barrett, "Entertainments," *LL* (March 1, 1918): 16–17. "Love's Garden of Roses," by Ruth Rutherford and Haydn Wood (London: Chappell, 1914), popularized by John McCormack; "Bird of Love Divine," by Haydn Wood and Kathleen Birch (London: Boosey, 1912); "God Send You Back to Me," by A. Emmet Adams and Douglas Furber (London: Newman, 1916).

39. *LL* (May 1, 1917): 12; *LL* (June 1, 1917): 14. These issues are not available on the "Trench Journals" database; I gathered this performance information from the "Songs Performed at Longleat during World War I" spreadsheet compiled by the Longleat House Archives staff in July 2015.

40. Examples of his spiritual columns are "Christmas Message" and "Chaplain's Notes," such as those in *LL* (December 1, 1917): 3, 4.

41. For example, see "Entertainments," *LL* (November 1, 1917): 8.

42. Ibid. "Sergeant of the Line," by W. H. Squire and Fred E. Weatherly (London: Boosey, 1908). Reverend Cocks performed this song on September 5, 1918, as well.

43. "Entertainments," *LL* (January 1, 1918): 8; Barrett, "Entertainments," *LL* (March 1, 1918): 13.

44. "B." [probably Barrett], "Entertainments," *LL* (February 1, 1918): 7; Barrett, "Entertainments," *LL* (March 1, 1918): 13. The three songs listed here were American ragtime hits, made popular by American star singers. "Just Try to Picture Me: Down Home in Tennessee," by William Jerome and Walter Donaldson (New York: Waterson, Berlin, and Snyder, 1915), was made popular by Al Jolson; "Auntie Skinner's Chicken Dinner," by Arthur Fields, Earl Carroll, and Theodore Morse (New York: M. Whitmark and Sons, 1915), was made popular by singer Ruth Royce, known as the "Princess of Ragtime"; and "That Naughty Melody," by George W. Meyer and Sam M. Lewis (New York: Geo. W. Meyer, 1913), was made popular by Billy Murray. See also Barrett, "Entertainments," *LL* (March 1, 1918): 16, 19.

45. Barrett, "Entertainments," *LL* (March 1, 1918): 16. "When Other Lips" from Michael William Balfe's *The Bohemian Girl* (1906). I thank Christina Bashford for pointing this aria out to me.

46. "Entertainments," *LL* (January 1, 1918): 8. "Echo" is a setting of Christina Rossetti's poem of the same name by Lord Henry Somerset (London: Chappell, 1906); "Neptune (Lord of the Sea I Am)," by Clifton Bingham and Stanley Gordon (New York: Chas. Shead, 1909).

47. Barrett, "Entertainments," *LL* (March 1, 1918): 20. Songs performed were "Long Live the King" ("The Veteran's Song"), by F. E. Weatherly and Stephen Adam (London: Boosey, 1902); "Jack Briton," by Fred E. Weatherly and W. H. Squire (London: Boosey, 1910); and "On the Road Called Santa Fe," by E. C. Potter and Charles T. Atkinson (publisher unknown, 1907). I have not been able to find information on "There Was No One to Harmonise," so it is possible these words are from the lyrics and not the title. The reference to the duet "The Twins" is probably to a musical setting of Robert Service's poem, but I have not been successful in tracking down any more information on it. According to the "Songs Performed at Longleat during World War I" document, the duet was performed again at Longleat in

September 1918 by Reverend Cocks and Sig. D. Williams and reported on by the *Lyre* the next month. See *LL* (October 1, 1918): 8–9.

48. Barrett, "Entertainments," *LL* (March 1, 1918). "Until," by Ed. Teschemacher and Wilfred Sanderson (London: Boosey, 1910), was made popular by John McCormack.

49. Barrett, "Entertainments," *LL* (March 1, 1918): 20. That men cross-dressed as women for Pierrot performances was not exclusive to Longleat. Carden-Coyne discusses this common practice in other hospitals and its social and gender implications. See Carden-Coyne, *Politics of Wounds*, 252–58.

50. Barrett, "Entertainments," *LL* (March 1, 1918): 20. "In the Old Plantation" most likely refers to the folk song "Hares in the Old Plantation."

51. Ibid., 19.

52. Ibid., 20.

53. "Entertainments," *LL* (November 1, 1917): 9. Songs performed were "Up from Somerset," by Frederick Weatherly and Wilfred Sanderson (London: Boosey, 1913); "Because," by Ed. Teschemacher and Guy D'Hardelot (London: Chappell, 1902); and "We'll All Have a Holiday in the Summertime," by Bert Lee and R. P. Weston (London: Francis, Day, and Hunter, 1916).

54. Barrett, "Entertainments," *LL* (March 1, 1918): 22–23.

55. John Mullen, *The Show Must Go On! Popular Song in Great Britain during the First World War*, Ashgate Popular and Folk Series (Farnham, UK: Ashgate, 2015).

56. Barrett, "Entertainments," *LL* (March 1, 1918): 20. In my monograph, I deal with the specifics of these songs and their transnational implications in more depth.

57. "B.," "Entertainments," *LL* (February 1, 1918): 7. The Longleat House archivists have identified this piece as the well-known encore Cavatina, op. 85, no. 3, by the German composer Joachim Raff.

58. "Entertainments," *LL* (November 1, 1918): 8.

59. J. G. Fuller, *Troop Morale and Popular Culture in the British and Dominion Armies, 1914–1918* (Oxford: Oxford University Press, 1991), 100. Here Fuller is citing P. Summerfield, "The Effingham Arms and the Empire: Deliberate Selection in the Evolution of the Music Hall in London," in *Popular Culture and Class Conflict, 1590–1914: Explorations in the History and Labour and Leisure*, ed. Eileen Yeo and Stephen Yeo (Brighton: Branch Line, 1981), 233. For examples of soldier shows in the United States and Canada, see Jeffrey Magee's chapter on Irving Berlin and Brian C. Thompson's discussion of Canadian performances at the front, both in this volume.

60. Fuller, *Troop Morale and Popular Culture*, 118, 124–25.

61. See Mullen, *Show Must Go On!*, 43.

62. John Mullen, "Why Singalong? The Meanings and Uses of the Singalong Chorus in First World War Music Hall" (paper presented at the "'Pack Up Your Troubles': Performance Cultures in the First World War" conference, University of Kent, Canterbury, April 27–29, 2016).

63. Private A. G. Barrett, "Imaginary Interviews," *LL* (March 1, 1918): 7.

64. A debating society had been formed at Longleat in October 1917. The elected officers were as follows: president, the Marquess of Bath; chairman, Reverend W. Cocks; vice

chairman, Gunner Vincent; committee: Lady Bath; Lady Kathleen; the matron, Sister Stokes; Mrs. Yard; Miss Farr; Corporal Kent; Lance Corporal Davies; Sergeant Smith; Private Perrin; Gunner Lover; and Driver Hammond; secretary, Miss Willans. "Debates," *LL* (November 1, 1917): 4.

65. "Debates," *LL* (February 1, 1918): 9–10. Compare the invectives generated by John Philip Sousa in the United States; see Patrick Warfield's chapter in this volume.

66. For a discussion of this debate as played out among critics and the national press, see Jane Angell, "Art Music in British Public Discourse during the First World War" (PhD diss., Royal Holloway University of London, 2013), 47–95; and Glenn Watkins, *Proof through the Night* (Berkeley: University of California Press, 2003), 33–37.

67. Fuller, *Troop Morale and Popular Culture*, 109–10.

68. Lady Kathleen Thynne to Lord Bath, November 12, 1918, papers of the 6th Marquess of Bath, Longleat House Archives, 5th Marquess of Bath 300. The Canadian Wet Canteen was most likely a mess serving the 103rd Company, Canadian Forestry Corps, working at the woodlands on the Longleat estate.

69. Stephen Greenblatt, "A Mobility Studies Manifesto," in *Cultural Mobility: A Manifesto*, ed. Stephen Greenblatt with Ines G. Županov et al. (Cambridge: Cambridge University Press, 2010), 251.

70. Reznick, *Healing the Nation*, 76.

71. Ibid., 86–87; Carden-Coyne, *Politics of Wounds*, 69.

72. Kay Kaufman Shelemay, "Musical Communities: Rethinking the Collective in Music," *Journal of the American Musicological Society* 64, no. 2 (2011): 350–51. A different, musically constituted community is discussed by William Brooks in chapter 9 of this volume.

73. Ibid., 367, 368.

74. Private A. G. Barrett, "Lantern Service," *LL* (March 1, 1918): 9.

75. Reznick, *Healing the Nation*, 65.

76. Ibid., 76.

77. "Editorial Notes: Freedom and Discipline," *Gazette of the Third London General Hospital* (October 1915): 3–4, quoted ibid., 70.

78. Reznick, *Healing the Nation*, 70.

79. Barrett, "Entertainments," *LL* (March 1, 1918): 13–14.

80. "Every Hospital's Own Gazette: A Great Success at Military Hospitals," *Hospital* (December 18, 1915): 257.

81. Reznick, *Healing the Nation*, 71.

82. "Things We Want to Know," *LL* (February 1, 1918): 12; "Things We Want to Know," *LL* (March 1, 1918): 9.

83. Editorial in *Gazette of the Third London General Hospital* (April 13, 1915): 1, quoted in Reznick, *Healing the Nation*, 67.

84. Reznick, *Healing the Nation*, 67.

85. "Editor's Notes," *LL* (March 1, 1918): 8.

CHAPTER 7

Women at the Pedals

Female Cinema Musicians during the Great War

KENDRA PRESTON LEONARD

The image of a white woman seated at a cinema organ, usually dressed in modest clothing and with her hair up, was a popular trope that developed early in the history of motion picture music, even when most theater musicians were still men. Advertisements for pianos, organs, sheet music, and other accoutrements of silent film accompaniment regularly featured illustrations of women at the keyboard (see figure 7.1). Later ads suggested that the job of cinema accompanist was a serious and respectable one for women, and it was compared positively with secretarial work, teaching, and nursing. The woman at the pedals—who truly came into her own when male cinema musicians were called up for service in 1917 when the United States entered the Great War—was the arbiter of morality and taste in the cinema, a performer and composer whose roles are inextricably entwined, a writer of patriotic songs, an inventor and innovator within the film industry.

The histories of these women are faded, far-flung, unpreserved, uncollected, unheard—an ironic fate considering that they provided sound for a supposedly soundless medium: music for and as motion, emotion, amusement, and cultural commentary. Although no census of cinema accompanists was ever taken, reports from trade and industry publications suggest that while white male musicians were in the majority in the early days of cinema accompaniment, women, both white and of color, soon equaled or outnumbered them. Women were particularly important as cinema accompanists during the First World War, when movie theater orchestras

LYON & HEALY'S EMPRESS

BELL ELECTRIC PIANOS

The newest, finest and most effective musical instrument for

MOTION PICTURE THEATRES

Operator not necessary, but may also be played by hand

Good Music Pays

The Rolls which operate this piano give the bell part the effect of artistic hand playing

Contains 24 Sheffield Steel Orchestra Bell Bars Also Mandolin Attachment

Figure 7.1. An advertisement for Bell Electric Pianos, showing the stereotypical woman at the pedals, published in *Motion Picture Magazine* 9, no. 1 (1915): 145.

were dissolved and male musicians left their positions to join the military.[1] There is no question that such women were often at the center of cinematic music making, particularly in smaller towns and cities and communities. Nor should there be any doubt about the importance of the work these women did. Their performances for newsreels, animations, live-action shorts, and feature films frequently served in multiple ways: to suggest, shape, and help define the musical tastes of the time; to educate listeners; to show how music could serve as a creative, narrative, and interpretative force in the cinema. But there has been little print dedicated to these important musicians and their work. As Ally Acker has written about women in other aspects of the film industry, "Women are as integral and transformative to the cinema as [well-known men], and yet their stories have consistently remained untold." The influence of these women, particularly during the Great War and its immediate aftermath, cannot be understated; as Acker continues, "More women worked in decision-making positions in film before 1920 than at any other time in history."[2]

Acker's claim certainly includes female musicians. As I will show here, women filled a number of roles in the American cinema music industry, particularly during the Great War. In addition to serving as cultural barometers for cinematic music and accompaniment, women were at the heart of innovations in cinema sound and composition. Yet the scholarly bibliography on women musicians in the silent cinema is essentially nonexistent. There are a number of reasons for this. In an era when women were often named only as "Miss [last name] or "Mrs. [husband's last name]" in print and those who wished to publish songs or other kinds of music still often had to do so under pseudonyms or with their first initials in place of their names in order to be considered seriously, only a limited number of female composers and performers were easily identified through or recognized for their work. Most research that has been done on silent film music has focused on male performers and composers active in New York and in Hollywood, in part because the trade magazines, house publications, and other necessary documents for study both were focused on activities in those places and were held by institutions there. These resources generally lack coverage of the activities of women in the profession.[3] In addition, film music scholars have focused on the primarily male cadre of published composers of silent film music active first on the American East Coast and later in Hollywood. The lack of information and research on women in silent cinema music is also due to an overwhelmingly canonized music history narrative, in which successful women musicians were somehow "extraordinary." Women working in cinema music came from a variety of ethnic, socioeconomic, and educational backgrounds and were not, in general, members of the elite, male-mentored group of female art-music composers and performers of the period, exemplified by Amy Beach and Maud Powell.

Further limiting research on female cinema musicians, much of the music from this period has not survived. In the late 1960s, MGM, among other studios, decided that it was not necessary to keep musical materials from the silent era and later periods and sent its entire music library to a landfill. Even the films for which these women composed, played, or created early recordings have not survived in great numbers: in 2013 a report by film historian David Pierce reported that of the more than 11,000 films made in America during the silent era, only 2,749 (about 25 percent) are still extant. Many of these still remain on nitrate stock, which is both highly flammable and rapidly disintegrating; we will lose a certain amount of that 25 percent before those films are ever preserved.[4] There is equally great loss in what experts on antiques term "paper ephemera." Sheet music that does credit women as the lyricists and composers goes uncataloged in archive basements or attics. Periodicals from the silent era demonstrating the activities of women in the cinema and film industry are discarded every day. Patents and other documents illustrating the creative and scientific contributions women made to the technology and practice of film accompaniment have disappeared into archives unseen by film historians and musicologists. And as is often the case with materials from segregated America, we have much less documentation about women of color than we do about white women.

It is important to both music and cinema history, therefore, to develop a basic history of who the women involved with music for silent films were, what roles they played, what we know about them and the music they played, and what we might do going forward to find and preserve more of their histories. Here I examine each of these roles in the context of the Great War with the purpose of providing springboards for further research.

Keyboardists

As the image in figure 7.1 suggests, women were often hired as film accompanists at the piano or organ for the sake of a theater's propriety even before managers seriously considered their musical abilities. A woman accompanist was viewed as an imprimatur of morality and cleanliness in a cinema. A properly "accomplished" pianist—in which "accomplished" broadly signified the gender (female), class (middle or above), and relative musical skill (a basic facility with the instrument and the ability to read music) of the performer—was a boon to any establishment wishing to distinguish itself as a proper place of family entertainment. As R. H. Pray observed in July 1914, a theater with a "slovenly outward appearance," and posters that were "of a vulgar and suggestive type," where music, "furnished by a piano and violin, gave vent with a tin-pan crash to all the ragtime pieces which were known as popular among the [young] people [mostly men] who visited the place" was put out of business as soon as "a large, neat and commodious build-ing," with a "pipe-organ, as fine as any church in the neighborhood could boast of, was installed, and good music beside this was also furnished in the way of an accomplished [female] pianist" opened in the same neighborhood.[5]

Once hired, cinema accompanists had a variety of tasks as part of their jobs. Very few films had full scores of either original or a mix of original and preexisting music created specifically to accompany them. (Perhaps the two most famous of these from the period before the US entry into the war in 1917 are the 1908 film *L'assassinat du Duc du Guise*, directed by Charles Le Bargy and André Calmettes, which had an original score by Saint-Saëns, and D. W. Griffith's 1915 epic, *The Birth of a Nation*, which was accompanied by a mix of preexisting and original music by Joseph Carl Breil.) Rather, the vast majority of movies distributed during this time were sent to theaters without any suggestions or indications for accompanying music. Thus, cinema accompanists were responsible for creating their own scores in whatever manner they preferred.

As Richard Abel, Rick Altman, Julie Hubbert, Martin Marks, and other scholars of silent film sound have documented, there were no standardized practices for sup-plying music for films. Music for accompanying films initially came from vaudeville music libraries, popular song, preexisting art music, and original compositions, only some of which were committed to paper. In the 1910s, publications of music expressly for film accompaniment began to proliferate, offering what is called genre music or mood music for actions, events, and emotions commonly found in film scenarios. Using published collections of genre music, called photoplay albums, cinema pianists, organists, or ensembles could patch together a handful of pieces to create a compiled score of generic pieces that provided music that broadly matched the action on-screen. These pieces provide the earliest documentation for the use of musical mimesis in films. Works for "hurry" or "gallop" were quick in tempo, mimicked the sound of hoof beats or heartbeats, and employed short note values, all of which suggested the associated speed of motion given in the title. In *Motion Picture Moods*, an enormous collection of generic pieces selected and arranged by film-score composer and arranger Erno Rapée, "Aeroplane" is represented by Mendelssohn's "Rondo Capriccio," in which a three-measure passage of rapidly alternating thirds in the piano's right hand is apparently meant to stand in for the sound of high-speed propellers; one entry for "Sea Storm" is Grieg's "Peer Gynt's Homecoming/Stormy Evening on the Coast," which musically imitates choppy seas through the use of alternating low and high As in the bass in sixteenth notes.[6]

At the same time, some performers improvised throughout an entire film, created their own motifs to use for each picture they accompanied, and composed entire scores that often went undocumented or committed to paper. Cinema organist Rosa Rio, for example, often had to accompany films without previewing them, so while she accompanied a movie for the first time, she worked to compose motifs or themes for the characters or events in the picture, upon which she would then improvise and elaborate in following showings, ultimately creating a consistent score that she would play from memory each time she accompanied the picture.[7] Other performers preferred to work from a list of suggestions for music, known as a cue sheet, which lists a film's major events or cues next to the title or incipit of a piece that would go well with the action. As the demand for music for film grew, studios began issuing cue sheets for individual films, prepared by in-studio composers or score compilers. The Edison Film Company began issuing cue sheets with all of its feature-length films in 1913,[8] Mutual Film Company did so in 1917,[9] and other companies followed. Around the same time, film magazines also began publishing cue sheets created by the editors of their music columns or music departments.[10]

During the 1910s and early '20s, only the most prestigious films with the largest budgets received fully original, completely synchronized scores for their presentation in cinemas. These "special scores," as they were marketed, generally eschewed preexisting music of any kind, although some did include a single notable preexisting theme or popular song, often for marketing purposes. The special score existed from the beginnings of film and film music, but, as Martin Marks notes, the genre blossomed in the United States between 1910 and 1914, and following the success of Joseph Carl Breil's fully synchronized score for Griffith's 1915 picture, *The Birth of a Nation*, more studios began producing full scores for their pictures.[11] Breil applied a Wagnerian approach to scoring his films, starting with his now lost score for *Queen Elizabeth* in 1912, assigning leitmotivs to characters and places as a means of connecting all of the elements of the film through the music and developing a coherent musical narrative that was carried throughout the score. This practice was immediately hailed as highly effective and widely adopted.

Nonetheless, as the cue sheets for even large-budget films produced during the 1920s indicate, the completely original and synchronized score remained far from the norm. Of the full-length film scores produced during the late teens and early twenties, many remained compiled scores with only a few original sections: that is, they were comprised of preexisting pieces that were connected to one another with original transitions and sometimes contained a new song or tune for a romantic or climactic scene. Photoplay albums and single-work generic music and cue sheets continued to be used by most motion picture accompanists until the coming of sound between 1927 and 1929, although original full scores became increasingly common as the 1920s progressed.

Most of the moving pictures of the 1910s were quite short, generally ranging between fifteen minutes and an hour, so the process of creating a musical accompaniment for a film could range from finding a single piece that would work for the entirety of a short film to compiling a list of up to thirty or more individual pieces from which brief passages would be used.[12] The vast majority of preexisting works collected for film accompaniment, whether in a publication for that purpose or by an individual performer, were almost uniformly classical in nature. Julie Hubbert has written that the classicization of moving picture music came about under the leadership of European-trained cinema composers and orchestra directors such as Samuel L. Rothafel (later Rothapfel) and Hugo Riesenfeld, but the highly gendered training of female pianists in the United States in the late nineteenth and early twentieth centuries clearly also played a role in this process.[13] Women whose upbringing during this period had included traditional piano lessons and who had been taught song and opera repertoire and short, descriptive, characteristic pieces that worked well in cinematic accompaniment were especially well prepared for the work. Such pianists also often had a repertoire of popular songs at hand, as music publishers marketed these for playing at home by women. It is ironic that women accompanists, initially hired for their gender and the social signifiers it conveyed, were uniquely qualified as cinema pianists, and, later, organists, partly because of the gendered treatment to which they had been subjected.[14]

The same gender essentialism that paradoxically helped create women as the ideal cinema accompanist carried over into their critical reception as musicians. Here women were hailed as indispensable to the success of moving pictures while simultaneously being labeled as "girls," a highly revealing term that speaks to their relative place in the hierarchy of power and influence within most cinemas. In an issue of *Motion Picture Magazine* from March 1914, Stanley Todd, a regular commentator on music for the cinema, described women as more emotional and passionate players, making them appropriate accompanists for film. Reporting from Denver, he noted that the "theatres are large, the entrances dazzlingly brilliant, and like as not you will find within a wonderful pipe-organ, ready in an instant to change its song of sadness to paeans of joy. It is in Denver, too, where a mere slip of a girl presides at the console of one of these great instruments, and each night plays, with her heart and soul, to the finest of screen projections. . . . In this way, music lends its valuable aid in interpreting the gamut of emotions, which only the picture can bring into play with that subtle power that has been one of its secrets of success."[15] J. J. Raymond described a theater manager who noted that good playing could bring in audiences for even poor pictures: "I've got a little girl in front of that music box that can shake out more ragtime a minute than any two others. The way that girl can hammer the ivory is marvelous." Some critics derided the "hammering" aspect of cinema players, but they could not deny the need for capable performers. Performers that were even better prepared, wrote Raymond, could do additional wonders: "Spend a few dollars more a week, get another violinist . . . make them look over the reels before they're put on at a regular show, and have them pick out the music that is best fitted to the pictures."[16]

Many managers found that a thoughtful, competent female pianist would draw in bigger and (socially) better audiences than many male organists or ensembles who were more interested in displaying their technical skills and less interested in the art of playing to the picture. Reporting on the success of the Madrid Theater in New York City, *Motion Picture News* noted that the "musical program of the Madrid is entrusted to Miss Lillian Greenberg, who is a graduate of a Leipsic [*sic*] conservatory of music. She has made the incidental music accompanying the pictures a matter of neighborhood comment."[17]

That women were "entrusted" with the musical accompaniments in a movie theater, including newsreels, shorts, and feature films, suggests that while they may have been looked upon as "girls" lacking in experience and wisdom, they were nonetheless responsible for crafting the tone in which audiences received news, enjoyed humorous animations, and understood drama and action on the screen. The evidence—letters from female accompanists to the popular film magazines' columns on photoplay music, published accounts of their scoring suggestions, reports on performance practice by critics, and reviews of accompanists across the United States—all testifies to the extent to which women were the arbiters of musical accompaniment in the cinema. Collections of cue sheets and other materials owned by professional female accompanists such as Claire H. Hamack and Adele V. Sullivan demonstrate that they frequently made changes to printed cue sheets and magazine recommendations to incorporate repertoire they already owned and knew. Accompanist Hazel Burnett compiled her own scores using sheet music and pieces cut from *Melody* and the *Etude* interleaved between pages of her photoplay albums.[18]

When the United States entered the war in April 1917, male musicians entered the military, and women were afforded additional opportunities as cinema musicians. In August 1918, *Wid's Daily* reported that the state of Wisconsin ordered "a general suspension of all orchestras," noting that this was "being done as a war measure to release every available man for war work. The theater managers came to a decision last week and will hereafter retain but one man in each house to furnish music."[19] *Moving Picture World* reported similar measures in Missouri in the article "Musicians Must Work or Fight." "Every professional musician who is not engaged in connection with legitimate concerts, operas or theatrical performances," read the act, "will be forced to enter other vocations or go to the front."[20] Women created scores and cue sheets for themselves as individual accompanists and as the leaders of cinema ensembles, improvised and composed new music for accompaniment, and engaged equally in the debates surrounding the kinds of repertoire best suited for motion picture accompaniment.

These debates about "appropriate music" could be exceptionally heated, and the energy expended on them came straight from the class anxieties of America's moneyed classes and traditionalists who strove to keep their society modeled as closely to European aristocracy as they could while building new dynasties in the United States. Having acquiesced to the fact that motion pictures were here to stay, women's clubs and other civic groups implored theater managers and musicians to use only "high-class" music in film accompaniment.

Cue sheets provided by female accompanists to the trade magazines and scoring suggestions made by women whose performances were hailed as "high class" indicate that "high class" equated with accompaniments using a mix of opera and ballet themes. The exception to this was the critical acceptance of a scattering of new generic works that served for scenarios specific to the new medium: "hurry" music, "mysterious" music, and similar specific generic pieces, then, were suitable in small amounts. Carrie Hetherington's suggestions—deemed "appropriate" by Sinn—for *The Clutching Hand* (1915) included works by Schubert, Gounod, Verdi, Wagner, Saint-Saëns, and, for short scenes, Zamecnik.[21] Kitty Meinhold, a cinema orchestra leader who programmed all of the music for pictures for her employer in upstate New York, wrote in 1915 that in creating the music for *Du Barry*, she used two works by Chaminade, selections from Gounod's *Faust*, the wedding march from *Lohengrin*, the march from *Aida*, a waltz from *Il Trovatore*, selections from *Lucia* and *Rigoletto*, and Elgar's "Salut d'amour."[22] Reviews show that accompanists used this combination of traditional orchestral and operatic repertoire and generic music that mimicked its harmonic language and form throughout the 1910s and 1920s for feature-length comedic and dramatic films, animations, and shorts.

For the first three years of the Great War, American cinemas offered just a handful of war movies; in fact, movies about the Spanish-American War remained more common than those about the European conflict. Films that were about the Great War were mostly imported from Europe, and for these film music critics recommended for the accompaniment the use of traditional, classically based "national" music such as national hymns, anthems, and dances.[23] At the end of 1917, though, after America had become involved in the war, studios suddenly found themselves in the business of producing war films, such as the fact-based memoir *My Four Years in Germany*, *The Legion of Death* (in which women fought in the trenches), and *Her Boy* (about the sacrifices of American mothers). While escapist films like *Tarzan of the Apes* and romances were also popular fare, the war film became an important part of cinematic offerings. The trade magazines' columns on music for the moving picture presented suggestions of serious, classical music for dramas and music from light opera or new music in classical styles for comedies.

There were no women writing regularly for publication on music for the silent film during this time. But male film music critics can provide us with a historical barometer of how art music was treated and used during 1917 and 1918, probably by both male and female accompanists who preferred it to improvising or new music. For war films, film music critic and columnist George W. Beynon wrote, "Patriotism plays a big part . . . and requires many patriotic marches."[24] Later, Beynon stressed the positive effects of cinema accompanists and orchestras leading audiences in singing patriotic songs before the main film began and during reel changes.[25] For *Lest We Forget*, which focused on the sinking of the *Lusitania* as the catalyst for America's involvement in the war, Beynon and Leon Perret compiled a score that included "The Star-Spangled Banner," used the soprano aria from Massenet's *Manon* as the primary theme throughout, employed "My Heart at Thy Sweet Voice" from *Samson and Delilah* as the film's love theme, used the overture to *La forza del destino* as music to signify German spies, and used "Le chant du départ" to characterize the French. Beynon also included the "Triumphal March" from *Aida*, Sousa's "Stars and Stripes Forever," and a number of melancholy Grieg pieces for atmospheric effect. Battles were accompanied by Wagner's "Ride of the Valkyries" and "The Tempest" from the overture to *William Tell*, a scene depicting the heroine killing a German would-be rapist is accompanied by the "Liebestod" from *Tristan und Isolde*, and, for a scene in which American soldiers are seen whistling, a popular song is rendered in whistles by the orchestra players.[26]

Many female accompanists followed this application of "high-art" music to the serious film, particularly war films. Reviews of women's performances for motion pictures provide documentation of their use of art music for war films.

Cora Tracey, a contralto employed at the Strand theater in New York, performed Victorian art songs in English to footage of troops in Europe;[27] Maleta Bonconi, a violinist in the Strand orchestra, offered contemporary art music by European composers Hubay and Drdla.[28] At the Rivoli, also in New York, female performers sang and played recent songs from England,[29] the "Marseillaise," and the "Waltz Song" from Gounod's *Mireille*.[30] The musical treatment of newsreels, however, offered a notable contrast to this approach. Newsreels were censored and normally showed positive images of the Great War: soldiers on parade, climbing out of trenches to make an attack or take ground, having tea, polishing their shoes, doing exercises, practicing with machine guns. When the wounded were shown, they were recuperating in bed, merrily reading comics or popular magazines and joking with their young female nurses. Musicians used popular songs, new generic music for the cinema, and improvised music to accompany the news, which always contained more entertainment or quirky news items than it did serious elements. Rick Altman writes, "March music was virtually *de rigueur* with the weekly," quoting accompanist and film music critic Eugene Ahern as saying that "I try to convey to the audience the idea of a band somewhere back of the crowd."[31] Altman holds that critics wanted newsreel music to "stress sound effects [and] descriptive music," and Raymond Fielding cites Samuel "Roxy" Rothapfel on using preexisting music for the newsreels:

> For the Topical Special, or as it is best known, the "Weekly," we play absolutely according to the scenes used, the national airs of different countries and little bits of marches that will fit the scene. Here, of course, we deviate from out regular adaptation and go back to playing the pictures.
>
> We pay a good deal of attention to this portion of our program and I attribute the wonderful successes of our Topical Review to the musical accompaniment.[32]

And as Fielding notes, some accompanists found material in photoplay albums useful: funeral marches; music for horse, automobile, or airplane races; and music for explosions or fire scenes were all appropriate for newsreels.

However, an interview with Harry Rosenthal, filmed in 1930, offers a different perspective, suggesting that much newsreel accompaniment was improvised, albeit drawing on individual performers' personal memorized libraries of music.[33] Rosenthal notes that newsreel music during this period was generally supposed to be upbeat and light, which is not unsurprising given that real footage was heavily censored to show positive images only and that some footage of the war was faked because camera operators were not allowed anywhere near the front lines or even general military installations; this is supported by research by Masha Shpolberg.[34] Thus, Rosenthal's improvisation—and likely those by many cinema accompanists—included quotes of popular or national songs, original material, sound effects, and variations on generic musical tropes.

Instrumentalists and Orchestras

The performers in all-women's orchestras for theaters have received treatment similar to that of keyboard performers. As Judith Tick has noted, all-women orchestras were nothing new at this time; several had been in existence as concert and touring groups since the 1880s.[35] Yet we know little about these ensembles and their individual members, especially after they became regular cinema ensembles. Their move into the cinema, like that of female pianists and organists, was ensured for social and moral reasons as well as their usefulness as novelties. All-female instrumental groups—sometimes also accompanied by a singer—were being used as promotions for cinemas in the early 1910s, if not before. In late 1913, a reporter for *Motion Picture News* described an all-woman orchestra used for the film *The Good Little Devil*: "The large stage at the Belasco Theatre was crowded with floral decorations, where were seated a large orchestra, comprised entirely of women, who rendered appropriate music that harmonized with the picture. In certain scenes the orchestra was silent and the audience was regaled with singing by an excellent quartet. The effect of the whole was one of much beauty."[36]

Caroline Nichols, who led the Boston-based women's orchestra the Fadettes, moved the group from vaudeville circuits to cinemas when she realized that doing so provided more regular schedules and incomes for her players. The Fadettes played for one of Rothapfel's cinemas in Minneapolis for six months in the mid-1910s; by the end of the decade, the vast majority of their engagements were for cinema accompaniment.[37] Like the players for *The Good Little Devil*, the Fadettes were regularly hailed as excellent musicians; although over the course of the group's existence Nichols was said to have trained more than six hundred women as professional orchestral musicians, we know the names of only a few.[38]

With the entry of the United States into the war, women suddenly became even more viable resources for cinema accompaniment and began replacing men in theater orchestras on a regular basis. *Motion Picture News* regularly listed the names of film stars and workers who had enlisted, and in 1918 *Wid's Daily* ran a story focusing on the work women were doing in cinema music. Titled "Rapf's All Women Feature," the film described a project in which women alone wrote, directed, produced, and accompanied a seven-reel film highlighting the work of women in the army, navy, and police forces. At screenings, "Rapf has made arrangements for a showing of the picture at one of the big Broadway houses and during its run the entire staff of the theatre will be composed of women, including the publicity staff, orchestra, and attendants."[39] As with female pianists and organists, female orchestral players were seen as improving the morals and class status of a cinema. Like keyboardists, they functioned as performers, chaperones, and arbiters of taste and values. While these roles were highly gendered, they also made headway for women's equality as professional musicians performing "high-class" art music.

In response to the calls for high-class or already canonized classical music, however, there was an equally vocal contingent of both keyboard and orchestral accompanists advocating for the use of new music for the new medium. Over the course of 1917–18, film music critics, writers, and, gradually, more and more music directors and orchestra leaders were slowly moving to the other side of the aisle in the old-music versus new-music argument. Beynon began publishing cue sheets by S. M. Berg that increasingly included music by Berg and his colleagues such as Sol Levy, Gaston Borch, Maurice Baron (who also published as Morris Aborn), Adolf Minot, Otto Langey, and Irénée Bergé (a man, despite any confusion over his name). Despite his own art-music score for *Lest We Forget*, Berg was endorsing cue sheets containing entirely new music for films by September 1918 (see figure 7.2).

"Inn of the Blue Moon, The."

Released by Sherry—Five Reels.

Prepared by S. M. Berg.

THEME I—Coquette Caprice............Allegretto Scherzando, Arensky
THEME II—Souvenir...................Tranquillo. ....Drdla
1. AT SCREENING...................THEME I
   2 min.
2. T. CHARLTON SLOANE...........May Dreams...........Borch
   3 min.   Andantino non Troppo Lento.
3. T. THE INN OF THE..............THEME II
   3 min.
4. D. DOROTHY THINKING OF........Intermezzo. ....Huerter
   4 min.   Moderato.
5. D. DISTRICT ATTORNEY..........Garden of Love...Ascher-Mahl
   4 min.   Caprice.
6. D. JUSTINE COMING. ....Dramatic Tension........Levy
   2 min.   Andante Molto.
7. T. THE MANUFACTURED. ....Heavy Misterioso........Levy
   1 min. 30 sec.   Andante Misterioso.
8. T. EARLY TO RISE...............THEME II
   1 min.
9. T. WHAT A BROKEN...............Under the Leaves......Thome
   4 min.   Poco Agitato.
10. T. WITH ADELAIDE'S ....THEME I
   3 min.
11. D. WHEN BOY BRINGS...........Kathleen. ....Berg
   2 min.   Valse Lento.
12. D. WHEN MAN TAKES...........Prelude. ....Jarnefelt
   2 min.   Moderato.
13. T. I'M NOT JUSTINE..............THEME II
   3 min.
14. T. BUT MOTHER, WE'RE.........Capricious Annette .....Borch
   3 min.   Characteristic Moderato.
15. T. BARNYARD HEROES...........March Burlesque........Gillet
   2 min.   Un peu Allegromente.
16. D. LETTER (IT IS LIKE)..........THEME I
   1 min. 30 sec.
17. T. MR. CHARLTON SLOANE.......Dramatic Andante No. 24,
   1 min. 30 sec.   Borch
18. D. AFTER JUSTINE LEAVES........Allegro Agitato........Kiefert
   2 min.   Allegro.
19. T. THE BALLERINA..........La Ballerina........Johnstone
   5 min.   Scottisch Characteristic.
20. T. THE THREE RUNAWAYS........THEME I
   2 min.
21. D. WHEN SISTERS LOOK..........THEME II
   2 min.
22. T. THE TWINS EXCHANGE........In the Bungalow.......Langey
   2 min.   Allegretto Intermezzo.
23. D. MAN ATTACKS GIRL...........Dramatic Allegro......Langey
   30 sec.   Allegro.
24. T. JUSTINE. ....THEME II
   30 sec.
25. D. MOTHER ARRIVES AT..........Legende. ....Friml
   3 min.   Moderato con Expressino.
26. D. AFTER FADE AWAY OF........THEME II
   1 min.
CHARACTER. ....Comedy-drama.
ATMOSPHERE. ....Rural.
MECHANICAL EFFECTS..............Watch picture.
SPECIAL EFFECTS.................None.
DIRECT CUES.....................None.
REMARKS. ....One theme only may be used if desired.

Figure 7.2. Film music critics slowly shifted from recommending classical art music for the accompaniment of film to new pieces written specifically for use in cinemas. Cue sheet for *The Inn of the Blue Moon* (1918), by S. M. Berg, published in George W. Beynon's "Music for the Picture," *Moving Picture World* 37, no. 11 (1918): 1580.

Performer-Improvisers and Performer-Composers

When cinema managers and critics of film music began to encourage the use of new music composed specifically for the medium, in addition to or in place of improvisations, they inadvertently created a new means for women to enter into composition. The female cinema musicians who used composition or composition-improvisation as their means of accompaniment were much like those who preferred preexisting music. They knew the same basic repertoire and were of the same socioeconomic class; they read the same trade publications and accompanied the same films; they were from the same geographical distribution. However, performer-improvisers strongly felt that the signifiers associated with preexisting music, particularly that from narrative works such as opera or ballet, brought unwanted cultural knowledge into the cinema. They wanted to provide music that was entertaining and communicative of a film's plot without over-shadowing the narrative on the screen. In 1915 Vermont, for example, Florence L. Currier prescreened all of the films she was to accompany, composing new musical themes for each character. Once she had created a set of basic themes for a film, Currier made detailed cue sheets for the whole movie, reiterating the themes as she saw fit and improvising, often using those themes as the basis for her improvisation. She did admit to occasionally using new generic music designed for cinema accompaniment much in the same way that accompanists who employed high-class music did—as necessary for storm scenes, battle cries, and other set pieces—but the majority of her scores were improvisations based on original ideas. In addition, Currier played the themes for each main character during the changing of reels in order to keep the musical connections fresh in the audience's mind.[40]

One of the most vocal proponents of original or improvised music was Alice Smythe Burton Jay. While she recommended that accompanists have both a thorough classical background and improvisatory skills, Jay was insistent that music for cinema accompaniment should closely fit the music to the action and emotions depicted on the screen without bringing any previous emotional associations with it. Jay's position, that "music to suit the picture must not conflict" with it either by mood or because of previous associations, was one that caused frequent argument in a time when many accompanists did not see any need to correlate the music with the action, or felt that "gigging" or "kidding" a film, in which music was used as a satirical commentary on the film, was more entertaining.[41] Jay participated in a heated exchange with composers, score compilers, publishers, and even equipment dealers. She made clear her own views on the need for matching, characteristic, instrumental music: "I fail to see where operatic selections fit any picture. . . . Opera brings the words to a person's mind, and seldom if ever fit the scene. . . . My idea of music is that tones from two notes to the entire scale express life in every sphere, and a person to improvise correctly must have a natural dramatic ability combined with the study of the great masters." However, she found some preexisting music useful in its place:

> Can we find any more fitting music for certain dance scenes than the Anitras [*sic*] Dance by Grieg or Asa's Death by the same master, suited to intense classical dramatic funeral scenes, like "Valse Parisian," by Lee S. Roberts, a modern composer, suited to light child or garden scenes. Two vastly different styles of composers, yet each one perfect in their place.
>
> . . . Why not select from the cue sheet, but be wise in your selection and do not fit a western drama with society music, or Traumerie [*sic*] to anything but a church scene.[42]

Jay and her suggestions were taken seriously; she received coverage in the trade journals equal to or more than many male composers, compilers, and accompanists did during the period between 1913 and 1918. She was so devoted to the creation of new music that fitted individual motion pictures that in 1916 she established the Symthe-Jay Music Company with offices in New York, Chicago, and San Francisco for the production of music rolls that could be played in automatic instruments such as the Fotoplayer instruments (about which more below).

Of the keyboard performers who followed Jay's philosophies of accompanying, perhaps the most famous in the United States was Rosa Rio, who died in 2010 at the age of 107. Rio began playing in her teens, mostly improvising her scores. In a 2006 interview with NPR, she said of her process:

> I didn't have a chance to see [the films] in advance. We had the new film; we ran it always on Monday mornings, generally a one o'clock show. And I faked it through. Then I would run out and get my music, or get ideas that I'd write down as I played. And then the next show, I did a good job. The next show I did a better job. By the time you played three shows a day, seven days a week, at the end of the week I really had it down perfect. And that was the end. And then I'd start over, all over from Sunday night, Monday again.
>
> . . . With the theater here, I generally think about it. I go to bed and I'll wake up around four or five o'clock in the morning with themes running through my head. And I'd grab a piece of paper and write down enough to, what I call a springboard.
>
> I enjoy being a part of a picture. I love going into a trance and being inspired by little tiny themes. I write out everything and memorize it.[43]

Rio's biography is a perfect example of the ways in which the expectations of an "accomplished" American woman, combined with the need for cinema musicians in the late 1910s and individual talent for composition and technical skills, came to influence the hybrid classical-improvisatory sound of American cinema. Born

Elizabeth Raub in 1902 in the American South, Rio was initially limited in her career choices. Rio's parents were vehement that being a performer in the cinema was not an acceptable occupation for a woman. However, as Margalit Fox wrote in Rio's *New York Times* obituary, "She persevered, and her parents relented a little. Playing in church would be fine, they decided. So would the genteel life of a children's piano teacher."[44] But when, at the end of her first year of classical piano studies at Oberlin College, the dean suggested she focus her efforts elsewhere, Rio enrolled at the Eastman School of Music, which had a program in silent film accompanying. "I had gone into Cleveland," she explained, and fallen in love with the motion picture palace:

> We had gone to one of the great theaters that they were building at that time. They were absolutely gold-gilded, red carpet, green carpet. . . .
>
> Being a southerner, I had never been into such a theater. And I was just floored. I don't know what the picture was today, and I don't think I was interested. But I heard a sound I had never heard before. I saw the pinpoint of a light grow larger and a console came from out of the pit, on the right hand side of the theater. And I heard theater organ for the first time in my life.
>
> I stayed for the second show just to hear it again. And when I walked out on the street, I looked up at the sky as if to say a prayer. I said thanks. I now know what I want to be in my life. I laugh and say, as long as I can play, lift me on the bench. I'll play. And I just couldn't be happier.[45]

Her combination of traditional in-home piano lessons, conservatory training, and natural imagination propelled her into cinema organist stardom.[46]

Such improvisatory practices also held true for war pictures, providing a path into composition (of popular or art-influenced music) for women who lacked formal composition training. One composer, described as "a soldier's mother," Mrs. A. S. Watt, "improvised the theme which is heard in her famous march . . . 'Pershing's March'" (see figure 7.3).[47] "Pershing's March" went on to become one of the top sheet music titles of the war, was endorsed by film music critics on both sides of the old music–new music debate, and became known across the country.

Violinist Helen Ware—not to be confused with the actor of the same name—also argued that improvisation is a form of composition and that improvisers, regardless of whether they consider themselves composers, were just that. Ware wanted to revive the tradition of classical improvisation in the manner of the Romantic composers and to see the movies benefit from original music arrived at by way of improvisation as practiced in the Romantic era. Born in 1887 in Philadelphia to communist organizer Ella "Mother" Bloor, Ware studied with Ševčík and Hubay in Europe, where she became an expert on Hungarian art and traditional musics. She made her professional debut in Budapest in 1912 and was the first American

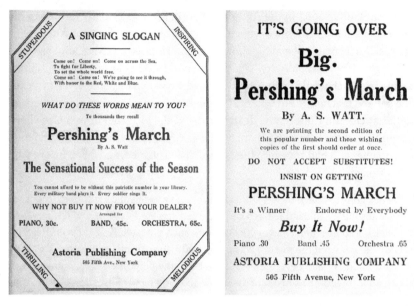

Figure 7.3. "Pershing's March" came out of film improvisation by Mrs. A. S. Watt. Like advertising for many pieces by women during this period, neither advertisement lists the full name of the composer, suggesting that the work is by a male composer. From *Moving Picture World* 37, no. 11 (1918): 1579 (*left*); and *Moving Picture World* 37, no. 13 (1918): 1891 (*right*).

violinist to tour Hungary. A frequent recitalist in concert with her husband, pianist Lazlo Schwartz, Ware toured the United States twice, playing the 1684 "Soames" Stradivarius, which she owned from 1912 until 1972.[48] Ware was positively reviewed by the *New York Times*,[49] hailed as one of the "world's greatest violinists" and the "Poetess of the Violin,"[50] and the natural successor to Maud Powell.

Ware's formally composed music—predominantly character pieces—was published by Carl Fischer along with that of Leopold Auer, Fritz Kreisler, and Maud Powell, but she, like Currier, Jay, and Rio, was foremost an exponent of improvisation in the cinema. Her advice was published in *Motion Picture Magazine* in 1919, where she, like Jay, argued for music and improvisation that followed a film's events and dramatic trajectory and helped convey the emotions portrayed on-screen by the actors. She wrote that she had originally become interested in improvisation as a musical skill because it had been a trademark of the European composers she studied, and she saw improvisation for film as a method of composing in itself, one that worked in parallel with viewing and understanding a film.

The other day, while viewing one of the Shakespearean classics thrown on the white sheet, my attention was distracted . . . by . . . a "movie pianist," who, truly inspired by the changing scenes and the dramatic play of emotions, fell into improvising in a most spirited and expressive manner. . . . Madame Remenyi . . . [t]he widow of the famous violinist[,] sadly commented on the fact that improvisation is a lost art in our days. . . . According to Madame Remenyi, Liszt, Chopin, and Rubenstein were the great masters in the art of improvising. . . . Since then, I have devoted considerable time to the study of this matter. . . .

If we proceed from the theory that improvising is the musical description of mental vision, or the expression of our emotions, then we are bound to appreciate the important part that the movie may play in the revival of this lost art. . . .

As the plot of the play unfolds . . . he enters into its spirit, and through the vision of it all his emotional powers are awakened, enabling him to express in music a grand, harmonious climax with as little effort as if reflecting in a gentle tonal picture the advent of the evening or the jingling of a mountain stream.

It is this logical conclusion that points to the wonderful possibilities which the movie reaches out to all aspiring musicians who wish to develop within themselves powers of improvising. . . .

With the mechanical device already on the market which would record the worthiest of these improvisations, such experiment may help us to discover many a slumbering talent of great composers-to-be. Our young artists would receive encouragement by realizing the fact that they are not merely parrots in the realm of music, but have ideas of their own and a new mode of expressing the worthiest within themselves.[51]

Ware's arguments that improvisation led to composition and that improvisers were composers in their own right suggest that many accompanists, particularly women, did not see themselves as creators of a new genre. Prior to the war, women published far less music than did their male accompanist counterparts, who often began their careers playing to the pictures and later left to become full-time composers of film music. There is little evidence that women followed this path from performer to (exclusive) composer. But although they were referred to or thought of themselves as accompanists rather than composers, women who created their own music for accompaniment were significant contributors to the development of the sound of the moving picture. Performers like Rio, who played in the largest picture houses for several hours a day, offered a consistent approach to scoring film, even if such scores weren't captured on paper. In silent film accompaniment, the line between improvisation and composition thinned, recalling the compositional practices of much earlier composers.

The sudden need for female musicians to replace men who joined the war effort, combined with the rapidly growing popularity of film, enabled many women to publish their compositions, which might not have been written or sold if not for film. Over the course of the silent era, more works by women composers—who may or may not have begun their musical careers as accompanists—were included in collections and sheet music offerings for the cinema than before the war, although they never came close to equaling the output by men. Nonetheless, it is possible to assemble a list of the more prolific female composers for the cinema, and more are being discovered as research in this area continues. Theodora Dutton (Blanche Ray Alden), Patricia Collinge, Irene Varley, and Alma Sanders all contributed to the published body of work designed to be used for accompanying films. Their works were included in photoplay albums of generic music alongside those of male composers, but as yet very little additional information is known about them beyond some basic biographical data. Dutton/Alden (1870–1934) is known for being the only female composer in the Suzuki Piano Repertoire; Collinge (1892–1974) was an Irish American actress who made her American stage debut in 1907, eventually appearing opposite Douglas Fairbanks onstage and in a number of sound films starting with *The Little Foxes* in 1941; Varley (1876–1975) appears to have been a pianist, originally from England, who registered a number of compositions with the US Copyright Office between 1917 and 1941;[52] and Sanders (1882–1956) composed songs in the 1910s and 1920s and nine full musicals that were produced on Broadway between 1918 and 1947, some of which set texts by her husband, Monte Carlo (Hans von Holstein). These women, their careers, and works deserve full research consideration, and they are undoubtedly just a few of the female performer-composers who wrote for silent film music and other genres in the first part of the twentieth century.

Other Contributions to Silent Cinema Sound

In addition to purely instrumental music for film accompaniment, many pieces intended for descriptive use in the cinema were published with a set of lyrics—usually related to a film or used as part of a film's intertitles—for the primary melody line, in the hopes that attaching a song or several songs to a particular film would make the sheet music for that film more marketable. Silent films were often promoted through the publication and sale of these songs for voice and piano: movie stars' photographs or stills from the film were prominently featured on the covers of songs to strengthen the connection between a film and the music.

The war effort encouraged women who had not previously composed for the cinema to do so. Indeed, the cinema constantly needed new music. Predictions by film music critics that that no one would be playing German music in concert halls or cinemas came true to a certain extent, and this was seen as particularly dire, as an enormous amount of the preexisting music packaged into albums for film accompaniment was German. There was, therefore, a tremendous need for politically acceptable music and generic music, and women contributed significantly to this repertoire, particularly in the form of songs. The resulting body of work includes a large subgroup that directly addresses the events in Europe through patriotic songs, marches, and dances.

The works of female songwriters whose works were performed in the cinema were well known during the war. Triangle Films even produced a five-reel feature featuring Alma Rubens as a New York songwriter in the 1918 film *The Love Brokers*. War songs by women tend to fall into several subgenres.[53] Some titles indicate the force of popular belief in the war by having narrators proudly announce the participation and sacrifice of their sons, husbands, or sweethearts. There were also calls for women to aid the effort. And yet another subgenre by women is narrated by young women waiting for their soldier boyfriends or husbands to return. But the importance of women's compositions does not lie in any radical divergence from mainstream songwriting or a in new sensibility applied to the war song. They are much like other war songs and conform with codes of women's war songs—the song of the lover/wife/sister/mother who yearns for/prays for/misses/mourns a man in the military—established by the Civil War. What is crucial is that such songs enabled female lyricists and composers to seek and receive some of the same performance opportunities and patronage enjoyed by male composers.

Women also contributed to silent film music through new inventions and innovations. In the period publications, two women in particular stand out: Alice Jay, the improviser-composer mentioned above, and Carrie Hetherington. Jay, in her zeal for attaching appropriate music to a film, rightly discovered that there was a market for music that was professionally matched to films and distributed in a way that did not allow for alterations to the cue sheet or poor performances. On the heels of the positive reception of Joseph Carl Breil's fully synchronized score for *The Birth of a Nation* in 1915, Jay announced that she would begin producing sound recordings synched to individual films. "Pictures will be screened in the factory," wrote a journalist on Jay's venture, describing the process in which Jay created an individual accompaniment for each film and had it replicated for playing in mechanical pianos, "and music made to fit the pictures prior to release." Jay herself composed and improvised themes and incidental music for individual film titles and recorded them using a Masteroll perforated machine.[54] (Saint-Saëns also recorded using this machine, and Arthur Nikisch and many other conductors, composers, and performers recorded using them as well. And player pianos are not quite dead as technology goes: you can even get John Adams's *Short Ride in a Fast Machine* on a piano roll.)

The *Music Trade Review* believed that this practice would surpass even Breil's foray into synchronized scoring accomplished through the distribution of full orchestral parts for a fully synchronized score for *The Birth of a Nation*. In a notice titled "Securing Suitable Music for the Motion Picture," its reporter wrote:

> Now comes Alice Smythe Jay, organist, of Aberdeen, State of Washington, with patents on a method for recording suitable music. The patents develop means for keeping the film operator and the music together by means of cueings displayed on the film. The inventor's claims include those of piano or orchestra scores developed from the record made by the musician while playing the picture in the first place. It should seem, therefore, that everything has been thought of.
>
> ... Certainly it appears that a step forward has been taken and that the long-prophesied art of synchronizing the film with suitable and universally available music has been worked out. How far it will be practical no one can say without seeing the whole process. But evidence is presented which appears to demonstrate that the idea is sound and that it can be made completely commercially practical [see figure 7.4].[55]

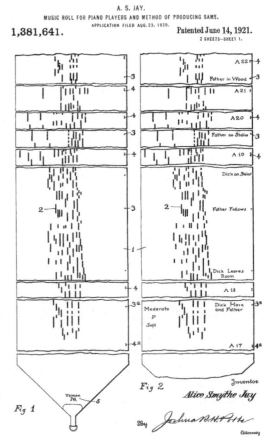

Figure 7.4. Alice Jay's patent application for her piano roll system for providing original synchronized music for individual films. From US1381641A, US Patent Office, patented June 14, 1921.

Jay officially went into business with Masteroll in 1915, when she recorded a score for *The Bank Messenger* and a selection of generic incidental pieces. However, according to Jay, Masteroll disagreed with her film-projection speeds and other details of her recordings, and the company destroyed some three hundred piano rolls—each for a particular film title—without Jay's permission. According to the *San Jose (CA) News*, "A nervous breakdown followed this incident and during the time [Jay] was ill the company ... did a flourishing business" using unharmed rolls made by Jay prior to her collapse.[56] Jay sued Metro-Goldwyn-Mayer, the eventual owner of Masteroll, for $1 million in damages, but she was unsuccessful. Nonetheless, cinema managers eagerly embraced Jay's method. Her proposed solution to poorly played accompaniments, nonsynchronized music, and theaters lacking the funds or desire to hire a live accompanist helped push the development and distribution of fully synchronized scores for film and the further exploration of sound-on-disc technology for providing music, sound, and speech for film.

Like Jay, Carrie Hetherington began her career as a performer-composer and cue sheet creator. Hetherington helped invent the American Photo Player Company's Fotoplayer (see figure 7.5). She described the instrument in *Moving Picture World*: "This instrument is composed of piano, reed-organ, pipe-organ, chimes, orchestral bells and all necessary drummers' traps; is played by regular 88-note player rolls, but has two separate tracker boards which enables the operator to make the quick changes without stopping the music. An expert operator can follow the picture so closely as to make a photoplay almost talk."[57]

As cinema orchestras began to shrink due to the war, Hetherington's remarkable instrument became popular, allowing a single operator to run a prerecorded roll, add in additional musical material using the keyboard as desired, and provide orchestral sounds, percussion, and sound effects. Hetherington's company made between ten and twelve thousand Fotoplayers between 1910 and 1928, and Hetherington was an important part of the instrument's success, traveling the country to provide demonstrations, oversee installations, and work with cinema managers to

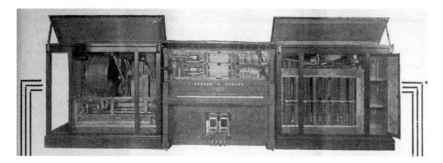

Figure 7.5. The American Fotoplayer as advertised in *Moving Picture World* 21, no. 3 (1914): 495.

customize their instruments.[58] Rolls for the Fotoplayer included popular marches and generic titles, such as "Mushy Music," "Fire! Fire! Fire!," "Drunk Soused Spree," "A Rustic Festival," and "The Roaring Volcano."

Conclusion

The information I present here is only the beginning of a much larger and deeper inquiry into the roles of women as cinema musicians. Already, it is clear that women played an important part in shaping the sound of the early cinema and the sound of patriotism during the Great War. Their accompaniments, which used already existing music, new compositions by themselves and others, and their own improvisations, shaped and helped define the musical sensitivities of the time. Accompanists created music and approaches to using music, and these became part of the audience's expectations for film music, established musical standards for film scores that would carry through into sound films, educated listeners as to different types of music and musical genres and to musical traditions relating to affect and meaning, and demonstrated how music could serve as a narrative and interpretative force in the cinema. Women designed methods of matching music to the action on the screen, developed ways of supplying cinemas with synchronized sound for pictures, and invented machines that allowed a single woman to represent the sounds of an orchestra for accompanying a film. Further research will undoubtedly uncover more documentation and materials related to women's musical careers in early film and the effects women's creativity had on cinematic music as a whole.

Notes

1. Reports on the dissolution, shrinking, or reconfiguration of all-male cinema ensembles and the firing or loss of male organists in theaters appear in 1917 and 1918, along with news that women are taking cinema musician jobs as men go off to war. References include George W. Beynon, "Music for the Picture," *Moving Picture World* 37, no. 8 (1918): 1120–21; George W. Beynon, "Music for the Picture," *Moving Picture World* 38, no. 13 (1918): 1521; "The Music and the Picture," *Motion Picture News* 16, no. 1 (1917): 143–45; "The Music and the Picture," *Motion Picture News* 16, no. 15 (1917): 2610–12; "The Music and the Picture," *Motion Picture News* 17, no. 16 (1918): 2439–42; "The Music and the Picture," *Motion Picture News* 17, no. 23 (1917): 3473–75; "Abandon Orchestras," *Wid's Daily* 5, no. 111 (1918): [3]; and "Among Ourselves," *American Organist* 2, no. 5 (1919): 212. Numerous newspaper articles and especially advertisements also document women's roles as cinema musicians, including those in the *Brooklyn Eagle, Chicago Defender, Chicago Tribune, Los Angeles Times, New York Evening World, New York Sun, New York Times, Portland Oregonian, Pittsburgh Post-Gazette*, and many others.

2. Ally Acker, *Reel Women: Pioneers of the Cinema, 1896 to the Present* (New York: Continuum, 1991), xvii, xviii.

3. While periodicals such as *Exhibitors Herald, Motion Picture Magazine, Moving Picture News, Moving Picture World, Universal Weekly,* and *Moving Picture Weekly* occasionally included news about, reviews of, and materials by female cinema organists, other forms of documentation suggest the wider scope of women's activities in film music. *American Organist* ran a number of articles and reviews by and about female film accompanists. Music periodicals for more general audiences, such as the *Musical Courier,* and music magazines aimed directly at women, including *Melody,* which specifically marketed itself as "for the Photoplay Musician and the Musical Home," frequently include mention of women cinema musicians. Advertisements in newspapers listing the musicians employed by various theaters attest to the numbers of women performing as film accompanists. For detailed indexing of these resources, see Kendra Preston Leonard, *Music for Silent Film: A Guide to North American Resources* (Madison, WI: Music Library Association and A-R Editions, 2016).

4. David Pierce, *The Survival of American Silent Feature Films, 1912–1929* (Washington, DC: National Film Preservation Board, with the Council on Library and Information Resources and the Library of Congress, 2013), 3.

5. R. H. Pray, "Good and Bad M.P. Theaters," *Motion Picture Magazine* 7, no. 6 (1914): 102–3. Material in brackets is from the original source, albeit in different lines, and added here for clarity and brevity. The term *accomplished* was overwhelmingly applied to women musicians of this period and rarely used to describe men.

6. Erno Rapée, *Motion Picture Moods, for Pianists and Organists [a Rapid-Reference Collection of Selected Pieces, Adapted to 52 Moods and Situations]* (New York: G. Schirmer, 1925), 2, 655.

7. *Weekend Edition Saturday,* "Making the Music for Silent Movies," NPR.org, http://www.npr.org/templates/story/story.php?storyId=5559593.

8. "Edison Issues Music Cues," *Motography* 10, no. 8 (1913): 291.

9. "Mutual to Provide Music Cue Service with Features," *Motion Picture News* 15, no. 12 (1917): 1847.

10. Early cue sheets in magazines include those by Ernst Luz for *Motion Picture News* in 1915, George W. Beynon in *Moving Picture World* starting in 1919, and L. G. Del Castillo in *American Organist* in 1922.

11. Martin Marks, *Music and the Silent Film: Contexts and Case Studies, 1895–1924* (New York: Oxford University Press, 1997), 62.

12. As musical accompaniment for moving pictures became more popular, cinemas often invested in sheet music anthologies containing generic pieces appropriate for typical movie scenarios. Theaters accumulated significant libraries of music, many of which were discarded or lost after the transition to integrated sound. For examples of these, see http://www.sfsma.org/ARK/22915/tag/album/.

13. Julie Hubbert, *Celluloid Symphonies Texts and Contexts in Film Music History* (Berkeley: University of California Press, 2011), 22.

14. Judith Tick, "Passed Away Is the Piano Girl: Changes in American Musical Life, 1870–1990," in *Women Making Music: The Western Art Tradition, 1150–1950*, ed. Jane M. Bowers and Judith Tick (Urbana: University of Illinois Press, 1986), 327.

15. Stanley Todd, "Music and the Photoplay," *Motion Picture Magazine* 7, no. 2 (1914): 94.

16. J. J. Raymond, "Why Exhibitors Fail," *Motion Picture News* 9, no. 1 (1914): 15, 50.

17. "His Three Rules," *Motion Picture News* 9, no. 12 (1914): 27.

18. Kendra Preston Leonard, "Cue Sheets, Musical Suggestions, and Performance Practices for Hollywood Films, 1908–1927," *Music and Sound in Silent Cinema: From the Nickelodeon to the Artist*, ed. Ruth Barton and Simon Trezise (New York: Routledge, 2018).

19. "Abandon Orchestras," *Wid's Daily* 5, no. 111 (1918): [3].

20. George W. Beynon, "Music for the Picture," *Moving Picture World* 37, no. 8 (1918): 1120–21.

21. Clarence E. Sinn, "Music for the Picture," *Moving Picture World* 24, no. 5 (1915): 717.

22. Kitty Meinhold, "Music for the Picture," *Moving Picture World* 23, no. 13 (1915): 1917.

23. S. M. Berg, "Music for the Picture," *Moving Picture World* 27, no. 3 (1916): 427–28.

24. George W. Beynon, "Music for the Picture," *Moving Picture World* 35, no. 7 (1918): 969.

25. George W. Beynon, "Music for the Picture," *Moving Picture World* 37, no. 5 (1918): 677–78.

26. George W. Beynon, "Music for the Picture," *Moving Picture World* 35, no. 8 (1918): 1093–94. Beynon mistakenly wrote *chanson* for *chant*.

27. George W. Beynon, "Music for the Picture," *Moving Picture World* 37, no. 4 (1918): 399–400.

28. George W. Beynon, "Music for the Picture," *Moving Picture World* 37, no. 8 (1918): 1120–21.

29. George W. Beynon, "Music for the Picture," *Moving Picture World* 37, no. 6 (1918): 843.

30. George W. Beynon, "Music for the Picture," *Moving Picture World* 37, no. 10 (1918): 1427.

31. E. A. Ahern, "Play with Your Brains as Well as Your Fingers," *Motion Picture News* 11, no. 7 (1914): 47, quoted in Rick Altman, *Silent Film Sound* (New York: Columbia University Press, 2004), 382. For other perspectives on marches as upbeat signifiers, see the chapters in this volume by Patrick Warfield and William Brooks.

32. Raymond Fielding, *The American Newsreel: A Complete History, 1911–1967*, 2nd ed. (Jefferson, NC: McFarland, 2006), 81.

33. Harry Rosenthal, "Music for the Silent Newsreels—Outtakes," Fox Movietone News Story 5-484, filmed March 11, 1930. Moving Image Research Collections Digital Video Repository, https://mirc.sc.edu/islandora/object/usc%3A23506.

34. Masha Shpolberg, "The Din of Gunfire: Rethinking the Role of Sound in World War II Newsreels," *NECSUS, European Journal of Media Studies* 3, no. 2 (2014), http://www.necsus-ejms.org/din-gunfire-rethinking-role-sound-world-war-ii-newsreels/#_edn14.

35. Bowers and Tick, *Women Making Music*, 329–31. Women's string orchestras were also widespread in Britain; see Christina Bashford's chapter in this volume.

36. A. D. M., "Belasco Sees 'The Good Little Devil' Film," *Motion Picture News* 8, no. 25 (1913): 23.

37. Anna-Lise P. Santella, "Fadette Ladies' Orchestra," *Grove Dictionary of American Music*, ed. Charles Hiroshi Garrett, 2nd ed. (Oxford: Oxford University Press, 2013), http://www.oxfordreference.com/view/10.1093/acref/9780195314281.001.0001/acref-9780195314281-e-2720.

38. Mary Brown Hinely, "The Uphill Climb of Women in American Music: Performers and Teachers," *Music Educators Journal* 70, no. 8 (1984): 31–35.

39. "Rapf's All Women Feature," *Wid's Daily* 5, no. 129 (1918): [1].

40. Florence L. Currier, letter to Clarence E. Sinn, "Music for the Picture," *Moving Picture World* 23, no. 1 (1915): 62.

41. Ernst Luz, "Music and the Picture," *Motion Picture News* 13, no. 3 (1916): 445.

42. Alice Jay, letter to "Music and the Picture," *Motion Picture News* 15, no. 11 (1917): 1739.

43. *Weekend Edition Saturday*, "Making the Music for Silent Movies."

44. Margalit Fox, "Rosa Rio, Organist from Silent Films to Soap Operas, Dies at 107," *New York Times*, May 14, 2010, http://www.nytimes.com/2010/05/15/arts/music/15rio.html.

45. *Weekend Edition Saturday*, "Making the Music for Silent Movies."

46. Rio made a career in the silents until the talkies arrived, both playing and composing, and then she went into radio and television. While she played for screenings of silent films her entire life, she also worked as an accompanist, often for Broadway shows, for government programs during the Second World War, and as the staff organist at NBC Radio and ABC Radio, where she played for *The Shadow* and various soap operas. With the revival of interest in silent films, Rio began playing for them once again both in live showings and on recordings, which were featured on DVD releases of silents.

47. George W. Beynon, "Music for the Picture," *Moving Picture World* 37, no. 9 (1918): 1269.

48. Jonathan Fuller-Maitland, "Helen Ware," in *Grove's Dictionary of Music and Musicians* (Philadelphia: Theodore Presser, 1922).

49. "Helen Ware in Violin Recital," *New York Times*, March 6, 1920, 9.

50. "City League Presents Famous Violinist," *Fort Wayne (IN) Daily News*, November 25, 1916, 10.

51. Helen Ware, "The Renaissance of Improvising," *Motion Picture Magazine* 8, no. 11 (1914): 79–81.

52. A. M. G., "Ruth Miller Delights Her Seattle Hearers," *Musical America* 26, no. 23 (1917): 19. Varley's works were also reviewed in at least one periodical: "Seattle Notes," *Music and Musicians* 3, no. 6 (1917): 11.

53. For a related discussion of women composers, genres, and significance, see William Brooks's discussion in chapter 9 of this volume.

54. Ernst Luz, "Music and the Picture," *Motion Picture News* 13, no. 6 (1916): 918.

55. "Securing Suitable Music for the Motion Picture," *Music Trade Review* 73, no. 9 (1921): [15].

56. "Woman Seeks Damages for Movie Patent," *San Jose (CA) News*, June 5, 1928, 11.

57. Carrie Hetherington, "Music for the Picture," ed. Clarence E. Sinn, *Moving Picture World* 20, no. 1 (1914): 50.

58. David Q. Bowers, *Encyclopedia of Automatic Musical Instruments* (New York: Vestal Press, 1972), 352.

CHAPTER 8

Empire, Nation, and Music

Canada's *Dominion Songbook*

BRIAN C. THOMPSON

C ompared with that of many of its allies and enemies, Canada's musical response to the First World War seems a modest one. The country produced no wartime hit songs like "Keep the Home Fires Burning" or "Over There" and no symphonic or choral masterpieces, either during or after the war. The most enduring artistic achievement to come from a Canadian as a result of the war was not a musical composition but John McCrae's lyric poem from the spring of 1915, "In Flanders Fields." In rondeau form, it is written from the perspective of the dead, who, in the final stanza, urge the reader to take up the fight. The poem first appeared on December 8, 1915, in the British magazine *Punch*, and it so effectively captured the moment that it inspired dozens of musical settings and, later, the annual wearing of poppies in remembrance of those who had died.[1] So powerful was McCrae's statement that if it was the only thing that one knew of Canadian sentiment about the world war as it was taking place, one might imagine an entire population marching stoically to the trenches. The dearth of memorable Great War music produced by Canadians, however, may give us a more accurate indication of the depth of their emotional engagement with the war. It most certainly tells us something about Canadians' cultural identity in the second decade of the twentieth century.

This does not mean that there was not a great deal of music making during the war, both in and out of the military. Canadians probably sang and played music as much as people anywhere, and Canadian historians and musicologists have made reference to the importance of music in World War I.[2] Yet music scholars have discovered little music of enduring quality or interest, despite their efforts. As Gayle Magee has noted in the most important study thus far of war-related Canadian popular songs, "The music for these songs is not particularly distinctive."[3] The *Canadian Musical Heritage* anthology series contains many examples of music published during World War I and relating to the war, while every history of music in Canada published over the past half century has touched at least briefly on music during the war.[4] Other notable publications include Edward Moogk's *Roll Back the Years: History of Canadian Recorded Sound and Its Legacy* and Jason Wilson's *Soldiers of Song*, a book and stage show that focuses on the Dumbells, a Canadian vaudeville troupe that began as an entertainment company within the military.[5] The place of popular song in the military is also the subject of military historian Tim Cook's article "The Singing War," which is based mostly on letters and memoirs and focuses on lyrics and subject matter.[6] In 2001 Library and Archives Canada commissioned two short articles related to that institution's sheet music collection.[7]

Further research on music in Canada during the war is certainly not hindered by a lack of resources or access. A wealth of sound recordings and sheet music from the era has survived, some of it published in the *Canadian Musical Heritage* anthologies mentioned above and many more accessible in digital form from libraries within Canada and the United States.[8] Scholars can draw on photographic archives and collections of ephemera as well as several important periodicals of the era. In Toronto the *Canadian Journal of Music* and the *Canadian Music and Trades Journal* provide detailed accounts of musical activities throughout the war years. Similarly, for Montreal, *Le passe-temps* and *Montréal qui chante* were published throughout the war, and *Le Canada musical* in 1917–18. For towns and cities across the country, newspapers provide a record of the daily events, and many have been digitized.

Turning now to the events of the war, on August 4, 1914, Great Britain declared war on Germany. The next day, Canada's governor-general and Queen Victoria's seventh child, Prince Arthur, Duke of Connaught and Strathearn, informed Canadians that they too were at war. Although the Dominion of Canada had been established in 1867, in 1914 its foreign policy was still decided by Britain.[9] When Britain declared war on Germany, it did not consult with the Canadian government. As British subjects, Canadians were expected to defend the empire. In all, Canada, with fewer than eight million people, would send nearly a half-million combatants overseas between 1914 and 1918.[10] More than sixty-seven thousand would die, while many more would return disfigured, disabled, or damaged psychologically.

The impact of the war on Canada and Canadian identity has occupied the thoughts of many historians over the past century. Some have claimed that the events of the war came to define Canada and to move it toward full nationhood. Others have focused on the deep divisions at home, most notably between English- and French-speaking Canadians, as a result of the implementation of conscription.[11] In this chapter, I explore the place of music both at home and abroad, searching for ways that it might reveal how Canadians experienced the war, both at home and at the western front. The chapter might be regarded as a search for an imagined "Dominion Songbook." My approach is partially chronological, allowing us to track the events of the war and the shifting attitudes toward it. And to some extent, I will focus on events in Montreal. Then Canada's largest and most cosmopolitan city, Montreal was the scene of euphoric celebrations at the start of the war and of heated confrontations over conscription three years later.[12]

Early Years of the War, 1914–1916

War on an epic scale was expected in the summer of 1914, and its arrival was greeted by some with relief. On the morning of Monday, August 3, Canadian newspapers reported on demonstrations in favor of supporting the war effort. A report in Montreal's *La patrie* described scenes of "patriotic fervor." Crowds sang "La Marseillaise" and "God Save the King" as they marched from the corner of Saint Catherine and Peel Streets to the French consulate at Viger Square.[13] On Wednesday a headline in another Montreal newspaper, the *Daily Mail*, read, "Canadian Cities Greet War News with Songs." The story reported on events from around the country. The newspaper's correspondent in Toronto wrote that crowds broke into cheers as the news of war was announced outside newspaper offices, "swelling into a vast chorus" as they sang "Rule Britannia" and "Red, White and Blue," and that night bands paraded through the streets.[14] In Ottawa, "Thousands stood in the streets before the newspaper bulletin boards and sang the National Anthem ["God Save the King"], the 'Maple Leaf Forever,' and 'O Canada.'" A report from Quebec City claimed that "English, French, and Irish" paraded together, but did not mention what they sang.[15]

In a separate article, the *Daily Mail* reported on a number of events that had taken place in Montreal.[16] Members of a matinee audience at the Orpheum Theatre were said to have cheered when they were informed of the declaration of war. They then stood and sang as the theater's orchestra played "God Save the King." Uptown, Colonel Carson informed the Grenadier Guards of the declaration. They then paraded out of their armory on Esplanade Avenue and down Park Avenue with their band, led by J. J. Gagnier, playing "Soldiers of the King."[17] Along the route, "flags were carried, and the cheering and singing was continuous." Along Saint Catherine Street, "flags of England, France and Russia were borne through the dense crowds by men held high on the shoulders of their fellows, and the most stirring war songs of the three countries were shouted at top voice by the surging mob. As it passed along, the crowd surged in from the rear and pressed forward, taking up the stirring tunes played by the Grenadier's band." The crowd had taken over the street, as "the roll of the drums had got into their blood and the music of the war tunes had stirred them." The Canadian government would quickly tap into this bloodlust to provide a military response in support of the empire.

On August 5, Colonel Samuel Hughes, the federal minister of the militia, announced that a Canadian Expeditionary Force would be assembled at a mobilization center at Valcartier, near Quebec City, and from there dispatched to Britain to serve within the imperial force. Recruiting stations were quickly opened across the country and did a brisk business, often with the aid of bands. In Montreal that evening, militia units filled the streets. On Craig Street (now Saint Antoine), crowds gathered outside the Drill Hall to see a parade of artillery. Uptown, there seems to have been a parade everywhere one looked, some of them likely resulting in scuffles. At one point, the Sixty-Fifth Regiment (the Carabiniers Mont-Royal), marching westward on Saint Catherine Street, came face-to-face with the Highland Brigade, marching eastward. After some hesitation, the band of the largely Francophone Sixty-Fifth struck up "O Canada" and turned left on Mansfield Street, only to encounter the Highland cadets.[18] In a curious side note to all of the patriotic music making in the streets of Montreal, at Dominion Park, an East End amusement venue, the Twenty-Second Regiment Band, previously known as Patrick Gilmore's Band, had opened their afternoon concert on August 4 with Franz von Blon's *Emperor Frederick March*, op. 56.[19] The band appears to have dropped that number from subsequent programs as it extended its engagement for another week.[20] Meanwhile, concerts of patriotic music were added to the programs at many of the city's theaters. And before the end of the month, the Théâtre Canadian-Français had opened a production of the drama *Le régiment* (figure 8.1).

More patriotic and national music was in the air than perhaps ever before. In Canada the national anthem was "God Save the King," but other songs had come to represent Canadians unofficially and informally. Alexander Muir, a schoolteacher from Toronto, composed "The Maple Leaf Forever," both words and music, in 1867, in response to confederation (figure 8.2).[21] The promising inspiration and jaunty tune helped to make "The Maple Leaf Forever" popular, but its celebration of the

Figure 8.1. An advertisement for *Le régiment*, published in *La patrie*, August 15, 1914.

conquering of New France in the name of the British Empire was always going to limit its appeal beyond Muir's circle of Orangemen.[22] There was never much hope of a French Canadian penning a translation or new poem to be sung to Muir's cheery melody. They already had "Vive la canadienne," a lively traditional song that had for decades served as an unofficial anthem for French-speaking Canada.

In the summer of 1880, French Canadians had a new *chant national*: "O Canada." The music had been composed by Calixa Lavallée, a professional musician then living in Quebec City, on commission from organizers of that summer's Catholic Congress, who saw it as an opportunity to create an anthem with the dignity of "God Save the Queen" (Queen Victoria then being in the forty-third year of her reign).[23] To Lavallée's music, Judge Adolphe-Basile Routhier wrote words celebrating French Canadian history and conservative Catholic values (figure 8.3). It was performed that summer and then largely forgotten until the beginning of the twentieth century. Within a little more than a decade, it was being played by brass bands throughout Canada and sung to several English texts (Robert Stanley Weir's 1908 text being the most successful), while the original French poem was included in anthologies of poems and lyrics.

Figure 8.2. "The Maple Leaf Forever." Words and music by Alexander Muir (Toronto: Harry Sparks Music, n.d.; originally published Toronto: the author, [1867]).

For many French Canadians, the demands of the British Empire were undoubtedly secondary to fraternal feelings toward France. This was reflected in recruiting posters (see p. 182), but also in the reporting and editorials of French-language newspapers and other print media. *Le passe-temps*, a mainstream Montreal periodical aimed largely at a female readership, became a robust supporter of the war effort.[24] Published twice each month, it featured cultural news and ten pages of light music in each issue. Whereas the cover normally featured a photograph of a popular singer, issue number 506, published on August 15, 1914, featured an

Figure 8.3. "O Canada." Music by Calixa Lavallée and words by Adolphe-Basile Routhier (Quebec City: A. Lavigne, [1880]), reprinted in *Le passe-temps*, no. 789 (May 1927): 70–71.

engraving (figure 8.4) of a French officer, saber raised, and the caption "France, en avant!" (Forward, France!). The caption indicated that actor and vocalist Damase Dubuisson performed the song at the Théâtre Chantecler, on Saint Denis Street. Inside, one found the song with the same title (words by Gaston Charles and music by Charles Tanguy), a choral arrangement of "God Save the King" on a French translation by Benjamin Sulte, and a march for piano by Amédée Roy titled *Canadiens, rallions nous!*[25] A regular columnist published an article in which he wrote that Europeans had brought the war upon themselves.[26] An advertisement on the last page drew readers' attention to patriotic songs published in previous issues of *Le passe-temps*. Many more would appear in the months and years that followed.

Figure 8.4. The August 15, 1914, cover of *Le passe-temps*, featuring Tanguy and Charles's patriotic song "France, en avant!"

Music in the Military

Methods of recruiting for the Canadian Expeditionary Force reflected the place of Canadians within the empire. The country's official flag was known as the Canadian Red Ensign, a design that in 1914 featured the Union Jack in the upper left corner and the coat of arms for each of Canada's territories and provinces in the middle right.[27] It was, however, the Union Jack that was used most often in English-language recruiting posters, while French-language posters sometimes made reference to Canadian kinship to France (see figures 8.5 and 8.6). On August 21, 1914, Hughes reported in the House of Commons that Canadian troops were part of the imperial army: "We have nothing whatever to say as to the destination of the troops once they cross the water, nor have we been informed as to what their destination may be."[28] For many of the volunteers, the situation likely seemed natural: in 1914, 70 percent of Canadian volunteers were immigrants from Britain.[29]

Running Canada's war effort fell largely to the minister of militia and defense, Samuel Hughes, an eccentric and larger-than-life veteran of the Boer War.[30]

Figure 8.5. "This is your flag." Recruiting poster for the Canadian Expeditionary Force, 1914–18. Toronto Reference Library Baldwin Collection.

Figure 8.6. "Canadien-Français, Enrolez-Vous." Recruiting poster for the Canadian Expeditionary Force, 1914–18. Rare Books and Special Collections, McGill University Library.

Mobilizing troops at Valcartier was Hughes's idea, as was the decision to disperse French Canadian recruits into regiments where they would be a minority and have to communicate in English. Mounted on horseback, Hughes addressed the first contingent of troops as they were set to depart from Valcartier with a long and rambling speech that included both poetry and song. The prime minister, Robert Borden, observed the speech and later noted in his diary, "Everybody [was] laughing at Sam's address."[31] It is unclear whether Borden was referring to members of his own circle laughing at Hughes, the troops, or both. The memoirs of William R. Jones, a young recruit who was present at the time, provide a detailed account of Hughes's farewell address.[32] It shows the poem recited to have been adapted from *Charles O'Malley, the Irish Dragoon*, Charles Lever's comic novel, set during the Peninsular War:

> And when with years and honors crowned,
> You sit some homeward hearth around,
> And hear no more the stirring sound
> That spoke the trumpet's warning.
> You'll sing and give one hip, hurrah!
> And pledge the memory of the day,
> When to do and dare you all were there
> And met the foe in the morning.[33]

The words, as Jones reported them, included some significant modifications. The fifth line had been changed from "You'll fill and drink, one Hip hurrah!" presumably so as not to encourage the use of alcohol, which Hughes had banned from Valcartier. The final couplet had been changed from "When, squadron square, They all were there / To meet the French in the morning."[34] After this, again according to Jones, Hughes then sang them the last verse of "Farewell to Lochaber," a Scottish ballad from the eighteenth century, attributed to Thomas O'Connellan:[35]

> I go then, sweet lass, to win honor and fame,
> And if I should chance to come gloriously hame,
> I'll bring a heart to thee with love running o'er,
> And then I'll leave thee and the homeland no more.[36]

If this bemused Hughes's listeners, some of the more innocent among them grew disquieted as he turned more directly to the fact that not all would return, something that many of the farm boys and students seem not to have considered.

Jones and his fellow recruits then set off for the Port of Quebec on horseback, "with bands playing." He survived the war and was met by the mayor of Toronto, a band, and a large crowd of friends and family as his train pulled into the station in April 1918.[37] In his memoir, he reported the favorite song of his company to have been "Sing Me to Sleep," a sentimental ballad from 1902 that was widely adapted by troops. Jones provided this tame excerpt:

> Far, far from Ypres, I long to be,
> Where German snipers can't snipe me,
> Down in my dug-out where worms creep,
> Waiting for someone to sing me to sleep.[38]

Other adaptations made reference to the "Boches" (Germans) putting them to sleep. The Second Battle of Ypres took place in the spring of 1915; it was the first major battle in which Canadian troops had been engaged and one of the first in which the Germans used chlorine gas.

Among the more interesting resources relating to music in the military are the song anthologies published during the war years. The collections did not usually include printed music, only song lyrics, on the assumption, it seems, that while most of the military personnel did not read music, they would sing along with a familiar melody and usually sang while on the march. One such collection was produced for members of the Sixty-Fourth Battalion, who were recruited from the East Coast provinces and departed for Europe on March 31, 1916. This songbook is divided into three sections. The first, "Songs of the 64th," included "The Boys from Nova Scotia's shore." The second section, "Ballads and Ditties," included "Auld Lang Syne," but also the French Canadian folk song "Alouette," possibly intended for Acadians in the battalion. The final section, "Patriotic Songs," contained eleven numbers, including "O Canada," the "Marseillaise," the "Russian National Anthem," and "God Save the King."[39]

Another anthology, simply titled *Regimental Songs*, was published in several editions and was quite eclectic in its selections. The 1914–15 edition opened with a page of advice from Lord Kitchener, followed by several new selections. The main part then opened with "Alexander's Ragtime Band," followed by "Alouette" (one of three French-language numbers). In addition to the usual marching songs ("It's a Long Way to Tipperary") and specifically Canadian numbers ("Canadian Boat Song"), it included quite a few songs by Stephen Foster, including "Old Folks at Home" and "Old Black Joe." The second part was titled "A Selection of Hymns for Use at Devine Service" and opened with a prayer by British field marshal Frederick Roberts.

The *Canadian Soldiers' Song Book* also appears not to have been intended for a specific contingent. On its cover (figure 8.7) was an engraving of Sir Galahad, clad in a red cloak, sword in hand, and looking skyward, based on a statue located on Parliament Hill, in Ottawa, and a quotation from Tennyson's *Idylls of the Kings*: "If I lose myself, I save myself."[40] Publishers of this anthology clearly believed that the

Christian ethos expressed by the knight could serve as inspiration for the volunteers. The entire passage reads:

> And Merlin call'd it "the Siege Perilous,"
> Perilous for good and ill; "for there," he said,
> "No man could sit but he should lose himself":
> And once by misadvertence Merlin sat
> In his own chair, and so was lost; but he,
> Galahad, when he heard of Merlin's doom,
> Cried, "If I lose myself, I save myself!"
> ("The Holy Grail," 172–78)

This was loftier material than was typically cited in this type of publication, and it would be interesting to know what the young recruits made of it. The songs themselves were quite diverse and collected under such headings as revue songs, parodies, home songs, and hymns. The group of national songs opened with "God

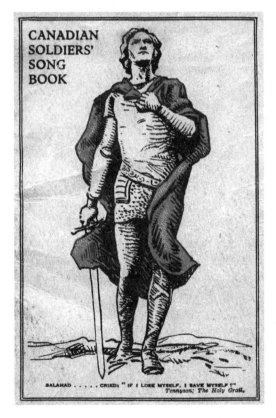

GALAHAD . . . . . CRIED: " IF I LOSE MYSELF, I SAVE MYSELF !"
Tennyson; *The Holy Grail.*

Figure 8.7. Cover of the *Canadian Soldiers' Song Book.* Published by the YMCA (ca. 1917).

Save the King" and "Rule Britannia" and included "O Canada" and "The Maple Leaf Forever," as well as the national anthems of France, the United States, and Belgium and the "Anglo-American Anthem" (the first verse of "God Save the King" followed by the opening of "America" ["My Country, 'Tis of Thee"]. There were also separate sections of English, Irish, Scottish, and even Hawaiian songs.

The one exclusively French Canadian regiment appears not to have had a published songbook, and it located its repertoire in other sources. The Royal Twenty-Second Regiment (or Twenty-Second Battalion) was created in the fall of 1914, when Arthur Mignault, a Montreal businessman, offered the Canadian government $50,000 to help raise a French Canadian regiment. The government accepted, and the troops departed for the United Kingdom on May 20, 1915. The regiment became known in English as the "Van Doos," an Anglicized version of the French *vingt-deux* (or *vingt-deuxième*). In September 1915, the regiment crossed the Channel to France as part of the Fifth Canadian Brigade and the Second Canadian Division. Among its officers was the future diplomat and governor-general Georges-Philéas Vanier, who arrived in France with the Twenty-Second Regiment on September 15, 1915. At an event marking the fiftieth anniversary of the creation of the regiment, in 1964, Vanier recalled that first day in France and the singing of Louis Fréchette's poem "Vive la France," the same poem that had inspired Roy's piano piece *Canadiens, rallions-nous!* The words had been set by a number of musicians, but the version by the bandleader Ernest Lavigne was best known and had been published in several versions, including one for male chorus (figure 8.8):[41]

O Canadiens, rallions nous,	O Canadians, let us rally
Et près du vieux drapeau,	And by the old flag,
Symbole d'espérance	Symbol of hope
Ensemble, crions à genoux:	Together on our knees we cry:
Vive la France!	Vive la France![42]

A solo version of Lavigne's setting had been recorded in 1910 by the well-known baritone Joseph Saucier.[43] After this, Vanier reported, the soldiers marched to the tune of "O Carillon," suggesting it was being played by musicians.[44] If so, it was likely the 1858 setting by Charles Wugk Sabatier of Octave Cremazie's "Le drapeau de Carillon," a thirty-two-stanza poem that tells of the French victory at Fort Carillon in 1758. In 1902 the poem had provided the starting point for a stage play by Laurent-Olivier David. Sabatier's setting of three stanzas from the poem had been published several times, once as recently as 1913.[45] Joseph Saucier had released a recording of "Le drapeau de Carillon" in 1915.[46] In recounting the story, in 1964, Georges Vanier appears not to have commented on the fact that the song commemorated a victory over the British.

Figure 8.8. Ernest Lavigne's setting of Louis Fréchette's poem "Vive la France!" (Montreal: J. E. Bélair, 1884).

Conscription, 1917–1918

While many aspects of life in Canada had continued with some normalcy, as 1917 arrived Canadians had been following the events of what was now called the Great War for two and a half years. Censors kept much of the worst of it out of print. Yet newspapers were still filled with stories from the war front and the names of the local soldiers who had perished. In 1915 Canadians had read of the battles at Neuve Chapelle and Ypres, the use of chlorine gas, and the sinking of the *Lusitania* and numerous other vessels. In June 1916, they learned that British field marshal Horatio Herbert Kitchener had perished at sea. In November Prime Minster Borden dismissed Sam Hughes from his cabinet, due in part to the procurement of faulty weapons. The Somme Offensive had begun in July and continued until late in the year, resulting in more than a million casualties. The new year brought the introduction of what was intended to be a temporary tax on personal income in Canada. In Russia there was revolution. And in Western Europe, US troops arrived. In France the four Canadian divisions fought together for the first time in what became known as the Battle of Vimy Ridge. Their victory, at a cost of more than ten thousand killed or wounded, would be used in the decades that followed as a symbol of national unity and identity.[47]

In much of the world, an atmosphere of mistrust grew more pronounced in 1917, the year in which Britain's royal family acknowledged the mood of the public and switched its name from the House of Saxe-Coburg and Gotha to the House of Windsor. In Canada, German names were looked on with suspicion. Many Canadians born in the Austro-Hungarian Empire were interned.[48] In 1916 the southwestern Ontario city of Berlin took the name of Kitchener (after the late British field marshal). The sound recording pioneer Emile Berliner chose not to change the name of his company, which he had established in Montreal in 1899. By 1914 he had a recording studio, a factory, and retail outlets in many towns and cities. He remained in business during the war, in part by producing numerous patriotic recordings in collaboration with RCA Victor and restricting his name to the fine print, as his company rode out the war on the public's appetite for the new technology.[49]

In other ways, cultural life continued normally. *Le Canada musical* made its debut on May 5, 1917.[50] In contrast to *Le passe-temps*, it reported mostly on opera and classical music. It also had an international perspective, reporting extensively on musical events in the United States and featuring a regular column on music in France. The cover page of its first issue featured news that the tenor Ugo Colombini was believed to have been killed at the front, a rumor that turned out to be true. There were also other reminders of the war, such as an article on the dominance of German music at the Metropolitan Opera.[51] But German music continued to be discussed in positive terms, just as both locals and visitors continued to play it. Indeed, with the exception of reports on fund-raising concerts, *Le Canada musical* seemed to go to great lengths to avoid discussing the war. Still, by mid-1917 the one political issue that could not be avoided was conscription. Even *Le Canada musical* found a related story, reprinting an article from *Musical America* on the opinions of well-known musicians on the issue of conscription.[52]

Recruiting had dropped to a trickle by 1916, and Prime Minster Borden was under pressure to come up with reinforcements. In mid-May, newspapers reported that the federal government had introduced a bill in the House of Commons aimed at raising a hundred thousand more recruits through conscription. The story in the *Montreal Gazette* carried a single large headline that included the number of recruits the government was aiming for and informed readers that the law was to be called the "Military Service Act of 1917."[53] Several pages in, it ran another story on the rallies and window smashing that had come in reaction to the legislation.[54] A crowd said to number ten thousand had listened to speeches in Lafontaine Park and then marched on newspapers that had supported conscription: *La presse*, *La patrie*, and the *Montreal Gazette*. The windows of the *Star* were saved only due to rioters' lack of planning. Rallies continued for several days and nights in Montreal and Quebec City. Reporting consistently mentioned the chanting of slogans and carrying of banners ("Down with Borden"), but none mentioned music, with perhaps just one exception. The weekly *Montreal Witness* of May 29 ran nearly a full page on the demonstrations and may have been the only one to mention music, in the context of a demonstration that took place in Quebec City:

> In a heavy downpour of rain at Montcalm Market, Quebec, on Thursday night, Col. Armand Lavergne addressed Quebec's second anti-conscription meeting, after a crowd marched to the offices of the *Quebec Chronicle* and *L'événement* and smashed the windows, jeering and shouting "Down with conscription," and singing "O Canada." About three thousand people braved the rain and cold and gathered on the Market Square just outside St. John's Gate. While waiting for the arrival of the speakers, they sang French-Canadian folk songs and shouted "Down with conscription," "Down with Borden; we shall strangle him," and "Down with *L'événement*."[55]

While we will never know whether this was the only group of protesters to sing, it is curious that only one newspaper seems to have mentioned it and fascinating that French Canadians used "O Canada" as a means of voicing their solidarity and opposition to the federal government.

Through the summer, newspapers reported extensively on conscription and the progress of the legislation in parliament, but for a while the streets were quiet. For some, thoughts had turned to the fiftieth anniversary of confederation. As Dominion Day fell on a Sunday in 1917, the first commemoration events were held in churches. In London, England, Dominion Day services were held at three churches. At the largest of these, the band of "an Honorable Artillery Company," led some six hundred troops, under the command of Colonel Barre, into Westminster Abbey. The *Montreal Gazette* reported that after mass, the band played "the solemn Te Deum following the mass and afterward the band played 'O Canada' and the National Anthem" ("God Save the King").[56] In Canada commemorations were left largely to local communities.[57] Toronto and Hamilton hosted parades that featured veterans of the Boer War. The march in Toronto ended at Exhibition Park, where the premier and other politicians spoke on the achievements of the past fifty years and a choir of three thousand schoolchildren sang "The Maple Leaf Forever," "Rule Britannia," "The Best Old Flag on Earth," and "God Save the King."[58] The ceremony on Parliament Hill, in Ottawa, opened with the singing of "O Canada," followed by "The Maple Leaf Forever" and, of course, "God Save the King."[59]

Newspapers reported soldiers in France celebrated Dominion Day 1917 by playing baseball and other sports.[60] Music was no doubt supplied for the occasion by the many bands employed just behind the lines. The military had for quite some time recognized the importance of providing diversions for soldiers at the front in the form of entertainers such as the Dumbells, who sang and performed comedy skits.[61] That same year, members of the military contributed to *Oh, Canada! A Medley of Stories, Verse, Pictures, and Music*, a collection published in London. The role of musicians at the front was the subject of an article by a correspondent for the *Montreal Gazette* as well. He reported listening to "a band from far-off Vancouver" playing a quartet from *Poet and Peasant* outside the officers' dining tent, in France, and on his subsequent conversation with the commander, Captain Edmund Burke, who commented on the importance of having musicians to help restore the mental abilities of soldiers. "Under the influence of music," he said, "listlessness gives way to interest, and then enthusiasm."[62] The reporter also noted that the musicians functioned as stretcher bearers.

Back in Canada, the Military Service Act became law, bringing demonstrators back out into the streets. Seeking a clearer mandate for implementation of the law, Borden called an election that took place in December. His Conservative Party won a majority but lost all of their seats in Quebec to the Liberals. In January the government began to enforce conscription. *Le passe-temps* and many other French-language publications remained supportive of the war effort while opposing conscription. Street protest continued through the early months of 1918, peaking over the Easter weekend, when troops fired on a crowd in Quebec City. At least four were killed, and dozens more were injured and arrested. The violence shocked the country and would have a lasting impact on Canadian politics.

By summer the tide of the war began to turn in the Allies' favor. With the Armistice, once again people spilled into the streets to sing and cheer. In its report on the spontaneous celebrations on November 11, 1918, *La patrie* reported that "national hymns sounded from everywhere." The most frequently heard were "O Canada" and "La Marseillaise."[63] Gradually, troops made their way back. Popular songs were published celebrating the victory and success of Canadian troops. The return of the Twenty-Second Regiment was a cause of celebration in Quebec. Actor Paul Ravennes cowrote the song "L'immortel 22ème Canadien-Français," which he performed in Montreal theaters.[64] In its November 16, 1918, issue, *Le passe-temps* printed "En avant!," the song of the Twenty-Second Regiment, by Joseph Vézina, as well as the music of "Rule Britannia," Lavigne's "Vive la France!" and C. A. Hammond's *In Memoriam (Charles Gill)*, dedicated to painter and poet Charles Gill, who had died on October 16 from the Spanish influenza.[65]

Surprisingly, though, little memorial music was composed during or after the war. Composer and organist Healey Willan (1880–1968), who had immigrated in

1913 to Canada from England to take up the position of organist and choir director at Saint Paul's Church on Bloor Street in Toronto, composed the motet "How They So Softly Rest."[66] The work was a setting of Henry Wadsworth Longfellow's "The Dead," a translation from the German poem by August Cornelius Stockman, and Willan dedicated his composition to members of Toronto's Mendelssohn Choir who had died during the war:

> How they so softly rest,
> All they the holy ones,
> Unto whose dwelling-place
> Now doth my soul draw near!
> How they so softly rest,
> All in their silent graves,
> Deep to corruption
> Slowly down-sinking!
>
> And they no longer weep,
> Here, where complaint is still!
> And they no longer feel,
> Here, where all gladness flies!
> And, by the cypresses
> Softly o'ershadowed
> Until the Angel
> Calls them, they slumber!

Unlike many of his fellow British immigrants who were of fighting age, Willan did not enlist. Influential Quebec composer Claude Champagne (1891–1965) composed *La ballade des lutins* (*The Ballad of the Elves*) in 1914 for the Band of the Canadian Grenadier Guards, of which he was a member, but he, like Willan, chose not to enlist.[67] Ernest MacMillan, the future conductor of the Toronto Symphony Orchestra, was a precocious teenager studying in Bayreuth in 1914 and found himself imprisoned in Berlin for the duration of the war. In 1918 he completed *England: An Ode*, his hourlong setting of Algernon Charles Swinburne's poem, for soprano and baritone soloists, chorus, and orchestra.[68] On his return to Canada, composition came second to his work as a performer and academic.

Some five hundred pieces of music relating to the Great War are contained in the collections of Library and Archives Canada.[69] Many are popular songs, churned out to meet the demands of the market. The war seems not to have inspired Canadians to create great or memorable music. Although conscription had many advocates in English-speaking Canada, Borden's appeal for a hundred thousand more troops resulted in no Canadian equivalent to Stephen Foster's "We Are Coming, Father Abraham."[70] More surprising, though, is that "In Flanders Fields" found no memorable setting by a Canadian composer, although J. Deane Wells's setting may have been the first published.[71]

The most successful work to have been inspired by the war was written sixty years after it ended: John Gray's 1978 musical stage play, *Billy Bishop Goes to War*, about the titular pilot. After its opening production in Vancouver, *Billy Bishop* was performed across the country and on Broadway (briefly), and it has since become a part of the theatrical repertoire in Canada. The pilot's actual achievements are unverified, a subject that the play sidesteps by having Bishop tell his own unreliable story, but there is little doubt that he was seen as a useful, if unlikely, symbol for the war effort. The play succeeded in part by conveying Bishop's determination to survive, but also by effectively capturing the sense of what it was to be a colonial member of the imperial military, most notably in the penultimate musical number, when Bishop is received at Buckingham Palace. The chorus of "The Empire Soirée" conveys both Bishop's excitement and his clear-eyed sense of place within the social order:

> You're all invited to the Empire Soirée,
> We'll see each other there, just wait and see;
> Attendance is required at the Empire Soirée,
> We'll all dance the dance of history.[72]

The final line of the chorus seems to echo into the final piece, as the play ends with Bishop giving a farewell speech to those departing for Europe in 1939.

Conclusion

Perhaps it is no surprise that Canada produced no great or enduring music at the time of or as result of World War I. For the most part, English-speaking Canadians reflected in their music their membership in the British Empire, singing "The Maple Leaf Forever" and performing British music at home and abroad. The war demonstrated that the Dominion of Canada was still a colony by nearly every definition of the word. For French-speaking Canadians, the war offered both an opportunity to show allegiance to the empire and a reminder of their marginal place in it. Yet they, too, had a musical repertoire that reminded them of who they were, and the music composed in honor of the Twenty-Second Regiment followed in a long tradition.

More than a decade after the Armistice was signed, in 1931, Canada took a large step from colonial dominion toward full independence from Britain with the passage of the Statute of Westminster. It would no longer have its foreign policy determined by the British Parliament. It would retain the Red Ensign as its flag for another three decades. The British monarch even now remains the head of state, and "God Save the King [or Queen]" has become the country's "Royal Anthem," performed at occasions when the queen or her representative is present. Although "O Canada" did not become the country's official anthem until 1980, it was in part through a 1936 performance of the song that Britain recognized Canada's independence. The setting was the unveiling of the memorial to Canadian troops at Vimy Ridge, by King Edward VIII. After the speeches and a performance of "God Save the King," the ceremony concluded with the playing of "O Canada," the order of the performances symbolically acknowledging Canadian independence.[73] The affirmation was repeated three years later, when George VI unveiled the National War Memorial, in Ottawa, and the ceremony once again concluded with the playing of "O Canada."

Notes

1. See Jennifer A. Ward, "American Musical Settings of 'In Flanders Fields' and the Great War," *Journal of Musicological Research* 33 (2014): 96–129.

2. See Jeffery A. Keshen, *Propaganda and Censorship during Canada's Great War* (Edmonton: University of Alberta Press, 1996); Tim Cook, "The Singing War: Canadian Soldiers' Songs of the Great War," *American Review of Canadian Studies* 39, no. 3 (2009): 224–241; and Gayle Magee, "'She's a Dear Old Lady': English Canadian Popular Songs from World War I," *American Music* 34, no. 4 (2016): 474–506.

3. Magee, "'She's a Dear Old Lady,'" 503.

4. See Frederick Hall, ed., *The Canadian Musical Heritage*, vol. 3, *Songs I to English Texts* (Ottawa: Canadian Musical Heritage Society, 1985); and Lucien Poirier, ed., *The Canadian Musical Heritage*, vol. 7, *Songs II to French Texts* (Ottawa: Canadian Musical Heritage Society, 1987). In *Music in Canada: Capturing Landscape and Diversity* (Montreal and Kingston: McGill-Queen's University Press, 2006), Elaine Keillor discusses the First World War's impact on institutions (135–38) and on popular song (187–93).

5. Edward B. Moogk, *Roll Back the Years: History of Canadian Recorded Sound and Its Legacy: Genesis to 1930* (Ottawa: National Library of Canada, 1975); Jason Wilson, *Soldiers of Song: The Dumbells and Other Canadian Concert Parties of the First World War* (Waterloo, ON: Wilfrid Laurier University Press, 2012).

6. Cook, "Singing War."

7. Elaine Keillor, "Writing for a Market: Canadian Musical Composition before the First World War" (Ottawa: Library and Archives Canada, 2004), https://www.collectionscanada .gc.ca/sheetmusic/028008-3200-e.html, and Barbara Norman, "Canadian Sheet Music of the First World War," *Sheet Music from Canada's Past* (Ottawa: Library and Archives Canada, 2001), https://www.collectionscanada.gc.ca/sheetmusic/028008-3300-e.html.

8. The websites of Library and Archives Canada and the Bibliothèque et Archives nationales du Québec both contain digital collections of printed and recorded music. US libraries with significant online resources of Canadian music include the Library of Congress and the Sheridan Libraries at Johns Hopkins University (Lester S. Levy Collection).

9. During negotiations that would lead to confederation, in 1867, the name "Kingdom of Canada" had been suggested but considered inappropriate. The idea of using "Dominion of Canada" has been attributed to Samuel Leonard Tilley, the premier of New Brunswick. It was accepted by Great Britain and subsequently used for several other colonies, including Australia, New Zealand, Newfoundland, and South Africa.

10. The most recent census, in 1911, placed the Canadian population at 7,204,838. *Fifth Census of Canada, 1911* (Ottawa: [Census and Statistics Office], 1912), vii.

11. One of the most recent books to argue that the war came to define Canada is Brian Douglas Tennyson, *Canada's Great War: How Canada Helped Save the British Empire and Became a North American Nation* (Lanham, MD: Rowman and Littlefield, 2015). For a nuanced exploration of what the war meant to those who fought in it, see Jonathan F. Vance, *Death So Noble: Memory, Meaning, and the First World War* (Vancouver, BC: UBC Press, 1997). The war's negative impact on relations between English- and French-speaking Canadians is explored in Gérard Filteau, *Le Québec, le Canada et la guerre, 1914–1918* (Montreal: Éditions de l'Aurore, 1977); Brock Millman, *Polarity, Patriotism, and Dissent in Great War Canada, 1914–1919* (Toronto: University of Toronto Press, Scholarly Publishing Division, 2016); and Geoff Keelan, "Canada's Cultural Mobilization during the First World War and a Case for Canadian War Culture," *Canadian Historical Review* 97, no. 3 (2016): 377–403. Hugh MacLennon explored the impact of the war and conscription on relations between English- and French-speaking Canadians in his novel *Two Solitudes* (Toronto: Macmillan, 1957).

12. The largest cities at the time of the 1911 census were Montreal (490,504), Toronto (381,383), Winnipeg (136,035), Vancouver (120,847), and Ottawa (87,082).

13. "L'enthousiasme dans la ville," *La patrie*, August 3, 1914.

14. Presumably, the song referred to as "Red, White, and Blue" was "Britannia, the Pride of the Ocean," and not the US version, "Columbia, the Gem of the Ocean," since the crowds were reportedly cheering for the empire.

15. "Canadian Cities Greet War News with Songs," *Montreal Daily Mail*, August 5, 1914.

16. "Great Enthusiasm in City Streets When War News Came," *Montreal Daily Mail*, August 5, 1914.

17. The regiment's band had been established in 1913, and Gagnier, a well-known professional musician, was selected to lead it. Membership in the regiment was otherwise almost entirely Anglophone. See Colonel F. S. Meighen, *Photographic Record and Souvenir of the Canadian Grenadier Guards Overseas Battalion "Eighty Seventh"* ([Montreal?]: n.p., 1916).

18. "Regiments on Parade Caused Enthusiasm along the Line of March," *Montreal Daily Mail*, August 6, 1914.

19. Von Blon's piece was billed as "Marche, 'Emperor Frederick.'" "Nos lieus d'amusements: Au Parc Dominion," *Le Canada*, August 4, 1914.

20. The extension of the engagement was noted in "Amusements," *Montreal Daily Mail*, August 8, 1914. The band continued to perform German music, including several pieces by Wagner.

21. See Magee, "'She's a Dear Old Lady,'" 479–81; and Helmut Kallmann and Andrew Mcintosh, "The Maple Leaf Forever," in *The Canadian Encyclopedia*, http://www.thecanadian encyclopedia.ca/en/article/the-maple-leaf-for-ever/.

22. The Protestant fraternal organization known as the Orange Order had a long history in Canada. Its annual July 12 celebration of William of Orange's victory at the Battle of the Boyne often resulted in brawls and sometimes in deaths.

23. See Brian Christopher Thompson, *Anthems and Minstrel Shows: The Life and Times of Calixa Lavallée (1842–1891)* (Montreal and Kingston: McGill-Queen's University Press, 2015), 217–27.

24. The entire run of *Le passe-temps* has been digitized by the Bibliothèque et archives nationales du Québec; see http://numerique.banq.qc.ca/patrimoine/details/52327/2272562.

25. The August 15 issue also included a romance, "Soupirs d'amours," and a simple piano piece titled *Eva valse*.

26. Jean Pic, "Horrible fléau!," *Le passe-temps*, no. 506 (August 15, 1914): 303.

27. The original provinces, in 1867, were New Brunswick, Nova Scotia, Ontario, and Quebec. Manitoba and the Northwest Territories were added in 1870, British Columbia in 1871, Prince Edward Island in 1873, the Yukon Territory in 1898, and Saskatchewan and Alberta in 1905. (Newfoundland would be added in 1949.)

28. Cited in Desmond Morton, "Exerting Control: The Development of Canadian Authority over the Canadian Expeditionary Force, 1914–1919," in *Men at War: Politics, Technology and Innovation in the Twentieth Century*, ed. Timothy Travers and Christon I. Archer (Chicago: Precedent, 1982), 7.

29. "Enthusiastic Reaction to War," Canada and the First World War, Canadian War Museum/Musée canadienne de la guerre, http://www.warmuseum.ca/firstworldwar/history/going-to-war/canada-enters-the-war/enthusiastic-reaction-to-war/. By 1918 the majority of recruits were Canadian born, but that may have been in part due to conscription, as many enlisted rather than wait to be called up.

30. Hughes was elected to Parliament in 1892, and in 1911 Prime Minister Borden selected him for the militia portfolio. He had served in the British army during the Second Boer War, in 1899, but had been dismissed for military indiscipline, which might have been a warning sign for Borden. Ronald G. Haycock notes, "Although Hughes was a sincere Canadian and a successful constituency politician, his erratic talents never matched the demands of high office during total war." Ronald G. Haycock, "Sir Samuel Hughes," in *The Canadian Encyclopedia*, http://www.thecanadianencyclopedia.ca/en/article/sir-samuel-hughes/. See also Historica Canada, *The Canadians: Sir Sam Hughes*, https://www.youtube.com/watch?v=FFOERFt-J2E.

31. Pierre Berton, *Vimy* (Toronto: Anchor Books, 2001), 42–43.

32. A transcription of Hughes's speech was quoted in William Ross Jones, *Fighting the Hun from Saddle and Trench* (Albany, NY: Aiken, 1918), 17–18.

33. Ibid., 20.

34. Charles Lever, *Charles O'Malley, the Irish Dragoon* (1841; reprint, London: Duvney, 1901), 353–54.

35. For information on O'Connellan, see Colm O'Baoill, "Two Irish Harpers in Scotland," in *Defining Strains: The Musical Life of Scots in the Seventeenth Century*, ed. James Porter (Berne: Peter Lang, 2007), 227–44.

36. Jones, *Fighting the Hun*, 20. In the last line, Hughes had replaced "Lochaber" with "homeland."

37. Ibid., 21 (quote), 266.

38. Ibid., 107.

39. Canada. Canadian Army, Battalion 64th, *Songs of the Sixty-Fourth Overseas Battalion, C.E.F.* (n.p., [1916]).

40. The statue commemorates the death of Henry Albert Harper, who drowned in 1901 while trying to save a young woman who had fallen through the ice while skating on the Ottawa River.

41. Lavigne's setting was first published in the "Supplément musical de *la patrie illustrée*" on June 24, 1884. The song had been contained in the 1908 program booklet for the three-hundredth anniversary of Quebec City. It was published separately around the same time by J. E. Bélair, who was also the publisher of *Le passe-temps*.

42. Fréchette's poem appears in the *Nouvelle lyre canadienne: Recueil de chansons canadiennes et françaises* (Montreal: Librairie Beauchemin, 1895), 110–11, as does "Le drapeau de Carillon" (18–19).

43. For information on Saucier, see *The Virtual Gramophone*, https://www.collections canada.gc.ca/gramophone/028011-1028-e.html.

44. Georges-Philéas Vanier, *Georges Vanier, Soldier: The Wartime Letters and Diaries, 1915–1919* (Toronto: Dundurn, 200), 61.

45. See Poirier, *Songs II to French Texts*, xvi–xvii. For a wider discussion of "Le drapeau de Carillon," see Natalie Rewa, "A Reflection of French-Canadian Nationalism: 'Le drapeau de Carillon,'" in *Historical Drama: Themes in Drama*, ed. James Redman (Cambridge: Cambridge University Press, 1986), 8:177–94.

46. *The Virtual Gramophone*, http://www.bac-lac.gc.ca/eng/discover/films-videos-sound -recordings/virtual-gramophone/Pages/Item.aspx?idNumber=1007621624.

47. Canadian War Museum, "The Battle of Vimy Ridge," http://www.warmuseum.ca/ cwm/exhibitions/vimy/index_e.shtml. For a discussion of the meaning of Vimy to Canadian identity at the time of its centenary and the decade leading to it, see Tony Keene, "Opinion: Vimy Was a Triumphant Battle, but It Was Hardly the 'Birth of a Nation,'" CBC News, April 8, 2017, http://www.cbc.ca/news/opinion/vimy-birth-of-a-nation-1.4060855; and Tim Cook, *Vimy: The Battle and the Legend* (Toronto: Penguin, 2017), 366–84.

48. See Keshen, *Propaganda and Censorship*, 7–11.

49. See "History of Canadian Record Companies," in *The Virtual Gramophone*, http://www .bac-lac.gc.ca/eng/discover/films-videos-sound-recordings/virtual-gramophone/Pages/ history-record-companies.aspx#TOC2b. RCA Victor also produced recordings of Canadian patriotic music. In 1915 the Victor Military Band recorded "O Canada" and "The Maple Leaf Forever."

50. See Hélène Paul, "'Le Canada musical' (1917–1924): Miroir d'une ville, reflet de deux continents," *Les cahiers de l'ARMuQ*, no. 13 (1991): 48–65. An earlier periodical also called *Le Canada musical* had been published in Montreal in 1866–67 and again from 1875 until 1881.

51. "En Amerique: La conquete musicale allemande," *Le Canada musical* 1, no. 18 (1918): 9. For American attempts to reposition German music and musicians, see Patrick Warfield's discussion in chapter 4 of this volume.

52. "Les musiciens et la conscription," *Le Canada musical* 1, no. 6 (1917): 8.

53. "Notice Given of Conscription Bill in House," *Montreal Gazette*, May 21, 1917.

54. "Conscription Is Condemned by Big Rally of Young Men," *Montreal Gazette*, May 21, 1917.

55. "Lavergne Will Be Shot or Go to Jail," *Montreal Weekly Witness*, May 29, 1917. Lavergne represented the constituency of Montmagny in the Quebec legislature, as a Nationalist.

56. "Confederation Commemorated in the Motherland," *Montreal Gazette*, July 2, 1917.

57. Among the federal government's modest contributions to the fiftieth anniversary of confederation was the issuing of a three-cent commemorative stamp featuring Robert Harris's 1883 painting *Conference at Quebec*, depicting the 1864 meeting at which the terms of confederation had been negotiated. The original painting had been destroyed in a fire in 1916 but preserved in a photograph.

58. "Imposing Jubilee Procession Today," *Toronto World*, July 2, 1917; "City Celebrates Jubilee to Tap of War Drum," *Toronto World*, July 3, 1917; "Canadian Veterans Parade at Hamilton," *Toronto World*, July 3, 1917.

59. "Confederation Commemorated in the Motherland," *Montreal Gazette*, July 2, 1917.

60. "Natal Day of Canada Celebrated at Front," *Toronto World*, July 3, 1917. For more on the playing of baseball by Canadian troops, see Andrew Horrall, "'Keep-a-Fighting! Play the Game!': Baseball and the Canadian Forces during the First World War," *Canadian Military History* 10, no. 2 (2012): 27–40.

61. For somewhat related soldiers' shows, see the chapters by Jeffrey Magee and Michelle Meinhart in this volume.

62. John Kidman, "Music Hath Charms to Soothe Soldier after Battle Din," *Montreal Gazette*, June 30, 1917. On music and healing, see the chapters by Christina Bashford and Michelle Meinhart in this volume.

63. "Montréal a fêté la grande victoire, hier," *La patrie*, November 11, 1918.

64. The song was published in *Montréal qui chante* and in a performing edition by J. E. Bélair. The words were by Léon Chevalier.

65. For more on the influenza epidemic and its chilling effect on music, see Deniz Ertan's chapter in this volume.

66. Healey Willan, "How They So Softly Rest," *Church Music Review* 488 (1917): 1–7.

67. See Timothy Maloney, "Claude Champagne's 'Ballade des lutins' / 'La ballade des lutins' de Claude Champagne," *Canadian Winds: The Journal of the Canadian Band Association* 10, no. 2 (2012): 24–25.

68. See three publications authored or edited by John Beckwith: "'And How Is Sir Ernest?,'" in *Music Papers: Articles and Talks, 1961–1994* (Ottawa: Golden Dog Press, 1997), 146–59; "Ernest MacMillan and England," *Canadian University Music Review / Revue de musique des universités canadiennes* 19, no. 1 (1998): 34–49; and *The Canadian Musical Heritage / Le patrimoine musical canadien*, vol. 18, *Oratorio and Cantata Excerpts / Extraits d'oratorios et de cantates* (Ottawa: Canadian Musical Heritage Society, 1995).

69. Norman, "Canadian Sheet Music of the First World War."

70. Stephen Foster set the poem James S. Gibbons had written in response to Abraham Lincoln's call for volunteers in July 1862.

71. J. Deane Wells, "In Flanders Fields" (Toronto: Whaley, Royce, 1917). Wells was an Australian musician, organist, and sheet music dealer living in Vancouver at the time. Wells's setting was followed in short order by Charles Ives's, discussed in Gayle Magee's chapter in this volume; John Philip Sousa also set McCrae's poem, as Patrick Warfield explains in this volume.

72. John Gray with Eric Peterson, *Billy Bishop Goes to War: A Play* (Vancouver, BC: Talonbooks, 1981): 98.

73. See Cook, *Vimy*, 262–68. No record seems to have survived of the band that performed at the Vimy Memorial inauguration.

CHAPTER 9

Of Stars, Soldiers, Mothers, and Mourning

WILLIAM BROOKS

Stars

When the United States entered the previously "European" war in April 1917, the country was ready to be united. The divisive neutrality of 1915 was well past, the controversies over preparedness a year later had been settled, two minor border wars with Mexico had prepared the citizenry for service on the home front and the military for reorganization into a truly national fighting force, and careful management of the news, coupled with increasingly impassioned oratory, had convinced most Americans that Germany was in the wrong and that the world "must be made safe for democracy."[1] Much of the country rushed to embrace symbols, slogans, and causes. Many of these were generated by government organizations such as George Creel's "Committee on Public Information"; others—songs, poems, pictures—were created by individuals working independently.[2] Still others came to occupy an indefinite space between private and public, authored and anonymous, and many of these were eagerly taken up and disseminated by communities seeking to express their solidarity.

One such symbol was the "service flag," an emblem to be displayed in the windows of the homes of families that had one or more members serving in the military.[3] As early as May 1917, the idea was reported to be "gaining in popularity,"[4] and between April and August 1917 at least six different designs were proposed by individuals scattered through the country, including James G. McIlroy (Cleveland), Robert L. Queisser (Cleveland), William H. Boorman (Jersey City), and Daniel E. Sullivan (Newport, Rhode Island).[5] From the start, the concept was a transnational affirmation of the alliance just joined by the United States. Japan had been a British ally since August 1914, and Sullivan cited as precedent a Japanese practice during the Sino-Russian War (1904–5), in which flags decorated the homes of families with sons in service. Boorman's design clearly recalls the Japanese ensign, and McIlroy, who probably was first to propose a design, had been the military attaché to the American embassy in Japan and was reported to have had the same practice in mind.[6] Queisser's design, on the other hand, was linked to British precedents; indeed, in England, the start of the war in 1914 had precipitated similar proposals to display placards and flags in honor of family members in service.[7] More generally, window displays—usually of lighted candles—had long been used in Britain and on the Continent to remember absent loved ones, a concept adapted for England's iconic war song "Keep the Home-Fires Burning" and in American spin-offs like "Place a Candle in the Window" and "Keep the Love-Light Burning in the Window." Occasionally, the candle and the flag were combined into a single text or image, as in "Keep the Beacon Light a-Burning Bright Beside the Little Service Star."[8]

McIlroy's design (figure 9.1, left) featured a blue bar on a white field surrounded by red,[9] and it was being widely discussed by June 1917.[10] But it was soon over-taken by Queisser's design (figure 9.1, right), which substituted a blue star for the blue bar. Queisser and McIlroy were both military men; McIlroy had held various postings since his time in Japan, and Queisser had served in the Mexican border crisis of 1916. In April 1917, McIlroy was recruiting officers for the new American Expeditionary Force in Cleveland, where Queisser was a longtime resident. In Dave Martucci's plausible reconstruction of events, McIlroy's flag was used primarily for recruiting purposes; Queisser then adapted it for public use, fusing McIlroy's design with the well-known icon of the "Tuberculosis Blue Star Campaign" that

Figure 9.1. Service-flag designs by James G. McIlroy (*left*) and Robert L. Queisser (*right*).

had begun in the Midwest in 1908, in which Queisser had been an active participant.[11] McIlroy moved on to other assignments after May, and he evidently made
no further use of his design; Queisser, though, was a very successful businessman,
and he mounted a substantial campaign on behalf of his "blue star" flag.[12] By the
end of June, his design was being commercially manufactured and advertised, and
by early July it had achieved a kind of official recognition in his home state.[13] By
September it was being used nationwide, and a widely disseminated photograph
depicted Theodore Roosevelt proudly standing below a large service flag bearing
four stars, one for each of his enlisted sons.[14]

On October 1, Queisser applied for a patent on his design, and it was granted
unusually quickly, on November 6.[15] Queisser thereupon began demanding a 10
percent royalty from service-flag manufacturers, and a national outcry ensued
despite his subsequent announcement that half the royalties would be donated to
the Red Cross.[16] The controversy continued into 1918, but by summer of that year,
despite continuing litigation, service flags were being freely manufactured in homes
and factories across the nation. The blue star had become common property, an
icon representing service and devotion. And as service flags became universally
accepted, the idea was redistributed to the Anglophone Allies—not so much to
England as to Canada, New Zealand, and Australia, with each country modifying
the design to suit its own iconographic tradition.

The full story of the service flag is more complex than can be related here, but
even this brief summary is more nuanced than most of the available accounts.[17]
The flag arose from the interaction of community, commercial, and governmental
interests, each claiming a certain kind of ownership of the idea and its associated values. In this the flag was entirely typical of many symbolic or expressive
responses to the war, whether images, texts, or songs. In particular, the music
that was created in response to the service flag also displayed, in its own way, the
interaction of commerce and community, professional and amateur, service and
self-interest.

Like the service flag, music publishing in 1917 was more complex than is often
portrayed. To fully understand how private and public interests interacted, it is
useful to distinguish between three types of publishers.[18] First, there was "Tin Pan
Alley," made up of commercial firms; these were concentrated in New York City
but also found in most large cities.[19] Second, there were "Kitchen Table" publishers—individuals widely scattered throughout the country who copyrighted and
self-published music written by themselves, family members, and sometimes
friends.[20] And finally, there were "Song Sharks"—individuals or firms that solic-
ited manuscripts or lyrics from would-be songwriters and published them for a
fee, supplying composed music or arrangements as necessary. Song sharks used a
variety of business models, from merely copyrighting a lead sheet to issuing proper

publications replete with illustrated covers; their fees were often exorbitant and they were frequently the targets of federal prosecution for mail fraud, but they also provided a service that allowed individuals to express deeply felt civic or personal concerns.[21]

The three types of publishers served different constituencies and had different agendas. Tin Pan Alley was made up of songwriting professionals concerned primarily with profit. It marketed songs nationwide, and it relied heavily on other segments of the industry—vaudeville, records, piano rolls—to make a song a hit. Kitchen Table publishers ranged from complete amateurs to professionals like organists and music teachers; some were semicommercial, in that they sought at least to recover their costs, but many were motivated primarily by personal interest or civic duty. Song sharks catered to amateurs exclusively, commonly amateurs with limited or no music literacy. Though they pitched their services as an opportunity to create the next great hit, a substantial portion of their clients had no such aspirations; they simply wanted their lyrics set to music for performance in their home community, and they were motivated above all by a desire for personal expression.

Between 1917 and 1921, at least 255 songs were written that make reference in some way to the service flag and its associated icons.[22] The number of titles drops off dramatically after September 1919 (there were none in October), so for present purposes data analysis will end with that month, by which 228 songs had been written. When publications are sorted into Tin Pan Alley, Kitchen Table, and

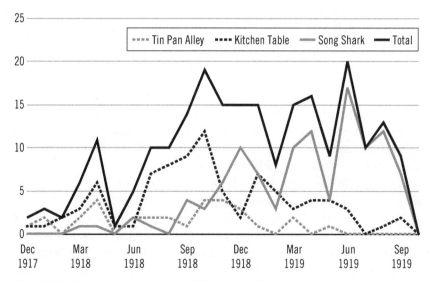

Figure 9.2. Publications by month, December 1917–October 1919.

Song Sharks, some revealing patterns emerge (figure 9.2). First, the total number of titles rose to a peak in October 1918, lessened slightly but remained relatively steady until another peak in June 1919, and fell away sharply thereafter. Second, Tin Pan Alley publications generally mirror the same overall pattern but are always a relatively low percentage of the total. Third, Kitchen Table publications form a generous portion of the whole until October 1918 and then make their own way in substantially reduced proportions. And finally, titles copyrighted by song sharks make up an increasing percentage of the whole over the entire period.

These patterns can be seen more clearly when the months are grouped into three periods (figure 9.3). In the first period (December 1917 through April 1918), Tin Pan Alley is more prominent than at any other time; in the second (May through October 1918), Kitchen Table publishers are in the ascendant; and in the third (November 1918 through October 1919), Song Sharks take over. The three periods correspond roughly to three topics associated with the service flag and star: soldiers, mothers, and mourning. Each prepares the way for the next: during the first, there is a gradual shift from soldiers to mothers; during the second, mothers are joined and surpassed by mourning. At the two junctures between the periods occur two different kinds of anomalies, as the country responds to changing circumstances. Each period also manifests a somewhat different distribution of three song types: march songs, waltz songs, and ballads.[23] And across the whole, there is a broad shift from lyrics written by and focused on males to those written by and focused on females.

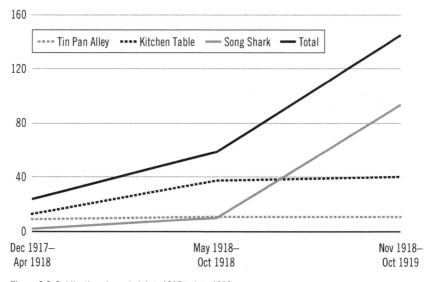

Figure 9.3. Publications by period, late 1917 to late 1919.

Soldiers

At the outset, the service flag was meant to be an expression of commitment, a public declaration of support for the war and for the soldiers. Even before April 1917, Tin Pan Alley had been churning out upbeat, enthusiastic expressions of allegiance and glory, and the service flag provided one more peg on which to hang patriotic sentiments. But it is easier to display an off-the-shelf flag than to write a song and have it edited and engraved, with covers and publicity designed and with a print run arranged, proofread, and produced; hence, although the service flag was in widespread use by October 1917, the first songs appeared only in December. The very first publication, "There's a Service Flag Flying at Our House," was issued by Joe Morris, a major Tin Pan Alley firm, and this patriotic effusion received the Alley's full promotional treatment: advertisements in *Variety*, plugs in trade journals, and recordings on both the Victor and the Columbia labels.[24]

As it turned out, this was the only service-flag song to be recorded or, indeed, so extensively promoted. But the Alley persisted: by the end of February, it had produced three songs, all by established composers and published by major firms. Four more had appeared from Kitchen Table publishers (two of these in manuscript). These seven songs were remarkably similar: men wrote all the lyrics, all but one focused on men (soldiers, fathers), and four of the seven were march songs. "Put a Star in the Service Flag for Me" (figure 9.4), written and self-published by Percy Stanford Miller, is typical of the genre (and of a vast number of wartime productions): a brisk, upbeat march, with a lyric written from the perspective of a departing soldier, the refrain includes clever quotations from "Over There" and "America."[25] Patriotic quotations established legitimacy and linked present to

Figure 9.4. A typical march song: "Put a Star in the Service Flag for Me," refrain. Percy Stanford Miller, music and words; copyrighted December 27, 1918 (Peekskill, NY: Miller).

past conflicts; they were pervasive in songs intended to boost morale and foster home-front support. But the Alley also produced songs in the two other styles: "Each Stitch Is a Thought of You" (figure 9.5) was a typical waltz song about a mother knitting clothes for her soldier boy, linked to the service flag only by the illustration on the cover, and F. Henri Klickmann's "There's a Little Blue Star in the Window" (figure 9.6) was a typical ballad written from the perspective of an unspecified parent.[26]

Figure 9.5. A typical waltz song: "Each Stitch Is a Thought of You," refrain. Billy Baskette, music; Al Sweet, words; copyrighted January 26, 1918 (New York: Leo Feist).

Figure 9.6. A typical ballad: "There's a Little Blue Star in the Window," refrain. F. Henri Klickmann, music; Paul B. Armstrong, words; issued before January 14, 1918 (Chicago: Frank K. Root).

In the two months that followed, most songs evidenced the same characteristics: they were marches authored by males and focused on soldiers. But there were intimations of change: the first lyric authored by a woman appeared in March 1918, with three more in April (figure 9.7); songs focused on mothers and families increased to three each in both March and April (figure 9.8); and waltz songs and ballads both gradually increased in number (figure 9.9).[27] Correlations also began to emerge: of the seven "mother" songs, only one was a march; of the four songs setting lyrics by women, three were ballads.[28]

In the meantime, public perception of the war was also changing. The flag-waving enthusiasm that followed the declaration of war in April 1917 and continued through the training and departure of the troops began to be reassessed after November 3, 1917, when the first American soldiers were killed. Almost

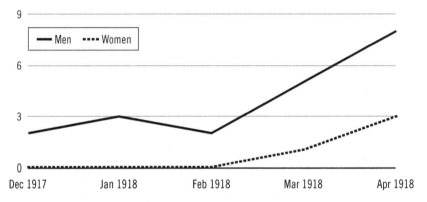

Figure 9.7. Lyric authorship by gender, December 1917–April 1918.

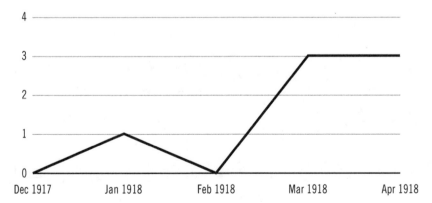

Figure 9.8. Songs about mothers or families, December 1917–April 1918.

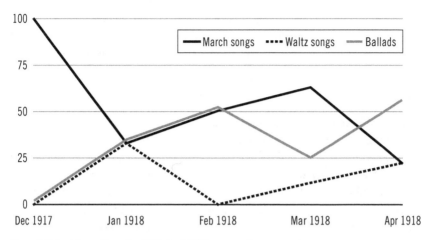

Figure 9.9. Song types, December 1917–April 1918, expressed as a percentage.

immediately, members of the public voiced concerns about proper symbols of remembrance. In Chicago the formidable activist and philanthropist Louise DeKoven Bowen argued that icons and memorials should emphasize glory rather than grief, and she proposed that military fatalities be honored with a gold star rather than with black for mourning.[29] The idea caught on quickly, and at the end of November the citizens of Frackville, Pennsylvania, added a gold star to a service flag honoring an early fatality.[30] By early 1918, the practice was widely embraced, and as American deaths continued to mount and gold stars replaced blue, service flags shifted from expressing resolve to signifying sacrifice or grief. Over the course of a few months, a standard icon evolved: a gold star, slightly smaller, was to be stitched over the blue one, so the gold was bordered by blue. In practice, though, the gold star was often a simple replacement.[31]

Four "gold-star" songs appeared in April; of these, the first were probably James A. Dillon's "There's a Service Flag in the Window" and F. Henri Klickmann's "When the Little Blue Star in the Window Has Turned to Gold," a transparent attempt to build on his January success.[32] Both songs point to the future in several ways: they are concerned with death and remembrance, the lyrics associate loss with motherhood, and neither is a march song (Klickmann's is a waltz song and Dillon's is a ballad). Both appeared when the star's appearance was still evolving, and Dillon's refrain actually implies a reversed icon:

> There's a service flag in the window,
> But it hasn't a star of blue.
> On its outer edge is a different star,
> Of a lighter and purer hue.

The other two April gold-star publications were also both ballads, a song type that would be even more popular than waltzes in the months to come. From May 1918 forward, service-flag songs, like the stars themselves, would be of a different hue.

Mothers

In May 1918, American songwriters—and, indeed, most Americans—appeared to be holding their breath. The German offensive in April had threatened Paris, American casualties were increasing, and prospects for a quick end to the war seemed remote. New war-related titles appeared at a much-reduced rate than in previous months, and service-flag titles plummeted: only one song was copyrighted in May, at the very start of the month. None then appeared until June 8, and through the month of June only five were issued. But as the news improved, business picked up, and through September and October, as the Armistice approached, the number of service-flag publications reached a new high (see figure 9.2).

The second period of service-flag songs (May to October 1918) differs in several key respects from the first. As already noted, Kitchen Table publishers dominate, and Tin Pan Alley recedes in importance (figure 9.2). The number of female authors increases to the extent that in September, briefly, men and women write the same number of lyrics (figure 9.10). The percentage of service-flag songs focusing on gold stars increases steadily, and in August it passes the 50 percent mark, to remain above that (with one exception) thereafter, and the percentage of songs focused on or written from the perspective of mothers or families also increases (figure 9.11).[33] Moreover, as figure 9.11 indicates, gold-star songs and mother songs appear to be

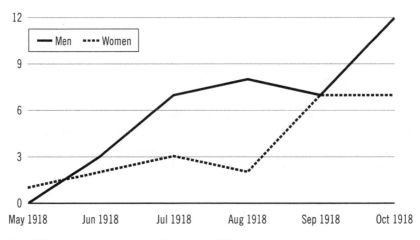

Figure 9.10. Lyric authorship by gender, May–October 1918.

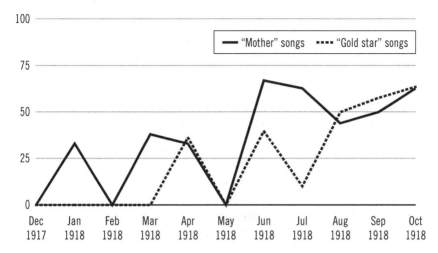

Figure 9.11. The percentage of mother songs and gold-star songs, December 1917–October 1918.

closely correlated, except for a notable departure in the month of July. And finally, songs are now primarily ballads, not marches, though the mix of song types appears to be comparatively volatile (figure 9.12).

As always, details and relationships are informative. The month of July, when the creation of service-flag songs regained its previous pace, was anomalous in two ways. First, the correlation between gold-star and mother songs breaks down for the only time: the proportion of mother songs remains essentially constant,

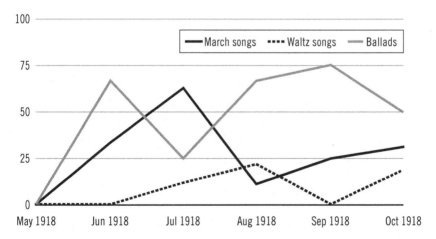

Figure 9.12. Song types, May–October 1918, expressed as a percentage:

while that of gold-star songs declines. Second, march songs surpass ballads, again for the only time in this period. The two anomalies result in part from a pair of July mother songs that are marches and are not gold-star songs (a third had appeared in mid-June). These closely resemble the march songs from earlier in the year; Florence Carleton Brewer's "My Service Flag," for instance, opens with a quote from "The Star-Spangled Banner" and goes on to a brisk duple-time march, with lyrics that evoke the Civil War song "We Are Coming, Father Abraham":

[Verse 1] The first star was for Jimmie, a soldier brave and true,
The next one was for Bobbie, a sailor boy in blue,
There's a stricken one that calls us to avenge a cruel wrong,
We're coming, Woodrow Wilson, now a hundred million strong.
[Refrain 2] So wave on Service Flag by the Red, White and Blue,
Ev'ry star that's in your banner means a warrior brave and true,
You're the Army, you're the Navy, you're a starry banner too,
And I'm praying, my soldier boy, my sailor boy, for you.[34]

This brief burst of motherly militancy resulted in part from two wartime developments. First, in June, American troops began to engage in battle under their own leadership; in July they would play a major role in the second battle of the Marne. The dispirited mood that had settled on the country after the April setbacks lifted, and there was a renewed sense of excitement and support, which, as always, was reflected in the music that was written. Second, mothers—and women in general— were finding their own voice and place in the war effort. Women served abroad in noncombat roles, and at home they took jobs that had been vacated by departing soldiers. Mothers needed no longer to be portrayed only in domestic settings, writing letters, knitting clothes, and praying for loved ones; they had a power to *act* that had previously been denied them.[35]

As mothers, rather than soldiers, became the focus of service-flag songs, there also began to appear an interplay between the general and the personal, sometimes manifested in a syntactic shift from third to first person. "I'll Ever Wear You, My Golden Star" opens with a descriptive verse ("In a cottage just at twilight sat a mother old and gray"), but in the refrain the mother speaks directly to the listener ("My golden star brings memories of baby ways, of childhood days").[36] Loss is collective but represented by individual experience. A related shift toward the universal occurs in a group of songs that also peaks in this period; these contain lyrics that situate the gold star in a broader Christian context. The first and most successful was Charles H. Gabriel's "Should the Stars in Your Service Flag Turn to Gold," with lyrics by Dora F. Hendricks: "Should the stars in your service flag turn to gold ... Creep close to God, and you will hear ... As soft and low, He whispers, 'Child, I know ... I, also, gave my beloved Son.'"[37] Between June and October, Gabriel's song was joined by six others with similar texts; only two appeared thereafter.

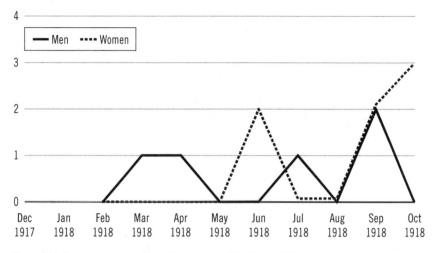

Figure 9.13. Song-shark lyricists by gender, December 1917–October 1918.

Finally, this period also saw the emergence of song sharks—largely in the shadows at this point, to be sure, but in increasing numbers. Only two copyrights were issued to song sharks before June 1918, but in June through October there were ten more. Data are less complete for song-shark publications, because slightly over half of their copyrights have not been digitized and are available only as physical copyright-deposit copies at the Library of Congress, many in manuscript only. Hence, assessment of topic or musical style is not reliable, but it can be noted that the male-female proportions of song-shark lyricists generally resemble those for service-flag songs as a whole, with only men represented in the first period and women emerging in the second (figure 9.13; compare figures 9.7 and 9.10).

Mourning

Though gold stars and motherhood were already linked in songs and in the public mind, it was only in the summer of 1918 that the phrase *gold-star mother* came into use.[38] Ceremonies and tributes brought bereaved mothers together, and informal associations began to be formed, with the first official organization established in August in the Greater Chicago area.[39] Although its stated purpose was "to lend comfort to the mothers and relatives of other war victims," the Chicago group devoted itself primarily to fund-raising up through the end of the year, celebrating its success—and raising more money—with a formal dinner on December 21, 1918.[40]

In the meantime, another historical watershed had been reached on November 11, when the Armistice took effect. Service-flag music—and the flag itself—again shifted focus; the music turned toward personal expressions of mourning, and the flag (and especially the gold star) became a symbol of remembrance. A third period emerged, distinguished from the second not by a resounding silence, as in May, but by new trends in publication, authorship, topic, and style. In the year that followed November 1918, song sharks came to dominate publication, and after May 1919 Tin Pan Alley disappeared altogether (figure 9.2). Most lyrics were now authored by women, with two exceptions, in December 1918 and March 1919 (figure 9.14). The majority of songs set either gold-star or mother lyrics—again excepting

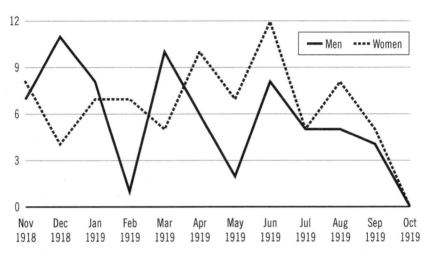

Figure 9.14. Lyric authorship by gender, November 1918–October 1919.

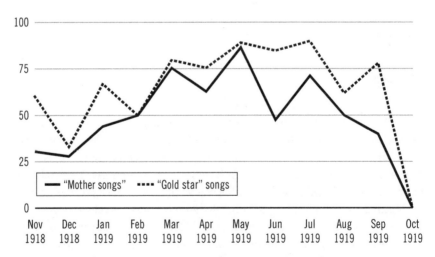

Figure 9.15. Percentages of mother songs and gold-star songs, November 1918–October 1919.

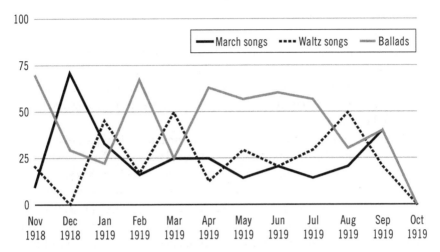

Figure 9.16. Song types expressed as a percentage, November 1918–October 1919.

December 1918—and the correlation between the two is well-nigh perfect (figure 9.15). Waltz songs were more common, and waltzes and ballads wholly eclipsed marches—once again with the exception of December 1918 (figure 9.16).

Details and relationships again help clarify the emerging trends. Tin Pan Alley remained a presence from October through December 1918 largely because, as the country contemplated peace and songwriters no longer had to buoy morale, memorial tributes to fallen soldiers acquired commercial value. The Alley adopted a public perspective, writing at a remove from personal loss; of its eleven publications, only one was a mother song. Typical was a "slow march" written by W. R. Williams:

> For the blue stars in the window
> Tell a story of their own,
> Of the soldiers for "Old Glory"
> For our Liberty and home.
> If the word comes "they have fallen",
> Then the blues are changed to gold
> And it's then we kneel in pray'r
> For the heroes "over there,"
> For that's the greatest story ever told.[41]

The surge in marches in December is only partly related. Of the five march songs, two set upbeat blue-star lyrics about soldiers—a throwback to the early excitement about America's entry into the war that probably reflects a comparable excitement about its end. Two more are by a song shark, Raymond A. Browne, who was inclined to write marches regardless of the lyric he was setting.[42] Male authors exceeded female ones in December partly because of the Tin Pan Alley publications; the surge in March, however, was in male authors of song-shark lyrics, and the available titles are too few to draw conclusions. In general, however, women were more common lyricists for song sharks, with the trend increasing throughout the period (figure 9.17).

The proportion of waltzes increases in this final period. In part that reflects the increased presence of song sharks, who favored waltzes and marches because the styles were so formulaic. But it also reflects the texts that they were given. Most of these were written by women, and many were first-person narratives, in a lyric style that had been associated with waltz songs since at least the paradigmatic "After the Ball" (1891).[43] A good instance is Lora V. Starret's "Star of Gold," set by Leo Friedman, with a text clearly modeled on Harris's (figure 9.18).[44] It's quite possible that some of the song-shark lyricists were gold-star mothers, though assembling that data exceeds the scope of this chapter; in any case, it seems clear that the same motivations—bonding with others who were bereaved, creating memorials for victims and heroes, and building hopes for a peaceful future—animated both these lyricists and those active in the emerging gold-star organizations.

When the data for all three periods are combined, some overall relationships are evident (figure 9.19). Women contribute a relatively small proportion of Tin Pan Alley lyrics and send a relatively large proportion to song sharks. Women's

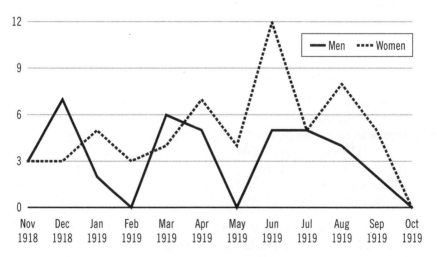

Figure 9.17. Song-shark lyricists by gender, November 1918–October 1919.

Figure 9.18. A song-shark waltz: "Star of Gold," verse and refrain. Leo Friedman, music; Lora V. Starret, words; copyrighted August 25, 1919 (Chicago: North American Music).

texts outstrip men's among gold-star songs, but the genders are roughly equal for mother songs. These relationships are correlated, since Tin Pan Alley produced proportionally fewer gold-star songs and proportionally more mother songs. The percentage of women composers is slightly higher among Kitchen Table publishers, and there are no women composers at all among the song sharks (figure 9.20).[45] In all circumstances, ballads dominate musical style; among Kitchen Table and Song Shark publications, marches come second, whereas in Tin Pan Alley, waltz songs have a slight edge. For gold-star and mother songs, the proportion of marches is markedly less, and for lyrics authored by men, the proportion of marches is relatively high (figure 9.21). There are no real surprises here, but the cumulative data do confirm the relationships that have been traced through the three periods separately.

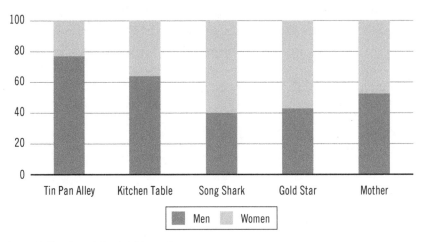

Figure 9.19. Lyricists (all periods) by gender.

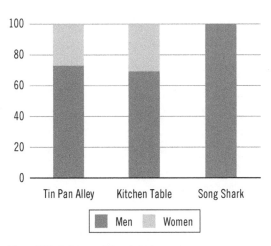

Figure 9.20. Composers (all periods) by gender.

Tin Pan Alley was a male domain, driven by profit; it produced music in conventional styles unless it could lay claim to a new niche or novelty; it eschewed topics when it thought demand was slack or public condemnation would result. Hence, in this instance, it produced primarily waltzes and ballads, written primarily by males, and it largely abandoned death and gold-star mother songs midway through 1918. Kitchen Table publishing was, in a sense, its polar opposite: women were more prominent, and publication was driven by civic concerns; styles were

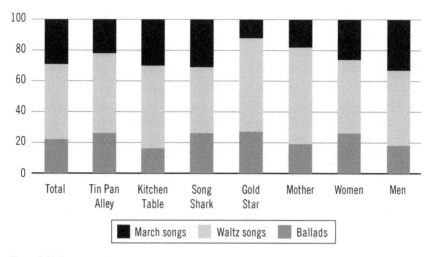

Figure 9.21. Song types (all periods).

chosen to enhance the message; and topics persisted as long as they were matters for public discussion. Hence, in this instance, Kitchen Table publishers issued ballads, waltzes, and marches in more equal quantities, with lyrics and music by women and men in more equal proportions, and they remained committed to memorialization well beyond the end of the war. Song sharks negotiated a strange sort of compromise between the poles: the operators were entirely male, but their lyricist clients were largely female; they wrote entirely formulaic music; and they responded to the needs of individuals who sought to express their personal feelings. During and after the war, they wrote songs having few or no distinctive stylistic features on topics that moved individuals to lyric expression: death and grief, in this instance.

The relationships between all these factors are typical of the workings of the popular music industry at this time. In addition to illuminating broader cultural issues, they exemplify the culmination of a phase in publishing and dissemination that peaked in the war years and was transformed in the following decade. After 1920 records replaced sheet music as the primary means of dissemination; film replaced vaudeville; broadcasts replaced pianos. Some attributes of the preceding era, such as gender roles, continued largely unchanged; others, like song sharks, were radically transformed. The Armistice, and the years that followed, marked more than the end of a world order; it marked the terminus of a certain kind of music making, and it brought a new music into being.

Aftermath

When the first American deaths occurred in November 1917, it became evident that the military had no real plan for dealing with the soldiers' remains. The problem was deferred when the government announced that, for the moment, soldiers would be buried in France but that their bodies might be repatriated at a later date. After the Armistice, the question again arose, and in the spring of 1919 the Quartermaster Corps began contacting next of kin with a questionnaire inquiring into the family's wishes. By the summer, the nation was embroiled in a very public controversy that was not really resolved until the construction of dedicated cemeteries at home and abroad in the 1920s.[46]

Gold-star mothers had a personal interest in the matter, of course. The first three fatalities of the war had by now attained an iconic stature, and their mothers became advocates for repatriation.[47] And families of less celebrated fatalities joined the crusade: "I am a gold star sister and my gold star mother waits for the body of her boy—who cannot come," wrote one in a letter to a newspaper.[48] Gold-star songs and mother songs joined together in comment. Lyrics made reference to French graves—sometimes approvingly, sometimes ambivalently or even critically. Justin B. Holmes, giving voice to a bereaved mother, offered a general blessing on the grave "where he sleeps in sunny France." Hilda Mobley wrote an appeal: "Dearest mother of France, we've left them in your care, / Place your emblem of love on their graves over there." Mary Winters was more specific still: "There's a wooden cross in Flanders, at the head of a soldier's grave / And it bears the name and number of the son whom this mother gave." And William J. Fradenburgh entered directly into the debate: "The mother bowed down with grief / because she can't place a wreath upon his grave in France."[49]

Gold-star organizations grew and consolidated, motivated in large part by concerns about cemeteries and memorials. In March Mrs. Oscar Vogl, president of the Chicago Gold Star Mothers, announced plans for an international organization, Gold Star Mothers of the World, noting that two additional chapters of the local organization had been formed in Kankakee and Milwaukee.[50] In April the Mothers of the Fifteenth Engineers greeted with acclaim the suggestion that memorial tablets be erected in honor of Pittsburgh's war dead.[51] And in June a parallel organization, Gold Star Mothers of America, was formed in Rochester, New York, motivated in large part by memorial ceremonies for newly interred soldiers.[52]

In 1919 the country remained directed outward, toward the formation of international organizations. General Pershing, supported by many gold-star mothers, argued that American dead should be reburied in Europe in new, beautifully designed cemeteries. The American Legion contemplated a world association of veterans; the International Red Cross renewed and expanded its transnational

agenda. And President Wilson stumped the country on behalf of his visionary League of Nations, through which a peaceful new world order would be
established.

All that changed in 1920. Wilson suffered a stroke on October 2, 1919, and he
and the League of Nations were defeated in the 1920 elections. The international
agenda of the American Legion was muted by a new "militant pacifism" that effectively precluded an effective contribution to its membership in the Inter-Allied Ex-
Servicemen Federation.[53] And the impetus for international memorial cemeteries
was blunted by renewed focus on the repatriation of bodies and the redesign of
Arlington National Cemetery in the United States.[54] Gold-star-mother organizations turned inward, their plans for an international presence not really reasserted
until after the formation of a truly national association in 1928.[55]

Gold-star songs also declined rapidly, from a dozen titles in November and
December 1919 to exactly the same number in all of 1920 and to even fewer per
year over the next decade. Music was changing; jazz was becoming the dominant
style, and recordings and films urged younger generations to become spectators,
not participants. There was little place for self-publication or for the printed ballads
and waltz songs that had characterized service-flag music. Prohibition, paradoxically, ushered in an era of self-indulgence and excess; the Roaring Twenties had
started.

It would take another war—or, more properly, the resumption of the war to end
all wars—to drag the county back into the international arena. In the meantime, the
national organization of gold-star mothers embarked on celebrated pilgrimages to
visit and refurbish European graveyards, memorialized the past, and contemplated
the future. When war resumed, blue-star and gold-star mothers were ready to take
up the cause again. They remain viable organizations even today, still bringing
together soldiers, mothers, and mourning in a cultural constellation that somehow
marries grief with resolve, empathy with militance—just as was done by the songs
that heralded their arrival during the Great War. In 2018, as the country embarks
on another, even more entrenched, isolationism and a new round of jingoistic
belligerence, and as the world tips inexorably toward nationalist fragmentation,
another war of even greater magnitude seems inevitable. The service flag has not
yet been laid to rest.

Notes

1. "Wilson's Address to Congress . . . April 2, 1917," in *President Wilson's State Papers and Addresses* (New York: Review of Reviews, 1917), 381.

2. George Creel, *How We Advertised America* (New York: Harper and Brothers, 1920); Stew-
art Halsey Ross, *Propaganda for War* (Jefferson, NC: McFarland, 1996); Celia Malone Kings-
bury, *For Home and Country* (Lincoln: University of Nebraska Press, 2010).

3. In an earlier usage, the phrase *service flag* referred to a flag actually used in service—that is, carried by the standard-bearer of a company—and often dedicated to that purpose by a politician or celebrity. As an instance, see "Company Asks Theda [Bara] for Flag," *Tacoma (WA) Times*, April 13, 1917, 6.

4. "City—Coalfield," *Bluefield (WV) Daily Telegraph*, May 19, 1917, 2.

5. Here and below I am deeply indebted to Dave Martucci (http://www.vexman.net), past president of the North American Vexillological Association, for sharing his research with me.

6. "Newport First to Adopt," *Newport (RI) Mercury*, July 13, 1917, 8; *Biographical Register of the Officers and Graduates of the U.S. Military Academy at West Point, New York*, supp. (Saginaw, MI: Seeman and Peters, 1910), 5:718; and Robert Douglas, "For Those Who Gave Their Best," *Leslie's Illustrated Weekly Newspaper* 123, no. 3221 (1917): 678. For Boorman's design, see Dave Martucci, "Service Flag (U.S.): More Info and Images," CRW Flags, http://www.crwflags .com/fotw/flags/us%5Esvc.html. In reality, the Japanese practice differed from Sullivan's description.

7. "Service Flags in Middletown," *Middletown (NY) Times-Press*, June 22, 1917, 3; "Put This Notice in the Window," *Daily Mirror* (London), October 27, 1914, 4.

8. "Keep the Home-Fires Burning," music by Ivor Novello, lyrics by Lena Guilbert Ford (New York: Chappell, 1917); "Place a Candle in the Window," music by Maxwell Goldman, lyrics by Fern Glenn (St. Louis: Buck and Lowney, 1918); "Keep the Love-Light Burning in the Window," music and words by Jack Caddigan and Jimmy McHugh (Boston: D. W. Cooper, 1917). Digitized copies of all three songs can be found at IN harmony, http://webapp1 .dlib.indiana.edu/inharmony/. "Keep the Beacon Light a-Burning Bright" (music by J. B. Robbins, words by Daniel F. Lawlor; Shenandoah, Pa.: Lawlor and Robbins, 1919) has been digitized by the Library of Congress at https://www.loc.gov/item/2009371652/.

9. See Martucci, "Service Flag"; images of McIlroy's, Queisser's, and Boorman's designs are available on the present publication's website.

10. "City—Coalfield"; "The Service Flag," *Holbrook (AZ) News*, June 8, 1917, 1; "Soldiers' Homes in City Will Be Marked," *Eugene (OR) Guard*, June 23, 1917, 10.

11. Dave Martucci, e-mail communications, December 24, 2016, and January 5, 2017. Queisser later claimed to have conceived his design in March 1917 ("Service Flag Designer Here," *New-York Tribune*, November 23, 1917, 6), but circumstantial evidence suggests this was more self-serving hindsight than fact.

12. "Queisser, Robert L.," in *The Book of Clevelanders* (Cleveland, OH: Burrows Bros., 1914), 216.

13. "Service Flags in Middletown," *Middletown (NY) Times-Press*, June 22, 1917, 3; advertisement, George H. Taylor Company, *New York Times*, June 26, 1917, 15; "A War Service Flag," *Piqua (OH) Daily Call*, July 3, 1917, 4.

14. "Flag Shows Teddy's Four Sons in War," *Wichita (KS) Beacon*, September 14, 1917, 9.

15. Queisser was well acquainted with Secretary of War Newton D. Baker, whose political career had begun in Cleveland; though Baker denied any involvement, it is likely the War Department facilitated the application. See [Chauncey Corey] Brainerd, "Service Flag Design Has Been Patented; May Make New One," *Brooklyn Daily Eagle*, November 25, 1917, 7.

16. "Patent Monopoly on Service Flag," *New York Times*, November 22, 1917, 24; "Service Flag Royalties Are Shared with Red Cross," *Boston Daily Globe*, November 24, 1917, 9; "The History of the Service Flag," *Outlook* 117, no. 17 (December 26, 1917), 668.

17. Most websites reduce the history to Queisser's contribution, and even substantive studies like that by Holly S. Fenelon, *That Knock at the Door: The History of Gold Star Mothers in America* (Bloomington, IN: iUniverse, 2012), tend to gloss over the details.

18. I have applied this distinction before. See William Brooks, "The Rehearsal," *American Music* 34, no. 4 (2016): 507–34, for a fuller discussion. A more nuanced set of categories is sometimes useful but is not needed in the present instance.

19. Commercial publishers included both "standard" and "popular" publishers, a distinction widely recognized at the time. For present purposes, I've subsumed both into the general category "Tin Pan Alley"; in practice, only a small handful of titles on the topics under discussion were issued by "standard" publishers.

20. Self-publication was a recognized practice at the time. See, for instance, Jack Gordon, *How to Publish Your Own Music Successfully* (Chicago: Jack Gordon, 1919). My thanks to Laurie Matheson for suggesting "Kitchen Table" as a phrase to complement "Tin Pan Alley."

21. For a typical warning against song sharks, see E. M. Wickes, *Writing the Popular Song* (Springfield, MA: Home Correspondence School, 1916), chap. 24.

22. A database containing details of these songs is available on this book's website, together with a brief explanations of the methods used. Compare this outpouring of songs, many of which mourned the deaths of loved ones, with the deafening silence that followed the even greater losses that resulted from the influenza epidemic; see Deniz Ertan's chapter in this volume.

23. A much more sophisticated set of song types appears in Wickes, *Writing the Popular Song*, chap. 2, but three broad categories suffice for present purposes.

24. Music by Al W. Brown, lyrics by Bernie Grossman and Thomas Hoier; a digitized copy is available from the Library of Congress at https://www.loc.gov/item/2014562047/. Copyright was registered on December 22, 1917, but the song was advertised in *Variety* on December 7; advertisements continued into March 1918. Brown and Hoier's song was plugged to show that Morris had "stolen a march on the rest of the boys" in "Joe Morris Has a Live Catalog," *Motion Picture News* 17, no. 3 (1918): 314. The song was recorded on December 27 by the Shannon Four on Victor 18434 (mx B-21294, released March 1918) and January 10 by the Sterling Trio on Columbia A2493 (mx 77621, released April 1918); for details, see *Discography of American Historical Recordings*, http://adp.library.ucsb.edu.

25. Miller's song was copyrighted on December 27, 1917, and issued by the Miller Publishing Company, Peekskill, NY; it has been digitized by the Library of Congress at https://www.loc.gov/item/2009440110/. March songs and marches are discussed in the chapters in this volume by Patrick Warfield and Kendra Preston Leonard.

26. "Each Stitch Is a Thought of You" is available from the Library of Congress at https://www.loc.gov/item/2013564581/. Klickmann's song (lyrics by Paul B. Armstrong) was published in Chicago by McKinley Music Company, under the imprint "Frank K. Root"; no copyright was registered, but a quarter-page ad in the *New York Clipper*, January 16, 1918,

35, warned pirates that McKinley was "the sole owners" of the title. Digitized copies can be found at IN Harmony.

27. Because some songs included in the database have not been available other than as copyright entries, song types are here expressed as percentages of the available songs rather than as absolute numbers.

28. "Mother" songs need not contain the word *mother* explicitly if the lyric is clearly written in a mother's voice or from a mother's perspective. Conversely, merely mentioning a "mother" in passing is not sufficient to classify the song as a "mother" song. An important factor is placement: the occurrence of "mother" in the verse is less convincing than an appearance in the penultimate line of the refrain (the "hook") would be.

29. "May Use Gold Star as Mourning Sign," *Decatur (IL) Herald*, November 13, 1917, 1.

30. "Gold Star in Service Flag for Dead Soldier," *Wilkes-Barre (PA) Times Leader*, November 30, 1917, 23.

31. Eventually, the service flag and its iconic stars were officially adopted by the military. They are still in use today, regulated under the Department of Defense's *Manual of Military Decorations and Awards*, DoD 1348.33-M, September 1996, Section C10.3. Thanks to Dave Martucci for this information.

32. Dillon's song was self-published, copyrighted April 10; a digitized copy is on the Library of Congress website at https://www.loc.gov/item/2014564253/. Klickmann's song again had lyrics by Paul B. Armstrong and was published by McKinley Music Company, Chicago; no copyright was registered, but internal evidence confirms that publication came on or after April 10, 1918. A digitized copy is at Mississippi State University, http://digital .library.msstate.edu/cdm/ref/collection/SheetMusic/id/3953.

33. Hereafter, "mother" songs are expressed as percentages of the available titles, to facilitate comparison with song types and with gold-star songs.

34. Brewer's song was self-published and copyrighted July 22, 1918; a copy has been digitized by the Library of Congress at https://www.loc.gov/resource/ihas.200199194.0/. "We Are Coming, Father Abraham," a poem by James Sloane Gibbons first published on July 16, 1862, was set by several composers and adapted and performed throughout the Civil War. See Irwin Silber and Jerry Silverman, *Songs of the Civil War* (New York: Bonanza Books, 1960), 92–93.

35. Women's roles were changing in many ways, of course; the chapters in this volume by Christina Bashford, Kendra Preston Leonard, and Michelle Meinhart all discuss related topics.

36. "I'll Ever Wear You, My Golden Star" (words and music by Avelyn Mae Kerr, copyrighted in manuscript on August 2, 1918) is at https://www.loc.gov/item/2014570265/.

37. Copyrighted on April 24, 1917, by the Rodeheaver Company, Chicago; a digitized copy is at Brown University, https://repository.library.brown.edu/studio/item/bdr:93242/.

38. The earliest appearance in print might be in "The Fourth of July Will Be Big Day in La Grande," *La Grande (OR) Observer*, July 2, 1918, 1: "All gold star mothers to ride in leading cars."

39. "The Gold Star Mothers," *Chicago Daily Tribune*, August 24, 1918, 6.

40. "Gold Star Mothers," *Chicago Daily Tribune*, December 22, 1918, 3.

41. W. R. Williams was a pseudonym for Will Rossiter. A digitized copy of "The Greatest Story Ever Told" (Chicago: Will Rossiter, copyright October 22, 1918) is available from the Library of Congress at https://www.loc.gov/item/2014564555/.

42. All three of Browne's service-flag songs are marches; his proclivities are evident at the Library of Congress website (https://www.loc.gov/collections/world-war-i-sheet-music/), which contains digitized copies of 695 war-related titles written by him.

43. Words and music by Charles K. Harris (New York: Charles K. Harris, 1891). Copyright was renewed and Harris's song reissued in 1919; a copy is at IN Harmony.

44. Published by North American Music Publishing Company, copyright August 25, 1919.

45. Pseudonyms were not uncommon, of course, and it is possible that some women wrote under male names or vice versa. However, I've used census records and similar sources to check the gender of the leading song sharks, and they are indeed all men.

46. See David W. Seitz's excellent dissertation for a full discussion: "Grave Negotiations: The Rhetorical Foundations of American World War I Cemeteries in Europe" (University of Pittsburgh, 2011).

47. Ibid., 279–81 and passim; "First Gold Star Mother Hopes for Return of Soldier's Body," *Green Bay (WI) Press-Gazette*, May 30, 1919, 6.

48. "Letters to the Editor: Gold Star Mother Waits" (signed "Gold Star Sister"), *Seattle Star*, June 5, 1919, 6.

49. "Just a Little Flag with One Bright Star of Gold" (words and music by Justin B. Holmes), Brunswick, ME: Justin B. Holmes, copyright June 15, 1919; "Our Star of Gold" (music by Burrell Van Buren, words by Hilda Mobley), Atlanta, IL: Hilda Mobley, copyright June 6, 1919; "Little Gold Star" (music by Leo Friedman, words by Mary E. Winters), Chicago: North American Music, copyright August 22, 1919; "The Star of Gold" (words and music by William J. Fradenburgh), Chicago: Delmar Music, copyright July 3, 1919. All four songs have been digitized and are available on the Library of Congress website https://www.loc .gov/collections/world-war-i-sheet-music/. "In Flanders Fields" was, of course, the most widely set lyric about French graves; for more on this poem and two of its settings, see the chapters in this volume by Gayle Magee, Patrick Warfield, and Brian Thompson.

50. "Want World Body of Gold Star Mothers," *Chicago Tribune*, March 5, 1919, 18.

51. "Memorial Tablets to Honor Fallen Men of Fifteenth, Unanimous Plan of Mothers," *Pittsburgh Post-Gazette*, April 23, 1919, 11.

52. "Gold Star Mothers Honor Dead Soldier," *Rochester (NY) Democrat and Chronicle*, June 2, 1919, 9; "Gold Star Mothers May Broaden Scope," *Rochester (NY) Democrat and Chronicle*, June 6, 1919, 23; "Invite Gold Star Mothers," *Rochester (NY) Democrat and Chronicle*, June 14, 1919, 17.

53. Stephen R. Ortiz, "Well-Armed Internationalism: American Veteran Organizations and the Crafting of an 'Associated' Veterans' Internationalism, 1919–1939," in *The Great War and Veterans' Internationalism*, ed. Julia Eichenberg and John Paul Newman (New York: Palgrave Macmillan, 2013), chap. 4 and esp. p. 55.

54. Seitz, "Grave Negotiations," chap. 5.

55. Fenelon, *That Knock at the Door*; John W. Graham, *The Gold Star Mother Pilgrimages of the 1930s: Overseas Grave Visitations by Mothers and Widows of Fallen U.S. World War I Soldiers* (Jefferson, NC: McFarland, 2005).

CHAPTER 10

The Beginning of the End of Something

DENIZ ERTAN

An American recalls the year 1918:

> It just simply divided my life, cut across it like that. So that everything before that
> was just getting ready, and after that I was in some strange way altered, ready. It
> took me a long time to go out and live in the world again. I was really "alienated," in
> the pure sense. It was, I think, the fact that I really had participated in death, that I
> knew what death was, and had almost experienced it.... Now if you have had that,
> and survived it, come back from it, you are no longer like other people, and there's
> no use deceiving yourself that you are.[1]

One might think that this is a soldier talking about the war. It is not. This is American writer Katherine Anne Porter (1890–1980) describing her experience of the
influenza pandemic as a watershed of profound awakening. She almost died—and
survived only to undergo a nightmare. Survival, it seems, did not diminish the
trauma of exposure. In her autobiographical fiction *Pale Horse, Pale Rider* (1939),
Porter wrote: "Opening [her eyes] again she saw with a new anguish the dull world
to which she was condemned, where the light seemed filmed over with cobwebs,
all the bright surfaces corroded, the sharp planes melted and formless, all objects
and beings meaningless.... There was no escape."[2]

    For millions of people, surviving the war and the disease did not offer relief or
redemption but rather made the world seem even bleaker than before. A great deal
of innocence was lost. The war and the epidemic altered music making, as two

fermatas—*points d'orgues*—in the lives and livelihoods of countless people. World War I—the war to end all wars—was meant to be the end of the old world order. The Armistice would mark and seal its end. But, writing about this period (autumn 1918–winter 1919), Porter's words are about descent: "This is the beginning of the end of something. Something terrible is going to happen to me."[3] These sickly times were stained by a downward spiral into uncertainty.

Modernity and the American character in particular were supposed to be about energy and optimism. Since its first appearance in 1893, Frederick Jackson Turner's influential frontier thesis had emphasized the American predispositions for toughness and individual freedom and the culture's preoccupation with the meeting point between savagery and civilization. His emphasis on a certain perpetual descent and ascent—a "continual beginning over again"—evinces not only the American predilections for aspiration and movement but also cyclical variations of progress and failure. Since its earliest days, the American temperament and history had gravitated toward revolution, rebirth, and renewal, often displaying a hunger for beginnings of beginnings, ever new. Thus, Porter's statement that "this is the beginning of the end" points to a disruption and impairment, a certain silencing. The cataclysm caught music makers unprepared, making many lives precarious. Like World War I, the influenza epidemic created a series of ruptures and trauma across the world, bringing imminent danger and giving rise to new forms of fear.

A Narrative History: Silent Noise

Europeans faced unspeakable brutalities during the war, whereas Americans were hit particularly hard by the virus. For Americans, the war had been "over there," but the virus was "over here"—the "Germs" had invaded home. The concept of "the nation" became quickly subjected to a noisy debate even in this crisis: the strain probably originated in Kansas,[4] but the Germans were to be blamed for what was called the "Spanish flu." Condemning the enemy fomented anger and perturbation, and many found it easier to continue to blame the Germans, whose agents were now supposedly busy with infecting all Americans. Dr. M. G. Parsons, a US Public Health Service officer for northeastern Mississippi, told a local paper, "The Hun resorts to unwanted murder of innocent noncombatants. . . . He has been tempted to spread sickness and death thru germs." Another story ran: "The Germs Are Coming. An epidemic of influenza is spreading or being spread, (we wonder which)."[5] When it was not the foreigner, then it was the outsider and the poor who were stigmatized—even though the virus recognized no class or race. Many neighbors, communities, and individuals stopped caring for each other.[6]

The combination of the end of the war and the rise of the epidemic signaled a great divide. Beneath the fault line, there was another schism, setting the private against the public. In *Pale Horse*, Porter observed the war and the uncertainty of the flu epidemic through the lens of the patriotic song "My Country, 'Tis of Thee." This is the same anthem that calls out loudly to let "freedom ring," "music swell the breeze," rocks break "their silence" and let "the sound prolong." Porter invokes "My Country, 'Tis of Thee" and "The Star-Spangled Banner" thus:

> Sweet land . . . oh, terrible land of this bitter world where the sound of rejoicing was a clamor of pain, where ragged tuneless old women . . . were singing "Sweet land of Liberty—"
>
> "Oh say, can you see?" their hopeless voices were asking next. . . . Now if real daylight such as I remember having seen in this world would only come again, but it is always twilight or just before morning, a promise of day that is never kept. What has become of the sun?[7]

From autumn 1918 onward, absences and silences increasingly overshadowed musical life.[8] In his emotional speech at a banquet in New York in May 1920, celebrated tenor John McCormack did not refrain from dwelling on transience, futility, and the many forgotten musicians affected by these years:

> The horrors of terrible war will all be forgotten in due time, and all that will remain will be the memory of the noble and valiant deeds of those who fought and bled and died "over there." Time will dim my powers as an artist and I shall join the long train of forgotten ones; but I hope that when that day comes, when I have said farewell, like the old Irish harper to his harp, and have laid it aside because my songs have all been sung, I hope, I pray that your affection for me, as a man, so beautifully expressed tonight, may still go on.
>
> How futile language is to express our deepest feelings! I am absolutely at a loss.[9]

Vast numbers disappeared into oblivion, and a torrent of humanity became wordless or incapacitated. Even the soldiers' letters—efforts to connect—were regularly censored by military officials for the sake of preserving civilian morale at home and hence deepened the divides (between the civil and the military) and the enforced silence.

Yet a significant part of the music written in the war-stricken West was proudly loud and triumphantly noisy. The response to the war was often a noisy exuberance, an explosion of musical activities, a series of blaring commemorations. But the epidemic was met with and endured in silence. Any noise it might have produced became internalized and musically inexpressible. Unlike the war, there was no heroism in this unutterable Silent Noise. An ultimate silence befell an estimated fifty million dead worldwide.[10] In Europe influenza deaths were only half those in

America. Music faltered, particularly when the epidemic surged across the United States. Much American music succumbed to inertia.

Since the beginning of the war, shortages (of resources and people) and cancellations (of events and activities) had left their mark on the music scene. But no one could have guessed that the disruptions would continue, let alone increase, after the Armistice. Editorials and clippings from American music newspapers from this period suggest that more rehearsals, concerts, seasons, tours, institutional and orchestral recruiting, and music lessons were canceled than they had been during the war years. Chicago experienced a particularly rough winter during the 1917–18 season, with dreadful weather conditions. *Music News* reported in January 1918, "Weather conditions in Chicago for more than a week have been so terrible that cancellations of concerts have been very prevalent. *Music News* has sent representatives place after place where closed doors and dark auditoriums have been encountered."[11] The rough season (between December 1917 and March 1918) forced many Americans to face, simultaneously, serious blizzards and coal shortages. Composer Felix Borowski reported "many 'snow bound' and 'cancellation' stories among musicians—born of the great blizzard."[12] It is possible that the effects of such hostile conditions increased the virulence of the circulating pathogen in the Midwest by inducing shifts in the strength, mutation, and spread of the infectious virus and, perhaps, by weakening people's immune systems.

Before the influenza emerged, cultural observers and music makers in the United States had seen the war years as an opportunity to heal the traumas that had persisted since the Civil War. Music during the war had to adjust and reinvent itself in character, purpose, and meaning. These transformations sometimes blurred residual boundaries and divisions, not only in society but also in music's own genres, styles, and functions. At least for a few years, such differences could be overcome; preferences intermingled. Helen M. Bennett observed, "There is an interesting catholicity of taste in music both at the front and in the factories and here at home in the camps. . . . [E]very man in the trenches and in the camp and every woman in the munition plant feels a distinct need for all sorts of music. Classic and popular, modern up-to-date stuff, and old favorites are all welcome by everyone."[13] Music did provide much bonding and healing: for the soldiers, it recalled home; for those at home, it helped commemorate loss—in Glenn Watkins's words, it "offered a heady mixture that traversed the entire landscape between heaven and hell."[14]

Categories that were created by the war—the distinction between soldiers and noncombatants, for example—were overcome as people joined forces through song. At times even national boundaries were transcended by the inherent power of music. At the very start of the war in 1914, in the famous "Christmas truce," German and English soldiers shared carols across no-man's-land. At the very end, two weeks before the Armistice, Bennett described a scene in which French and American people came together:

> Soldiers sing. Women toiling in the munition plants in France grasp eagerly at the noon hour relief when in the Blue Triangle Foyers of the Y. M. C. A. they can listen to the victrola or to some one-time professional, now a factory worker, drawing dulcet strains from the piano or violin. The second line of defense in this country also sings. Boys in camp ask for musical instruments and sheet music. Glee clubs and banjo clubs spring into life. . . . And back in the quiet home towns, in the little cities and villages scattered far apart . . . the older people and children get out their song books which the War Camp Community Service has issued and gather together for a community sing. Never was a war so vocal. The allied troops sing each other's songs. American boys with a French accent so newly born that it is unrecognizable shout the Marseillaise, and the French respond with their own version of our national anthem, singing vigorously "Le Drapeau Etoile."[15]

Indeed, never had a war been so vocal. Bennett continues with an illustration of dialogue and translation at work: "Energetic young girls . . . want[ed] to learn the English words of Tipperary, or gather around the piano to beg for dance music"; it was "not uncommon to hear the group singing the Star Spangled Banner in two languages."[16] Such interchanges, which allowed local communities to form and dissolve, were only one symptom of the emerging internationalism that would appear at the end of the war in a world experiencing the trauma of a pandemic.

Disruptive Episodes: "Groping in the Dark"

While the buzz of the war effort in America continued on weeks and months after the Armistice, grief began to surface as the virus shattered dreams and efforts to bring about sociocultural harmony. John Philip Sousa was one of the thousands of attendees at the Chicago parade on November 10, 1918, where he encountered a great number of amputee war veterans—an event that he described as "one of the most moving experiences of his life." Immediately afterward, he became ill with influenza.[17] He survived, probably because of his age. The young and the strong were particularly vulnerable. The deaths among those aged twenty to forty were almost five times higher than among those aged forty-one to sixty. Stretching roughly from September 1918 to 1921, in raw numbers the influenza epidemic killed more people than any other outbreak in history—even the fourteenth-century plague.[18] Symptoms often included violent shaking, intense pain, bleeding, paralysis, depression, hysteria, and insanity.

The epidemic closed theaters, halls, churches, schools, music clubs, and other public places in the United States. People moved away from each other, avoiding conversation. They fled policemen and medical people, who wore ghostly surgical masks. Many communities, social sectors, and public services broke down, especially during the second wave of the epidemic: "Many local governments collapsed, and those who held real power in a community—from Philadelphia's bluebloods to Phoenix's citizens' committee—took over . . . but generally failed to keep the community together."[19] As the epidemic undermined many aspects of community life, it did much damage to interpersonal dialogue and trust. In some places (for example, Prescott, Arizona), it became illegal to shake hands.[20]

Perhaps the tensions of the war had already prepared the ground for such a psychosocial breakdown, but *Music News* described the epidemic as more detrimental than the war. Charles E. Watt wrote on January 3, 1919:

> For four years we have been groping in the dark. . . .
> This is not due altogether to the war. . . . [D]uring the present season, when the agony of war thought has been somewhat lifted from the public mind, music has been the chief sufferer through the untoward health conditions which have existed throughout this country.
> No one outside the profession will ever know the trials, the disappointments, the delays, the changes, the cancellations, the postponements and the general confusion and loss which have resulted from the epidemic of influenza.[21]

Critic Joseph De Valdor described the high-level impact of the epidemic on musical America as early as October 1918: the epidemic had "affected the musical life of the country in a way which the war in itself [had] never done."[22]

Many critics and journalists struggled to continue writing about things that were no longer happening. Herman Devries wrote in the final days of October 1918: "The critical inkwell is yawning ineffectually and the critic is 'marking time' these troublous days. Hardly had the musical season begun with a promise of many fresh pleasures and old ones renewed than the municipal order to close theaters and concert halls puts a quietus on our activities and we are at the mercy of the 'flu.'" The battle with sickness resembled the war in France, implied Devries, who used martial imagery to capture the mood of the times: "The enemy is facing a grim battle and our goodly army of hardworking doctors and nurses soon will Chateau-Thierry them into a complete rout. And since I am using military metaphor, in praise of our gallant American men, it seems fitting that we once more pen a plea for those Americans who triumph in peace."[23]

Yet fighting with heroism and "triumph in peace" were no longer options. The leading scientists and doctors raced to find a cure but had neither time nor success. Like American music culture, American medicine had had a heavily Germanic (and French) grounding and was seeking scientific autonomy and world leadership. In describing the Johns Hopkins Medical School as it was in 1904–5, Henry James used war and the military as metaphors. But he also perceived human ailments and the medical experience by analogy with music: "The grim human alignments that became, in their cool vistas, delicate 'symphonies in white,' and, more even than anything else, the pair of gallant Doctors who ruled, for me, so gently, the whole still concert, abide with me, collectively, as agents of the higher tone."[24]

Literally and metaphorically, the pandemic emerged as a personal, collective, and international invasion—a kind of rape to society's bodily structure and socio-cultural parts. As theaters, concert halls, churches, clubs, and restaurants normally constituted the primary venues of cultural exchange and communication, the virus, as the enemy, fed on social motives, habits, and desires: the pandemic was a disease born out of crowds and human relationships. No one would have guessed that attending the opera could be life-threatening or even deadly. De Valdor wrote in February 1920, at a time when, since the start of the year, eleven thousand epidemic-related deaths had occurred in New York City and Chicago alone:[25] "The influenza is raging in New York with great fury. The Lexington Opera House, with its poor ventilation, is a danger to public health. Currents and drafts greet you mercilessly. Under such conditions the public refuses to have its health ruined by an opera house which is not good at the best for the presentation of operas."[26]

Despite the general sense of sociopolitical relief that followed the end of the war, for many Americans these years proved to be highly unsettling and alarming. Fear was rife. Anyone, anywhere, anytime could become sick and die. Cleofonte Campanini, who was principal conductor and director of the Chicago Opera Association (1915–19), developed a "bad cold" that then turned into pneumonia. He died in December 1919. In the *Chicago Tribune*, critic Edward Moore described the period following Campanini's death as "a time of distress": it did "not seem possible that the Chicago Opera could continue."[27]

Many notable figures were affected: Franklin Roosevelt, President Woodrow Wilson, Walt Disney, and Georgia O'Keeffe. All these caught the virus but survived. Lonnie Johnson, a pioneer of American blues and jazz, lost ten of his siblings to the epidemic.[28] American soprano Saba Doak's "wide circle of friends throughout the country [were] shocked on Monday [December 9, 1918] to read of [her] death . . . in Chicago"; Doak was described as "a soprano of beautiful voice and fine personality" who had "devoted her entire time to concert singing and had made numerous tours with various bands and orchestras."[29] Wisconsin-born composer Charles Hambitzer (1876[?]–1918), Gershwin's mentor, died.[30] So did New York composer Charles Tomlinson Griffes (1884–1920).

Case Studies: "Deep Silence" and "Jesus Coming"

Griffes is often remembered for what he might have written or become "if . . ." He was, in a sense, the all-embracing American composer, open to a striking range of ideas, styles, and cultural domains. Like Walt Whitman—whose work he admired and set to music (for instance, in *Salut au monde*)—his talent and vision were unfinished, adventurous, and youthful. His tendency to move from one context to another was not only an early manifestation of multiculturalism but also, like Whitman's ever-expanding universe and reinventive poetics, indicative of a continual quest for self-definition. In Griffes one can detect a diversity of musics: late-nineteenth-century German Romanticism, musical Orientalism, French impressionism, ultramodernism, and various inflections of folk and world music. Wagner, Scriabin, Stravinsky, and Debussy were among the composers who helped mold his musical directions and synthesis. In several of his works, Griffes experimented with composing in a "Japanese style," once even writing for a koto.[31] During the last years of his life, Griffes was writing music that was increasingly bold in conception, using free forms, dissonant harmonies, and obscure impressionistic tonalities, with a heavy emphasis on color.

Three Poems of Fiona MacLeod, op. 11 (1918), exemplifies Griffes's contradictory mixture of fiery nervousness and subdued reticence: the music is erratic, varied, and restless. In a letter written a few months before his death in December 1919, Griffes quoted a sentence that appears at the top of the original poem: "There is an old mystical legend that when a soul among the dead woos a soul among the living, so that both may be reborn as one, the sign is a dark rose, or a rose in flame, in the heart of the night."[32] His remark makes reference to "The Rose of the Night," which is the final song in *Three Poems of Fiona MacLeod*. The text reads in part:

> Deep silence of the night,
>   Husht like a breathless lyre,
> Save the sea's thunderous might,
>   Dim, menacing, dire,
> Silence and wind and sea, they are thee, O Rose of my Desire!
>
> As a wind-eddying flame
>   Leaping higher and higher,
> Thy soul, thy secret name,
>   Leaps thro' Death's blazing pyre!
> Kiss me, Imperishable Fire, dark Rose, O Rose of my Desire!

The song is strikingly prophetic of what was to come. In an accurate, sensitive musical performance, Griffes's painting of such words as *night*, *silence*, *pyre*, and *fire* can be powerfully—if not devastatingly—evocative. The text is saturated with imagery forewarning tragedy and ruin; in the context of world events, the word *pyre* might have evoked the funeral rites for the nearly twenty million people who died in South Asia from the epidemic.[33] The ending of the music is also suggestive, in that there is neither triumph nor defeat but only uncertainty—frozen or eternal, a feeling of floating into some kind of emptiness.[34]

How did composers and songwriters who survived the influenza treat the subject? With silence. Whether out of disbelief, ambivalence, or avoidance, there was no musical expression of grief for the dead or for the survivors. Perhaps treating and expressing trauma musically was not intrinsic to American culture, especially in the absence of any affirmation of heroism or self-assured optimism. Perhaps grief muted aspiration. The noise that had agitated and celebrated the war years was transformed into its opposite: muffled, inarticulate muttering. The heroic psychology of the prewar years and of the American experience of the Great War was now replaced by a humbling helplessness. While it had been easy to glamorize the war, the epidemic left Americans with no control and without anything to glorify. The majority chose introversion and silence; some evaded truth through denial. Most songwriters tended to sidestep controversial topics. The handful of songwriters who were bold enough to treat the epidemic in their songs often turned to humor. "The Man Who Put the Germ in Germany," which was written by Nora Bayes, Sam Downing, and Abe Glatt in 1918, prophesied the outbreak a few weeks before the virus entered its epidemic stage. Its tongue-in-cheek humor played with words thus: "But the world is now aflame / At the 'Hell' in Wilhelm's name, / The man who put the 'Germ' in Germany." Despite its proud and upbeat delivery, the song ends with a hint of uncertainty and speculation: "Now that our boys are in France, / If they just get half a chance / They'll disinfect that 'Germ' in Germany." Unfortunately, it would soon be those very boys who, failing to disinfect themselves, would fall victim to the new enemy.

Those who chose pretense or denial joined in, consciously or unconsciously, with the authorities of suppression. The Wilson administration had already been censoring information during the war. Disillusionment, fueled by such practices, intensified the mood of mistrust and the sense of weariness among many Americans, so much that many placed self-preservation above civic duty. Porter's heroine Miranda asked, "We dare not say a word to each other of our desperation, we are speechless animals letting ourselves be destroyed, and why? Does anybody here believe the things we say to each other?"[35] Both the war and the epidemic imposed a systematic sanitization on the expression and dissemination of thought in cultural and communal life.

There was some resemblance between this form of censorship and the generally derogative attitude toward early jazz, ragtime, and blues. Many official and conservative groups in the United States of America had subscribed to the need to curb and expunge jazz music and dancing in public spaces since the emergence of New Orleans's "hot jazz" about a decade earlier. This "brothel music" was especially repugnant to those who held the view that bad habits (such as drinking) and physical and social diseases were fostered by jazz music and dance. Sadly, closed and crowded spaces were exactly what both jazz and the influenza virus needed in order to develop, thrive, and spread. It is highly likely that the mutation that produced the virus was born because of the war. The latter prepared the ground for the former—thanks to the unprecedented concentration and cross-Atlantic movement of thousands of confined soldiers after 1916. A torrent of humanity with diverse immunity profiles and gene pools became the perfect breeding ground. At the same time, jazz and the blues were much more successful than art music in offering some relief to soldiers and civilians alike. As complex fusions in themselves, these "hot" musical styles were highly effective in connecting people and consolidating spaces between classes and cultures. Moreover, as an intrinsically American musical genre of grief and mourning, the blues suited well the subject of the influenza epidemic. Nevertheless, very few songwriters and composers tackled the topic, and when they did it was mainly through memory and observance, usually years or decades later. Some of these songs include "Too Late Too Late Blues (The Flu Blues)" (Frances Wallace and Clara Burnston), "The 1919 Influenza Blues" (Essie Jenkins), and "Jesus Is Coming Soon" (Blind Willie Johnson).

"Jesus Is Coming Soon" was recorded by Blind Willie Johnson (1897–1945) in 1928. As a musician whose life was heavily impacted by poverty, disability, and illness, Johnson recalls a country touched and shaken by God through the epidemic. The vehemence and religious intensity of his voice amplify the song's intriguingly static drive, momentum, harmonic structure, and form. The music possesses a certain zeal and vitality that is, however, ominous and stifled. Its tone is almost numbed. There is no climax, but Johnson sang it like the preacher that he was. The text of "Jesus Is Coming Soon" recalls the country's exposure, vulnerability, and complete powerlessness:

> [refrain] We done told you, our God's done warned you, Jesus comin' soon;
> We done told you, our God's done warned you, Jesus comin' soon.

> In the year of 19 and 18, God sent a mighty disease.
> It killed many a-thousand, on land and on the seas.

> [refrain]

> Great disease was mighty and the people were sick everywhere.
> It was an epidemic, it floated through the air.

> [refrain]

> The doctors they got troubled and they didn't know what to do.
> They gathered themselves together, they called it the Spanish flu.

> [refrain]

> Soldiers died on the battlefield, died in the counts too.
> Captain said to the lieutenant, "I don't know what to do."

[refrain]

Well, God is warning the nation, He's a-warnin' them every way
To turn away from evil and seek the Lord and pray.

[refrain]

Well, the nobles said to the people, "You better close your public schools.
Until the events of death has ending, you better close your churches too."

[refrain] . . .[36]

A Fractured History: Transnational Frontiers

During the war, then, the country felt itself empowered on a grand scale. Its experience was characterized by noise, energy, anger, pride, and propaganda. On the positive side, "Liberty Sings," which were weekly community events held across the United States, involved all possible social programs and demographic groups—children, barbers, factory workers, and even bankers. Patriotic music was played and heard almost incessantly (and usually loudly), while more official performances were required to begin with a "Four-Minute Man" speech. However, sad songs or realistic portrayals of death and destruction were not allowed. Many individuals and cultural observers who transcended nationalist agendas—such as Porter—were (sometimes silently) disgusted by the noisy war effort and the tacky dynamics of flawed or shallow war songs. This portion of the population detested such bombast because its musical manifestations were invasive, lacked profundity, failed to honor truth, and pronounced the death of individual autonomy. The patriotic citizen had outstripped the private self.

In contrast, the virus stripped everyone of any sort of power—even a leader of the very top rank, like President Wilson.[37] Science had failed; morale was low; the death toll kept rising. The virus led to a grand silencing. Porter writes:

> The whole humane conviction and custom of society, conspired to pull her inseparable rack of bones and wasted flesh to its feet, to put in order her disordered mind, and to set her once more safely in the road that would lead her again to death. . . . [O]ne foot in either world now. . . . No more war, no more plague, only the dazed silence that follows the ceasing of the heavy guns; noiseless houses with the shades drawn, empty streets, the dead cold light of tomorrow.[38]

The war and the epidemic produced contrasting emotional responses but similar physiological results. Soldiers who survived suffered shock, frayed nerves, and exhaustion. The term *shell shock*, which was coined during World War I, came to embody a cluster of symptoms such as tremors, amnesia, and muteness, all caused by a psychological breakdown. Analogously, the virus was extremely fast, spreading and killing in a matter of hours. It appeared "with electric suddenness, and, acting like powerful, uncontrolled currents, produce[d] violent and eccentric effects. ... [I]ts presence [was] startling."[39] The unforeseeable long-term side effects on the survivors were caused by the disturbance and exhaustion of the nervous system and brain, ranging from agitation and violence to dementia, hallucination, and various kinds of mental illness. The virus could destroy brain cells and alter behavior or cause temporary psychosis.[40] All these characteristics of the epidemic may also bring to mind the way (ultra)modern music was received at the time: as an unexpected anomaly—sudden, treacherous, mutable, and shattering all prior aesthetic contracts. Ultramodernism was dreaded and resisted by many critics and concertgoers, who used labels such as "anarchy," "plain noise," or "orgiastic abandon."[41] Many saw it as a metaphor for the invading "other." Moreover, "ultramodern" composers such as Leo Ornstein, Henry Cowell, and Edgard Varèse were not just adamant individualists but also internationalists. The flu virus had emerged out of Kansas only to become an international traveler; so, too, through cross-border operations and exchanges with the Allies and the aliens, World War I had altered the texture of international life forever.

The story of the influenza epidemic is a relentless account of moral, social, and cultural calamity. The war and the influenza tested individual and national limits on several different levels, bringing them to the edge of psychosocial frontiers. Like the mythic frontier, the influenza challenged the borders that define humanity. Writing in 1920, Frederick Jackson Turner defined the frontier almost as if it were an infection forming "the outer edge of the wave—the meeting point between savagery and civilization":[42]

> At the frontier the environment is at first too strong for the man. He must accept the conditions which it furnishes, or perish, and so he fits himself into the Indian clearings and follows the Indian trails. Little by little he transforms the wilderness, but the outcome is not the old Europe, not simply the development of Germanic germs, any more than the first phenomenon was a case of reversion to the Germanic mark. The fact is, that here is a new product that is American. At first, the frontier was the Atlantic coast. It was the frontier of Europe in a very real sense. Moving westward, the frontier became more and more American. As successive terminal moraines result from successive glaciations, so each frontier leaves its traces behind it, and when it becomes a settled area the region still partakes of the frontier characteristics. Thus the advance of the frontier has meant a steady movement away from the influence of Europe, a steady growth of independence on American lines.[43]

In Turner's view, the frontier was "productive of individualism," with a tendency to be "anti-social," which produced "antipathy to control."[44] The end of the frontier meant that there was no place left for new territories; the physical and psychological boundaries for anyone who wanted to stay outside or on the margins of the society had been sealed off not so long ago, in 1912. Psychologically, geopolitically, and musically, the American frontier opened up and extended to Flanders Fields in 1917—even though artists and artworks could no longer travel freely. The dichotomy between "over here" (America) versus "over there" (Europe) became a new frontier.

But while Europe was weary, America was ready for new, extended forms of autonomy and ascendancy. Internationalism began an upward sweep in the months following the Armistice. Yet even though this was the beginning of the new role of world leadership for the United States of America, its composers did not necessarily feel ready or nourished enough. Although in international arenas the country was priding itself on its impressive population of world-renowned musical virtuosos, American compositions appeared to fall short. When the influenza epidemic emerged as the latest and the most cataclysmic psychosocial frontier for Americans, it marked a watershed beyond which would rise a new, bolder, and, arguably, more "American" music, beginning in 1923.[45] Only after that year did the viral mutation of the influenza finally fade away.[46] The meaning of the frontier thus kept shifting and transforming—in the spirit of ever-new beginnings.

A frontier both marks an end and points to a beginning. The Great Migration, the closing of the frontier in 1912, World War I, and the epidemic were all manifestations of death and rebirth. American intellectual Randolph Bourne regarded the war as the killing of a nation by and for the state and as a suicide: "That terrible war *en masse* of the national State, that exploitation of the nation in the interests of the State, that abuse of the national life and resource in the frenzied mutual suicide, which is modern war."[47]

A sense of having lost direction also prevailed among many postwar composers, bringing with it questions such as "What does it mean to be a composer now? To which arena shall I belong (local, national or international)? How should I sound? What do *I* want?" More often than not, there were no easy answers. Musical interests, explorations, and loyalties of this generation of music makers wavered between progressive and universal ideals and the constraints of local-national-global circles. The attempts at reconciliation sometimes resulted in cracks and losses, at other times in consolidation and success. The pressures revealed in editorials at the time saturated the front pages of American music magazines with emotionally charged—yet humanistic and universal—content. Practice, habit, and aesthetics could easily collide with political ideology and national identity, jeopardizing an artist's integrity and commitment to art for art's sake. At the same time, the world's sickness was too complex and had cut too deep. In January 1923,

John Dewey, who had taught Bourne, was still thinking about sickness: "It may be doubted if the consciousness of sickness was ever so widespread as it is today. . . . The interest in cures and salvations is evidence of how sick the world is."[48]

Bourne was the prophet and architect of the concept of transnationalism. He deeply understood that modernity so far had proved to be an unstable battleground over transient powers. As nations and cultures fought for a new local and global order, their wars led to an intensification of the exchange and intermingling of musical styles, genres, and tastes. The United States of America already exemplified such an amalgamation. The interchange of the national and the transnational in cosmopolitan America, Bourne observed, was characterized by "a weaving back and forth, with the other lands, of many threads of all sizes and colors."[49] One can also understand modernity through the lens of handicap, sickness, and immobility; Bourne not only welcomed modernism but was also a pioneer in disability studies. A recurring motif within early-twentieth-century modernist aesthetics probes the limits of civilization and savagery, the threshold between soundness and sickness or madness. In Europe the fascination with commedia dell'arte figures such as Pierrot and Petrushka points to a preoccupation with the question of what it means for humanity and the individual to be half dead, half human. The metaphor—and, indeed, the purport of existence—extends to the ambiguous territories of muteness (being a puppet or an animal) and reasoned discourse (producing scientific knowledge). As some of the drawings and paintings of Egon Schiele, Edvard Munch, and Arnold Schoenberg reveal, the human face and body marked new forms of expression, amplified through fragmentation, distortion, deformation, disfigurement, and sickness—all modernist motifs. It is interesting to note that during the epidemic years, foremost modernists Schiele, Gustav Klimt, and Guillaume Apollinaire died of the influenza; other European thinkers Franz Kafka and Walter Benjamin caught the virus but survived.

Bourne's perspective on wordlessness and incapacity was in part a by-product of his own disability and assessments of physical deformation. Psychosocial marginalization and personal helplessness were intimately linked with his vision of America and the modern world. In 1918 he pronounced the free individual to be a myth: "You have not affected the world you live in. . . . Your moral responsibility has been a myth, for you were never really free enough to have any responsibility. While you thought you were making headway, you were really being devoured. . . . You have a picture of great things achieved, but Time laughs his ironical laugh and rolls you in dust. . . . There is fear, which makes you misinterpret the unfamiliar and haunts you with its freezing power all through life."[50] Very shortly after, Bourne died of the influenza. He was thirty-two years old.

Notes

1. "Katherine Anne Porter: An Interview," *Paris Interview* 29 (1963): 87–114, cited in Joan Givner, *Katherine Anne Porter: A Life* (London: Jonathan Cape, 1982), 126.

2. Katherine Anne Porter, *Pale Horse, Pale Rider: Three Short Novels* (New York: Harcourt, Brace, and World, 1936), 259–60, 263–64.

3. Porter, *Pale Horse, Pale Rider*, 215.

4. John M. Barry, *The Great Influenza: The Epic History of the Deadliest Plague in History* (New York: Viking, 2004), 456.

5. Dr. M. G. Parsons to Rupert Blue, surgeon general of the United States, September 26, 1918, National Archives, entry 10, file 1622, Record Group 90, cited in Barry, *Great Influenza*, 343. On the demonization of Germans and German culture, see also Patrick Warfield's chapter in this volume.

6. See Barry, *Great Influenza*, 334–35, 337, 396, 398.

7. Porter, *Pale Horse, Pale Rider*, 256–57.

8. In chapter 9 of this volume, William Brooks discusses a similar shift in the tenor of songs about fallen soldiers in the same period.

9. John McCormack, "Speech Delivered by Mr. John McCormack at the Banquet Tendered to Him by a Number of His Fellow Citizens at the Waldorf Astoria, New York, Tuesday Evening, May 4, 1920," *Music News* 12, no. 20 (1920): 28.

10. Barry explains, "In 1918 the world's population was 1.8 billion, only 28 percent of today's. Yet the 1918 influenza virus killed a likely 50 million and possibly as many as 100 million people." Barry, *Great Influenza*, 452.

11. [Watt], "[Editorial] Passing Comment," *Music News* 10, no. 3 (1918): 1–2.

12. [Watt], "[Editorial] Passing Comment," *Music News* 10, no. 4 (1918): 1.

13. Helen M. Bennett, "The Song and the Soldier," *Music News* 10, no. 43 (1918): 1. In chapter 7 of this volume, Michelle Meinhart notes the wide mix of repertoire and styles performed by soldiers and staff in the hospital at Longleat.

14. Glenn Watkins, *Proof through the Night: Music and the Great War* (Berkeley: University of California Press, 2003), 7.

15. Bennett, "Song and the Soldier."

16. Ibid.

17. Paul E. Bierley, *John Philip Sousa: American Phenomenon* (Englewood Cliffs, NJ: Prentice Hall, 1973), 81. See also Patrick Warfield's chapter in this volume.

18. Barry, *Great Influenza*, 4–5, 238–39.

19. Ibid., 225–26, 395. According to Barry, San Francisco was a rare exception; its leaders told the truth, and the city responded heroically.

20. Ibid., 347.

21. Charles E. Watt, "[Editorial] Passing Comment," *Music News* 11, no. 1 (1919): 3.

22. Joseph De Valdor, "Aurore La Croix, Boston Pianist, Makes Striking Debut at Aeolian Hall," *Music News* 10, no. 43 (1918): 22–23.

23. Herman Devries, "U.S. Musicians Need Only a Chance: A Plea," *Music News* 10, no. 44 (1918): 10.

24. Henry James, *The American Scene* (London: Chapman and Hall, 1907), 319.

25. See Barry, *Great Influenza,* 396–97.

26. Joseph De Valdor, "First Week of the Chicago Opera in New York," *Music News* 12, no. 6 (1920): 24–25.

27. Cited in Ronald L. Davis, *Opera in Chicago: A Social and Cultural History, 1850–1965* (New York: Appleton-Century, 1966), 124–25 (original source not identified).

28. Frank Cullen, Florence Hackman, and Donald McNeilly, *Vaudeville, Old and New: An Encyclopedia of Variety Performers in America* (New York and London: Routledge, 2007), 572.

29. [Watt], "[Editorial] Passing Comment," *Music News* 10, no. 50 (1918): 1–2.

30. See William G. Hyland, *George Gershwin: A New Biography* (Westport, CT: Greenwood Press, 2003), 39.

31. See Joseph Horowitz, *Classical Music in America: A History of Its Rise and Fall* (New York: W. W. Norton, 2005), 232.

32. Arthur E. Scherr, liner notes for New World Records 80273. See also Fiona MacLeod, *Poems and Dramas* (New York: Duffield, 1911), 251.

33. Barry, *Great Influenza,* 365.

34. Frank Bridge and Charles Ives wrote similarly striking responses to an earlier, more specific tragedy: the sinking of the *Lusitania*. Aspects of their styles are discussed by Christina Bashford and Gayle Magee in the first two chapters of this volume.

35. Porter, *Pale Horse, Pale Rider,* 218–19.

36. Johnson's lyrics are adapted from the transcription at http://www.oldielyrics.com/lyrics/blind_willie_johnson/jesus_is_coming_soon.html.

37. President Wilson's influenza, which he contracted in Paris in April 1919, during the heated negotiations at Versailles, may have changed the course of twentieth-century political history. Soon after he recovered, he gave in to the crushing demands of Great Britain, France, and Italy, which may have prepared the ground for the rise of National Socialism in Germany. See Barry, *Great Influenza,* 386–88.

38. Porter, *Pale Horse, Pale Rider,* 259–60, 263–64.

39. Major George A. Soper, "The Influenza-Pneumonia Pandemic in the American Army Camps during September and October, 1918," *Science* 48, no. 1245 (1918): 454, quoted in Barry, *Great Influenza,* 313.

40. Barry, *Great Influenza,* 379, 240, 381.

41. Walter Anthony, "Rosen Proves Normal in His Music Tastes," *Music News* 11, no. 12 (1919): 24; Charles E. Watt, "Miss Cole's Second Concert," *Music News* 9, no. 13 (1917): 10; James Huneker, writing in the *New York Puck*, April 17, 1915, as cited in "Leo Ornstein, Master Pianist," *Music News* 8, no. 43 (1916): 12.

42. Frederick Jackson Turner, *The Frontier in American History* (New York: Henry Holt, 1921), 3.

43. Ibid., 4.

44. Ibid., 30.

45. During the 1922–23 season, the New York Philharmonic launched an "Americanization" project. The years 1923–24 saw the following: James P. Johnson's song "The Charleston" debuted in 1923 on Broadway; the country's "dean" of music critics, Henry Edward Krehbiel, who represented the German-American music culture, died; Juilliard School of Music was founded; Varèse's *Hyperprism* was premiered in New York and described by

Lawrence Gilman of the *New York Herald Tribune* as "an ultra-modern work" (cited in Louise Varèse, *A Looking-Glass Diary*, vol. 1, *1883–1928* [(New York: W. W. Norton, 1972], 224); the League of Composers was established; the publication of *Modern Music* began; the National Origins Act restricted immigration severely, resulting in an increased nativist and "Anglo-American" insistence; Aaron Copland returned to New York from Paris; and Paul Whiteman gave the first concert of his tour of "Experiment in Modern Music" at the Aeolian Hall, on February 12, with George Gershwin playing the piano in the premiere of *Rhapsody in Blue*.

46. See Barry, *Great Influenza*, 391.

47. Randolph Bourne, "Unfinished Fragment on the State (Winter, 1918)," in *Untimely Papers* (New York: B. W. Huebsch, 1919), 166.

48. John Dewey, "A Sick World," *New Republic* 33 (January 24, 1923): 217, quoted in Barry, *Great Influenza*, 393.

49. Randolph Bourne, "Trans-national America," in *The History of a Literary Radical and Other Essays*, ed. Van Wyck Brooks (New York: B. W. Huebsch, 1920), 297.

50. Randolph Bourne, "Old Tyrannies (a Fragment, Written in 1918)," in *Untimely Papers*, 15–16.

Postlude: Not an End

WILLIAM BROOKS, CHRISTINA BASHFORD, AND GAYLE MAGEE

The Great War—the "war to end all wars"—ended nothing. In fact, the social and political consequences of the war, as well as the musical ones, continue to resonate even today. After a fifteen-year hiatus, during which the great powers nursed their wounds and grudges, the run-up to the continuation started: Adolf Hitler took power in Germany. And after World War II, there was Korea . . . and Algeria . . . and Vietnam . . . and Iraq . . .

World War I ended with the Armistice of November 11, 1918, though the terms of the peace would take six months to negotiate. In the months that followed, it became clear that popular music in the United States had been permanently altered: styles had changed; dissemination had begun to shift to broadcasts and recordings rather than sheet music; marketing was becoming attached to soloists and bands rather than to composers. Notated scores for home performance were giving way to improvisations captured on records; the public was being reconstituted as listeners rather than amateur music makers. All these trends, which surged ahead in the 1920s, were signaled, if not initiated, during the war years: the first six commercially successful jazz records, for instance, by the Original Dixieland Jazz Band, were recorded in the six weeks that immediately preceded America's entry into the war and popularized at the height of the conflict.

The war years saw the last, greatest flowering of self-published titles by amateur composers: more than thirteen hundred titles relating to the war were copyrighted by amateurs between 1914 and 1920. These individuals were motivated not by profit or fame but by civic duty, by the desire to "do their bit" for the war effort—by writing music rather than (or in addition to) volunteering, sending supplies, or raising money. In the decade to come, they and the next generation would become consumers rather than creators; it was not until the folk revivals of the 1940s and 1950s that amateur musicians would again find a way to raise their voices on behalf of the collective good.

Wilson had argued that the war would "make the world safe for democracy," and in negotiating the Treaty of Versailles and proposing a visionary League of Nations as an instrument to preserve peace, he attempted to extend a progressive political agenda to the world as a whole. But he suffered a stroke, the treaty and the league went down to defeat, and the progressives lost the 1920 election. In the next decade, America would turn its back on Europe: it refused to join international organizations, it sealed its borders, and it severely limited immigration. It removed many of the mechanisms that the progressives had put in place to regulate the economy and care for the country's underclasses. Racism, lynchings, and bigotry surged. The rich got richer; nine years later, an overheated, underregulated economy would plunge the country into the Great Depression.

 In the 1920s, Britain attempted to reach out to Europe with international veterans' organizations, economic alliances, and social action. It had its place at the League of Nations, which was up and running without the United States, though that body would prove incapable of stopping the aggressions from Germany and Italy that were to come in the 1930s. Meanwhile, anxiety about the prospect of another war against France remained high, and British relations with both Germany and the United States were tended to with care.

Musically, the aftermath of the war in Britain occupied classical composers for several years, during which time several significant responses to the conflict emerged from those who had experienced it. These ranged from Vaughan Williams's "Pastoral" Symphony (1922), which contemplates the carnage of the battlefield and the senseless loss of humanity, to Bliss's *Morning Heroes* for orator, chorus, and orchestra (1930), written in memory of those (including his brother) who died and evoking much of the emotional pain and psychological scars that war engenders, and later to Vaughan Williams's cantata *Dona Nobis Pacem* (1936), the text for which includes a celebrated parliamentary antiwar speech made during the Crimean War and would later seem like a prescient warning about what lay ahead.

Canada signed the Treaty of Versailles as an independent, sovereign nation and served as a founding member of the League of Nations. As one Canadian commentator described it, "The next great achievement of the human society, heralded by the League of Nations in all its ramifications, is what I venture to call nothing less than the beginnings of a new International Civilization."[1] In 1931 Canada, Australia, and New Zealand became independent nations with control over their militaries through the Statute of Westminster. It made no difference. In September 1939, when Britain declared war on Germany, Canada followed suit. More than a million Canadians fought during the Second World War, in an increasingly diverse and inclusive military. By the last year of the conflict, Canadians of African, British, Chinese, French, and Japanese descent were fighting in nonsegregated battalions alongside what was, as in the Great War, a disproportionately large contingent of First Nations soldiers.[2] Nearly one hundred thousand Canadians died or were wounded.

 Meanwhile, Britain's problems were mounting. As early as 1919, black African dockworkers who had loyally served the war effort in Glasgow, Liverpool, and Cardiff found themselves the target of white racism; violence and xenophobia escalated.[3] In the 1930s, unemployment soared to unheard-of levels, and in India civil disobedience campaigns set off alarms in (the British) government. But the deepest consternation arose from what was happening in Europe: under Hitler, and still seething at its treatment by the terms of the Treaty of Versailles, Germany was rearming and expanding its territories. British policy, which, above all else, sought to avoid the slaughter of war, was one of appeasement, and it was popular with a fair segment of the population. In September 1938, the British Conservative prime minister, Neville Chamberlain, along with French prime minister Édouard Daladier, signed an agreement with Hitler, acquiescing to his recent invasion of German-speaking Czechoslovakia. Chamberlain came home falsely believing—and insisting—it guaranteed "peace for our time."

 Charles Ives saw most of this coming, and he lived long enough to witness the tragic sequel of World War II. In the aftermath of the 1920 election, he wrote a bitter indictment of the American retreat from progressive thought, "November 2, 1920," setting his own text to music. His lyrics are a litany of ills that resonate still today: money interfering with democracy, an electorate led by headlines only, politicians who distort the truth. But at the end, he reaffirms his faith: progressivism—belief in freedom and dignity for all, in a society that promotes the welfare of all—will return. And when war came again,

Ives returned to his 1917 song "He Is There," to recast it as a call for a "People's World Nation." Ives kept his faith that progressivism would return and that it would eventually triumph.

As we write these words in September 2018, the centenary of the Armistice approaches. In a world that seems so little changed by a hundred years of conflict, we can only hope that Ives was right.

William Brooks
Christina Bashford
Gayle Magee

Notes

1. Reverend C. A. Seager, "Canada and the League of Nations," address to the Empire Club of Canada, Toronto, April 24, 1924, transcript online at http://speeches.empireclub .org/62653/data.

2. R. Scott Sheffield, "Indigenous Peoples and the World Wars," in *The Canadian Encyclopedia* (Toronto: Historica Canada, 2016), https://www.thecanadianencyclopedia.ca/ en/article/indigenous-peoples-and-the-world-wars/; "Japanese Canadians Serving in World War II," http://nikkei-tapestry.ca/servir_dans_la_guerre-serving_in_war-eng .html; Mathias Joost, "Racism and Enlistment: The Second World War Policies of the Royal Canadian Air Force," *Canadian Military History* 21, no. 1 (2015): 17–34.

3. See Jacqueline Jenkinson, *Black 1919: Riots, Racism, and Resistance in Imperial Britain* (Liverpool: Liverpool University Press, 2009).

Contributors

CHRISTINA BASHFORD, COEDITOR: Bashford's main research interests are in performance history and musical culture in nineteenth- and early-twentieth-century Britain. She is the author of *The Pursuit of High Culture: John Ella and Chamber Music in Victorian London* (2007) and is currently working on a book about violin culture in Britain, ca. 1880–1930.

WILLIAM BROOKS, COEDITOR: Brooks's research focuses on the music of Charles Ives and John Cage, as well as contemporary American composition. Author of the two "overview" chapters in *The Cambridge History of American Music*, in 2015–16 he was appointed the Lloyd Lewis Fellow in American History at the Newberry Library, Chicago, for a research project exploring the sheet music of World War I.

DENIZ ERTAN: Ertan is the author of *Dane Rudhyar* (2009) and articles on Carl Ruggles and others. She is the recipient of several research fellowships, including Adrienne Block, Newberry Library (Chicago), Leverhulme, and Rothermere American Institute (Oxford). Her current research focuses on American music during the period 1908–23.

BARBARA L. KELLY: Kelly's research focuses on late-nineteenth- and early-twentieth-century French music and culture. She is the author of several publications, including two monographs, *Tradition and Style in the Works of Darius Milhaud* (2003) and *Music and Ultra-Modernism in France: A Fragile Consensus, 1913–1939* (2013), and has edited three essay collections, most recently *Music Criticism in France, 1918–1939: Authority, Advocacy, Legacy*, with Christopher Moore (2018).

KENDRA PRESTON LEONARD: Leonard's research focuses on music and screen history, the musical representation of the English early modern period on-screen, and the use of preexisting art music for silent cinema. She is the author of *Shakespeare, Madness, and Music: Scoring Insanity in Cinematic Adaptations* (2009) and *Music for Silent Film: A Guide to North American Resources* (2016).

GAYLE MAGEE, COEDITOR: Magee's research focuses on the music of Charles Ives and film music, particularly the British heritage film and the New Hollywood era. She is the author of *Charles Ives Reconsidered* (University of Illinois Press, 2008) and *Robert Altman's Soundtracks* (2014).

JEFFREY MAGEE: Magee writes about music in the United States, especially jazz, musical theater, and popular song. He is the author of *Fletcher Henderson: The Uncrowned King of Swing* (2005), which won the Irving Lowens Award for Best Book in American Music from the Society for American Music and an award for excellence in historical recorded sound research from the Association for Recorded Sound Collections, and *Irving Berlin's American Musical Theater* (2012).

MICHELLE MEINHART: Meinhart's research focuses on music, memory, and trauma in late-nineteenth- and early-twentieth-century Britain. Currently, she is completing a monograph titled "Music, Healing, and Memory in the English Country House, 1914–1919." Her publications include "Memory and Private Mourning in the English Country House during the First World War" in the *Journal of Musicological Research* and essays in various edited collections. She is also coediting a special issue on music and trauma for the *Nineteenth-Century Music Review* and editing the volume *A "Great Divide" or a Longer Nineteenth Century? Music, Britain, and the First World War*.

BRIAN C. THOMPSON: Thompson is the author of *Anthems and Minstrel Shows: The Life and Times of Calixa Lavallée, 1842–1891* (2015), on the composer of "O Canada." He is a specialist in nineteenth-century and Canadian music.

PATRICK WARFIELD: Warfield is a specialist on the music of John Philip Sousa and musical life in Washington, DC. He is the author of *Making the March King: John Philip Sousa's Washington Years, 1854–1893* (University of Illinois Press, 2013).

Index

Note: **Boldface** page numbers refer to illustrations.

"1919 Influenza Blues, The," 233
"41eme Battalion R.C.F., Le," 7

Aborn, Morris, 160
Adams, Byron, 17
Adams, John, 52–53, 167
Afghanistan, 37
African American soldiers, 11n22, 118–19, 120
"After the Ball," 214
Ahern, Eugene, 158
Alden, Blanche Ray, 166
Algeria, 241
Allies. *See under* World War I; *and specific countries*
"Allies March to Freedom, The," 5, 16
"Alouette," 184
"Alsace Lorraine," 7, 10n18
"America" ("My Country, 'Tis of Thee"), 46, 186, 204, 226
American Defense Society, 88
Anderson, Alan, 98
Anderton, Margaret, 29
Anglophone Canadians, 5, 192, 201

Apollinaire, Guillaume, 237
Armistice Day, 190, 192, 208, 211, 217–18; celebrations on, 91, 121, 134, 138, 190; centenary of, 244; United States after, 84, 225, 227–28, 236, 241
Arthur, Prince, 175
Ashwell, Lena, 116
Auer, Leopold, 164
"Auld Lang Syne," 184
"Auntie Skinner's Chicken Dinner," 134
Australia, 4, 118, 141, 194n9, 198n71, 201, 243; soldiers from, at Longleat House, 116, 127, 129, 130, 136, 139

Bach, J. S., 67, 138
ballade des lutins, La (*The Ballad of the Elves*), 191
Bargy, Charles Le, 152
Baron, Maurice, 160
Barrett, A. G., 131, 135
Basquette, Billy, **205**
Bath, Lady and Lord. *See* Thynne family
Bathori, Jane, 65–69, 72n47
"Battle Cry of Freedom, The," 50
Bayes, Nora, 232
Beach, Amy, 151
"Beauty of the Guards, The," 128, 135
"Because," 136

Beethoven, Ludwig van, 61

Belgium, 3, 5, 6, 15–16, 18, 62; soldiers from, at Longleat House, 116, 127, 129, 130, 141. *See also* Debussy, Claude: and Belgium

"Belgium Forever!," 6

Benjamin, Walter, 237

Bennett, Arnold, 59

Bennett, Helen M., 227–28

Berg, S. M., 160, **160**

Bergé, Irénée, 160

Berlin, Irving, 8–9, 77, 97–111, 115; *Alexander's Ragtime Band* (film), 99, 107, 109–10; "Alexander's Ragtime Band" (song), 99, 104, 184; "Bevo," 103; "Ding Dong," 102–3; and draft, 9, 99, 102; "For Your Country and My Country," 8–9, 11n23, 108, 110; "Gee, I Wish I Was Back in the Army," 111; "God Bless America," 53n1, 107–8, 110; *Holiday Inn* (film), 110; "(I Can Always Find a Little Sunshine in) The Y.M.C.A.," 106, 109; "Kitchen Police (Poor Little Me)," 106, 110; "Ladies of the Chorus," 109; "Mandy [Sterling Silver Moon]," 102, 111, 113n31; minstrelsy and, 101–4, 108–9, 111; "My British Buddy," 97–98; "Oh! How I Hate to Get Up in the Morning," 9, 97, 102, 105–6, 114n44; "The Ragtime Razor Brigade," 103; "Send a Lot of Jazz Bands over There," 104–5; "Stay Down Here Where You Belong," 8, 11n23; "Tambourine Drill," 102; *This Is the Army* (*T.I.T.A.*, stage show), 98–99, 108–11; *Watch Your Step* (stage show), 99; "We'll Follow the Old Man," 111; "We're on Our Way to France," 106–11; "What a Difference a Uniform Will Make," 103; "White Christmas" (song), 110; *White Christmas* (film), 99, 110–11; *Yip Yip Yaphank* (stage show), 9, 97–111, 112n13, 113n31

Berliner, Emile, 188

Berlioz, Hector, 61, 67

"Best Old Flag on Earth, The," 6, 189

Beynon, George W., 157, 160, **160**

Biff-Bang!, 100

Billy Bishop Goes to War, 192

"Bird of Love Divine," 134

Blackburn, Thomas W., 48

blackface, 101–2, 111. *See also* minstrelsy

black soldiers, 11n22, 118–19, 120

Bliss, Arthur, 117, 242

Bloor, Ella "Mother," 163

blues, 119, 230, 232–33. *See also* jazz

Boer War, 9, 46, 80; veterans of, 6, 120, 181, 189, 190n30

Bonconi, Maleta, 158

Boorman, William H., 200

Borch, Gaston, 160

Borden, Robert, 183, 187–90, 191, 195n30

Borowski, Felix, 227

Boston, 50, 80, 159,

Boston Symphony Orchestra, 75

Botrel, Théodore, 8

Boughton, Rutland, 25

Bourne, Randolph, 236–37

Bowen, Louise DeKoven, 207

Bower, James M., 82

"Boys from Nova Scotia's Shore," 184

"Boys of the Ocean Blue, The," 128, 137

Breil, Joseph Carl, 152, 153–54, 167

Brewer, Florence Carleton, 210

Bridge, Frank, 8, 19–20, 115; Lament for string orchestra (H. 117), 16–17, 19–30, **24**

Britain, 2–5, 15–17, 121; and Canada, 6, 175, 177, 181, 192–93, 243; and European Allies, 1, 17, 239n37; and Germany, 3, 5, 18, 32n19, 175; and League of Nations, 242; and *Lusitania*, 17–21; military, 79, 97; music in war zones, 116–17; musicians in wartime, 116, 142 and passim; postwar economy, 243, 244n3; postwar musicians in, 242; royal family, 188; and United States, 7–8, 17, 239n37; war songs in, 118, 123n8, 147n55, 200; wartime economy and industries, 115; women in, 4–5, 8, 21, 26–30, 115–16, 172n35. *See also* Longleat House; *Longleat Lyre, The*; *Lusitania* (ship); *and individuals by name*

Britten, Benjamin, 33n29

Brooke, Rupert, 30, 33n29

Browne, Raymond A., 214

Bryan, Alfred, 118

Burke, Edmund, 190

Burnell, Ciara, 17

Burnett, Hazel, 156

Burnston, Clara, 233

Busser, Henry, 64

Butler, Antonia, 20

Butterworth, George, 19, 117

"Call of the King, The," 6
Calmettes, André, 152
Cammaerts, Emile, 15–16
Campanini, Cleofonte, 230
Camp Upton, Long Island, 99, 102, 103, 105, 108–9. *See also* Berlin, Irving
Canada, 1, 2, 4, 90–91, 174–98, 201; and Britain, 6, 175, 177, 181, 192–93, 243; English-French tensions, 5, 120–21; First Nations and Métis soldiers, 120, 123n16, 243; and France, 6, 177–81, **181**, 186–88, **187**, 190; and Germany, 175; and League of Nations, 243, 244; and *Lusitania*, 8, 17, 32n18; military, 5–7, 123n16; music in war zones, 147n59; music publishing in, 4–6, 7, 9n7, 10n12; music recordings in, 118; postwar, 243; soldiers from, at Longleat House, 116, 127, 129, 130, 138, 139, 141; and United States, 175, 186, 188; War Measures Act, 6; women in, 5. *See also* Anglophone Canadians; "Dumbells" (vaudeville troupe); Francophone Canadians; "In Flanders Fields" (poem); *and individuals by name*
"Canadian Boat Song," 184
Canadian Expeditionary Force (CEF), 5–6, 120, **181**; at Second Battle of Ypres, 18, 46, 120, 144n15, 184, 187
Canadian Soldiers' Song Book, 184–86, **185**
Caplet, André, 64, 65
Carlo, Monte, 166
Carpenter, John Alden, 82
Carr, Thomas M., 25
Caruso, Enrico, 118
Casino Saint-Pierre, 64
Castle, Irene, 99, 103
Castle, Vernon, 77, 99
Chamberlain, Neville, 243
Chaminade, Cécile, 156
Champagne, Claude, 191
Champagne, Eusèbe, 7
Chaplin, Charlie, 77, 87
Chapman, Audrey, 27, 36n62
Charles, Gaston, 180
Chicago, 80, 82, 84, 87, 88; and influenza, 227, 228, 230; and memorials, 207, 211, 218; and silent film, 162
Chopin, Frédéric, 165
Cincinnati, 80, 87

clergy, at Longleat House, 127, 139
Cleveland, 80, 87, 163, 200
Cocks, Reverend W., 128, 130, 134, 135
Cocteau, Jean, 64
Cohan, George M., 101, 103; "Over There" (song), 87, 106, 118, 122–23n8, 174; quotations from "Over There" in other works, 50, 104–5, 204, 250; "Yankee Doodle Boy," 106
Coleridge-Taylor, Samuel, 134
Coles, Cecil, 19, 117
Collinge, Patricia, 166
Colombini, Ugo, 188
Concerts Colonne-Lamoureux, 61
conscription: in Britain, 20, 115, 138; in Canada, 121, 176, 187–90, 195n29. *See also* Berlin, Irving: and draft
"coon songs," 103, 119, 130. *See also* minstrelsy
Copeau, Jacques, 65
Cortot, Alfred, 69
Cowell, Henry, 235
Creel, George, 199
Cremazie, Octave, 186
Croiza, Claire, 65, 69
Crompton, Catherine, 19–23, **22**, 29
Crompton, Gladys, 19–22, **22**
Crompton, Paul, 19–21
Crosby, Bing, 110
cross-dressing. *See* impersonation, theatrical
cue sheets, 153–56, 160–62, **160**, 167, 169
Currier, Florence L., 161, 164

Daladier, Édouard, 243
Damrosch, Walter, 90
Daniels, Josephus, 87
Daughters of the American Revolution (DAR), 77–78
David, Laurent-Olivier, 186
Debussy, Claude, 31n8, 58–72, 115, 231; and Belgium, 58, 62, 69; *Berceuse héroïque*, 58–61; *Chansons de Bilitis*, 65; *En blanc et noir*, 59–61; *Fêtes galantes*, 65; musical discretion, 59–64; *Noël des enfants qui n'ont plus de maison*, 8, 58–70; *Ode à la France*, 60, 71n11, 71n31; *Pelléas et Mélisande*, 63; *Pièce pour piano pour l'Œuvre du "vêtement du blessé,"* 59–60; *Le Promenoir de deux amants*, 65; Sonata for cello and piano, 59–61, 65; *Trois ballades de François Villon*, 65

Destinn, Emmy, 77
De Valdor, Joseph, 229, 230
Devries, Herman, 229
Dewey, John, 237
Dillingham, Charles B., 76–77, 80
Dillon, James A., 207
Disney, Walt, 230
"Dixie," 50
Doak, Saba, 230
Dockstader, Lou, 101
doctors, 18; and social order, 139. *See also*
    influenza; medical therapies
"Done We Harold? Yes, Reggie, we do!," 135
"Down Home in Tennessee," 134
Downing, Sam, 232
"drapeau de Carillon, Le," 186
draft, military. *See* conscription
Drdla, Franz, 158
Dressler, Marie, 87
Dubois, Théodore, 3
Dubuisson, Damase, 180
Duce, Geoffrey, 1, 2
Dufy, Raoul, 64
"Dumbells" (vaudeville troupe), 1, 175, 190,
    193n5. *See also* vaudeville
Dutton, Theodora, 166

"Each Stitch Is a Thought of You," 205, **205**
"Echo," 135
"Eine feste Burg," 61
Eisenhower, Dwight, 98
Elgar, Edward, 15–16, 25–26, 59, 137, 156
"En avant!," 190
England: An Ode, 191
Europe, James Reese, 119
Evans, Edwin, 20, 21, 22

Fadettes, The, 159
Fairbanks, Douglas, 87, 166
Fare, Florence, 17
Farrar, Ernest, 30n4
"Fatherland, the Motherland, the Home of
    My Best Girl, The," 7
Féart, Rose, 65, 69, 72n40
Feist, Leo, 79
"feste Burg, Eine," 61
film music. *See* silent film music; *and specific
    titles under* Berlin, Irving
Finck, Herman, 10n10

First World War. *See* World War I
Fischer, Carl, 164
Foreman, Lewis, 18
"For King and Country," 4
Forman, Justus Miles, 42
Foster, Stephen, 184, 191
Fotoplayer, 162, **169**, 169–70
Fradenburgh, William J., 218
Fralick, F. A., 17
France, 7, 11n22, 18, 60, 82, 118, 145n34; and
    Canada, 6, 177–81, **181**, 186–88, **187**, 190;
    and European Allies, 1, 4, 5, 18, 177, 186,
    239n37; and Germany, 3, 8; and India,
    9n6; and League of Nations, 242; and
    United States, 3, 6, 186, 218, 228–29, 232.
    See also individuals by name
Franck, César, 67
Francophone Canadians, 5, 7, 118, 177–81,
    186, 192; and conscription, 121, 176,
    187–90
Fréchette, Louis, 186, **187**
Friedman, Leo, 214, **215**
Friend, Howard, 102

Gabriel, Charles H., 210
Gagnier, J. J., 177
Gary, Hampson, 78
George V, King, 6
German Americans, 3, 7, 42, 87–90, 239n45.
    See also jingoism
Germany, 18, 76; and Britain, 3, 5, 18, 32n19,
    175; and Canada, 175; declaration of war,
    3; and France, 3, 8; gas warfare, 18, 120,
    184, 187; and *Lusitania*, 44; and Mexico,
    57n47, 118; postwar, 239n37, 241–43; and
    United States, 18, 80, 118, 157, 175. *See also
    individuals by name*
Gershwin, George, 230, 239–40n45
Gill, Charles, 190
Glasgow, 243
Glasgow Ladies' String Orchestra, 27
Glatt, Abe, 232
Glogau, Jack, 78–80, **78, 79**
"God Bless Our Empire," 6
Godet, Robert, 63–64, 68
"God Save the King," 177, 193; performances
    of, 3, 137, 176, 189; publications of, 180,
    184, 185–86; quotations of, 6
"God Save the Queen," 178, 193

"God Send You Back to Me," 134
"gold star" traditions, 121, 207–19
Good-Bye Bill, 100
Goodman, Benny, 109
Gounod, Charles, 156, 158
Graff, George, 78–80, **78, 79**
Gray, John, 192
Great War. *See* World War I
Greenberg, Lillian, 155
Greinert, Charles, 3
"Gretna Green," 135
grief: as process, 25. *See also* "gold star" traditions; "In Flanders Fields" (poem); influenza; *Lusitania* (ship)
Grieg, Edvard, 153, 157, 162
Griffes, Charles Tomlinson, 230–31
Griffith, D.W., 152, 153
Grovlez, Gabriel, 65, 72n47
Gurney, Ivor, 19, 30n4, 117, 122n7

Hahn, Reynaldo, 65
Haley, Jack, 109
Halle, Adam de la, 66
Hamack, Claire H., 155
Hambitzer, Charles, 230
Hamilton, Edward, 10n8
Hammond, C. A., 190
Hardy, Thomas, 59
Harkness, Robert, 4, 9n7
Harlem Renaissance, 119, 123n14
Harris, Sam H., 101
"Hats Off to the Flag and the King," 6
Healy, Danny, 102
Helmer, Alexis, 46
Henderson, Alfred E., 80
Hendricks, Dora F., 210
Hetherington, Carrie, 156, 167, 169–70, **169**
Higgins, Bobby, 101–2
Hindmarsh, Paul, 17
"Hinky Dinky Parley Vous," 128
Hippodrome, 76–78, **78**, 80, 82, 137
Hitler, Adolph, 241, 243
"Holiday, in the Summertime," 136
Holmes, Justin B., 218
Holst, Gustav, 25
Holstein, Hans von, 166
hospitals, military. *See* Longleat House; military hospitals
Howells, Herbert, 30

Howland, F. A., 47–48
"How They So Softly Rest," 191
Hubay, Jenő, 158, 163
Hubbard, Elbert, 19
Hughes, Samuel, 177, 181–83, 187, 195n30
Humphrey, E., 130, 133
Huss, Mark Amos, 17

Ide, George E., 47
"I Didn't Raise My Boy to Be a Soldier," 7
"I'll Ever Wear You, My Golden Star," 210
illness, 224–25, 234–36. *See also* influenza
"immortel 22ème Canadien-Français, L'," 190
impersonation, theatrical, 100–101, 102, 109, 130, 147n48
India, soldiers from, in British army, 4, 144n11
"In Flanders Fields" (poem), 1, 73, 120, 174, 191. *See also* Ives, Charles; McCrae, John; Sousa, John Philip
influenza, 91, 115, 120–21, 190, 224–40
In Memoriam (Charles Gill), 190
insurance industry, 41, 43–53, 94n20, 121
International Mercantile Marine (IMM), 39–40
"In the Old Plantation," 135
"In the Sweet Bye and Bye," 39–40, **40**, 43, 50–51, **51**
Iraq, 37, 241
Ireland, 17, 18, 19, 37; soldiers from, 118, 129
Italy, 5
"It's a Long Way to Tipperary," 6, 117, 137, 184, 228
"It's the Wrong Way to Tickle Mary," 117
Ives, Charles, 3, 37–57, 115, 123n18; "From Hanover Square North," 8, 38–43, 45, 52–53, 239n34; "He Is There," 50, 244; "In Flanders Fields" (song), 38, 45–46, 50, 73, 121, 198n71; and insurance industry, 41, 43–53, 94n20, 121; "Nov. 2, 1920 (An Election)," 243; Second Orchestral Set, 38; "The Things Our Fathers Loved," 50–52, **51**; "Tom Sails Away," 50; *The Unanswered Question*, 52

"Jack Briton," 135
James, Henry, 229–30
Japan, 4, 5, 77, 120, 200, 231, 243
Jay, Alice Smythe Burton, 161–62, 164, 167–69, **168**

jazz, 104–5, 109–10; and influenza, 230, 232–33; and postwar United States, 119, 121, 219, 241

Jenkins, Essie, 233

"Jesus Is Coming Soon," 233–34

jingoism, 8–9, 75, 87, 97, 90, 219

Joan of Arc, 118. *See also* Debussy, Claude: *Ode à la France*

"Joan of Arc, They Are Calling You," 118

Johnson, Blind Willie, 233–34

Johnson, Lonnie, 230

Jolson, Al, 99, 103

Jones, William R., 183–84

"Just Try to Picture Me: Down Home in Tennessee," 137

Kafka, Franz, 237

Kansas City, 80

Keillor, Garrison, 101

Kelly, Frederick Septimus, 30

keyboardists. *See* silent film music

King Albert's Book, 58

Kitchener, Horatio Herbert, 184, 187, 188

Kitchen Table publishers, 201–4, 208, 215–17

Klickmann, F. Henri, 205, **205**, 207

Klimt, Gustav, 237

Korea, 241

Krehbiel, Henry Edward, 239–40n45

Kreisler, Fritz, 75, 93n4, 164

Laloy, Louis, 60, 64

lamentation. *See* Bridge, Frank: Lament for string orchestra (H. 117)

Lane, Hugh, 19

Langey, Otto, 160

Lanham, McCall, 45–46

Lauder, Harry, 116

Lavallée, Calixa, 178, **180**

Lavergne, Armand, 189

Lavigne, Ernest, 186, **187**, 190

League of Nations, 219, 242, 243

Lee, Guy F., 85

Lestang, Paule de, 65

Lever, Charles, 183

Levy, Sol, 160

Lewis, William, 45

Liberty Loans, 49–50, 84, 87–88

Library of Congress, 2, 9n1, 211

Liszt, Franz, 165

Liverpool, 3, 17, 243

loans: Liberty Loans, 49–50, 84, 87–88; Victory Loan Campaign, 57n43, 84, 91, 94–95n23

London, 4, 19–21, 41, 73, 115; music published in, 4–5, 17, 190, ; performances in, 16, 20, 27–29, **27**, 97–98; referenced by soldiers, 128, 135; wartime celebrations in, 189; zeppelin raids over, 18

London Palladium, 97–98

London Symphony Orchestra, 16, 25

Longfellow, Henry Wadsworth, 191

Longleat House, 116, 127–48, **132**; soldiers at, 116, 127, 129, 130, 136, 138, 139, 141

Longleat Lyre, The, 116, 127–48, **132**

"Long Live the King," 135

Lorraine, La, 3

"Love's Garden of Roses," 134

lullament. *See* Bridge, Frank: Lament for string orchestra (H. 117)

"Lusitania" (piano piece), 17

Lusitania (ship), 3, 7–8, 77, 117, 187; musical commemorations of, 16–23, 27–28, 37–44, 50–53, 157. *See also* United States: entry into war

"Lusitania Two-Step" (piano piece), 17

"Lycidas" (Milton), 17

MacMillan, Ernest, 191

Madison Square Garden, 80

Mallarmé, Stéphane, 64

"Manhattan Beach, The," 85

"Man Who Put the Germ in Germany, The," 232

"Maple Leaf Forever, The," 176–78, **179**, 192; performances of, 176, *189*; publications of, 186

"Marche l'humanité," 7, 10n15

marches, 76, 91–92, 206, 209–10, 213–17. *See also* Sousa, John Philip

"Marseillaise, La," 184; performances of, 3, 158, 176, 190, 228; quotations of, 46, 61

Marshall, Thomas, 87

Masefield, John, 117

Massenet, Jules, 157

Mauritania (ship), 31n16, 39–41

McAdoo, William Gibbs, 46–50, 84, 87

McCormack, John, 226

McCrae, John, 45–46, 74, 92n1, 120–21; death of, 55n31, 73, 121. *See also* "In Flanders Fields" (poem)

McIlroy, James G., **200**, 200–201
medical therapies, 29, 36n67, 229–31, 234–35
Meinhold, Kitty, 156
Melba, Nellie, 77
Mendelssohn, Felix, 88, 153, 191
Messager, André, 59
Mexico, 57n47, 118, 199, 200
Mignault, Arthur, 186
military hospitals, 18, 116, 127, 129, 139 (*see also* Longleat House); for Indian soliders, 144n11; magazines from, 131–32, 140–42, 144n20, 145n27 (see also *Longleat Lyre, The*)
Miller, Percy Stanford, 204, **204**
Milo, Georges (George Marchant de Trigon), 7
Minot, Adolf, 160
minstrelsy: ad hoc, 100; Irving Berlin and, 101–4, 108–9, 111
Miura, Tamaki, 77
Moberley, Reverend, 26–27
Mobley, Hilda, 218
Moffett, William A., 82, 87
Montjovet, Jeanne, 64, 65, 72n47
Montreal, 46, 73–74, 186; and conscription, 188–89; music periodicals in, 175, 179–80, **181**; music published in, 120, 186–87, **187**; music recording in, 188; wartime performances in, 90–91, 120, 176–77, 190
Moogk, Edward, 175
Moore, Edward, 230
Morgan, J. P., 39–40
Morris, Joe, 204
Morton, Leslie, 18
Muck, Karl, 75, 93n4
Muir, Alexander, 177–78, **179**
Munch, Edvard, 237
Murphy, George, 98
music therapy, 25, 29–30
Mutual of New York, 41
"My Country, 'Tis of Thee," 46, 186, 204, 226
"My Old Kentucky Home," 50
Myrick, Julian, 41, 45, 50
"My Service Flag," 210

"Naughty Melody," 134–35
"Neptune," 135
neutrality, 7–8, 18, 50, 117, 199. *See also* Sousa, John Philip: and neutrality

"Neutrality Rag," 7, 10n17
Newmarch, Rosa, 20
New York, 3, 5, 37–47, 49–53, 65; harbor, 39–41, 79, 120; and influenza, 230; and the *Lusitania*, 7–8, 17–19, 21–22, 37–44, 51–52; postwar, 226; and silent film, 151, 155, 156, 158, 167; in sound film, 109–10. *See also* Tin Pan Alley publishers
"New York Hippodrome, The," 76–77
New Zealand, 4, 194n9, 201, 243; soldiers from, at Longleat House, 116, 127, 129, 130, 141
Nichols, Caroline, 159
Nikisch, Arthur, 167
noise, 225–26, 232, 234, 236
"Nothing to Wear," 128
Novello, Ivor, 15, 174, 200
nurses, 18, 129–30; in newsreels, 158; as performers, 134, 135, 139; and social boundaries, 136, 139, 140–41

O'Callaghan, Clare, 25
"O Canada," 178, **180**, 184, 186, 193; performances of, 176, 177, 189, 190. *See also* Lavallée, Calixa
"O Carillon," 186
O'Connellan, Thomas, 183
O'Keeffe, Georgia, 230
"Old Black Joe," 184
"Old Folks at Home," 184
"Old Oaken Bucket," 85
"One Man Band, The," 128
"On the Banks of the Wabash," 50
"Onward, Christian Soldiers," 117
Orchestra of Queen Alexandra's House, 27
organists, cinema, 149, 152–63, 168–70. *See also* silent film music
Ornstein, Leo, 77, 235

pacifism, 33, 45, 50, 219
"Pack Up Your Troubles," 15
Paderewski, Ignacy Jan, 16
Parker, Horatio, 39
Parry, Hubert, 25
Parsons, M. G., 225
Perham Artistes, 136
Perret, Leon, 157
Pershing, John J., 6, 92, 163, **164**, 218
Phelps, William Lyon, 42
Phillips, Sidney, 89–90

pianists, cinema. *See* silent film music
piano rolls, 169, 202
Pickford, Mary, 87, 102
Pierrot Troupe, 135–36
Porter, Katherine Anne, 224–26, 232, 234
Poulet, Gaston, 65
Powell, Felix, 15
Powell, George, 15
Powell, Maud, 151, 164
Power, Tyrone, 109
preparedness, 44–45, 117–18, 199. *See also*
   Sousa, John Philip: and preparedness
Primrose, George, 101
Prince's Hall, **27**
progressivism, 7, 85–86, 236, 242–44
Promenade Concerts, 16, 28, 31n10. *See also*
   Queen's Hall
Puccini, Giacomo, 128, 134, 156
Punch (magazine), 55n31, 73, 121, 174. *See also*
   "In Flanders Fields" (poem)
"Put a Star in the Service Flag for Me," 204,
   204

Quebec City, 6, 176–78, 189, 190
Queen's Hall, 16, 22, 28. *See also* Promenade
   Concerts
Queisser, Robert L., **200**, 200–201

race, 4, 77, 102–3, 118–20, 144n11, 231, 235,
   243
Radnor, Countess of, 26–27, **27**
ragtime, 75, 103–5, 119, 134, 137, 146n44; and
   influenza, 232; and silent film scores, 152,
   155. *See also* Berlin, Irving
Rapée, Erno, 153
Raub, Elizabeth. *See* Rio, Rosa
Ravel, Maurice, 32n28, 36n67, 63, 65; *L'Enfant
   et les sortilèges*, 63
Ravennes, Paul, 190
Raymond, J. J., 155
Reagan, Ronald, 98
"Red Rose of England," 128
"Reveille," 106
revues, musical. *See* Berlin, Irving
Riesenfeld, Hugo, 154
Rio, Rosa (née Elizabeth Raub), 153, 162–65,
   173n46
Roberts, Frederick, 184
Roberts, Lee S., 162

Rogers, Will, 77
Roosevelt, Franklin, 230
Roosevelt, Theodore, 76, 82, 88–89, 117, 201;
   and hyphenation debate, 42, 88
Rosenthal, Harry, 158–59
"Roses of Picardy," 137
Rossini, Gioachino, 157
Rostand, Edmond, 65
Rothafel (Rothapfel), Samuel L., 154, 158, 159
Routhier, Adolphe-Basile, 178, **180**
Roy, Amédée, 180, 186
Royal College of Music (RCM), 20, 21, 33n35
Royal Northern College of Music, 2
Rubens, Alma, 167
Rubens, Paul, 4–5, 10n9, 15
Rubenstein, Anton, 165
Ruby, Harry, 107–8
"Rule Britannia," 6, 176, 186, 189, 190
Russia, 4, 5, 131, 177, 184; revolution, 188;
   Sino-Russian war, 200

Sabatier, Charles Wugk, 186
Saint-Saëns, Camille, 152, 156, 167
Saint Sulpice (church, Paris), 65
Salfen, Kevin, 17
Salmon, Jacques, 65
Sanders, Alma, 166
"Sands of the Desert, The," 128
"Santa Fe," 135
Satie, Eric, 65
Saucier, Joseph, 186
Scarlatti, Domenico, 67
Schiele, Egon, 237
Schoenberg, Arnold, 237
Schubert, Franz, 156
Schwartz, Lazlo, 164
Scriabin, Alexander, 231
"Sergeant of the Line," 134
service flag, 199–201, 204, 208–13
Ševčík, Otakar, 163
Shaftesbury Theatre, 16
"Should the Stars in Your Service Flag Turn
   to Gold," 210
silence, 117, 122, 225–26, 230–34
silent film music: Chicago and, 162; New
   York and, 151, 155, 156, 158, 167; ragtime
   and, 152, 155; vaudeville and, 152, 159;
   Wagner and, 153–54, 156, 157, 158; women
   and, 119, 149–73

Silverman, Sime, 99, 101–5
"Silver Threads among the Gold," 102
"Sing Me to Sleep," 183–84
Smith, Kate, 110
soldiers: advice to, 89, 90; depictions of, 50, 120, 158 (*see also* Berlin, Irving); families of, 119, 167 (*see also* "gold star" traditions); fund-raising for, 77; and influenza, 234–35; insurance for, 44–49; letters and private writings by, 139, 144n14, 226; as musical revue cast members (*see* Berlin, Irving); music as therapeutic for, 29, 190, 227; nonwhite, 4, 11n22, 118–19, 120, 123n12, 123n14, 123n16, 144n11, 243; as song topic, 203–4, 206, 213–14. *See also under* Longleat House; *and specific countries*
soldiers' press. See *Longleat Lyre, The*
Somme Offensive, 187
Song Sharks (music publishers), 201–3, 211–17
"Song That Reached My Heart," 128, 135
Sousa, John Philip, 73–96, **86**, 115, 157, 228; "Boots," 80–81, **81**; and Great Lakes Naval Training Station, 82–87, 91; "In Flanders Fields," 8, 73, **74**, 91, 92n1, 121, 198n71; "March of the States, The," 77; and neutrality, 8, 75–82, 87, 89; and preparedness, 8, 75–79; "The S.S. Forever," 85; "The Stars and Stripes Forever," 89–90, 157; tours in Canada, 73, 90–91; tours in United States, 74; "Wake Up, America," 78–80, **78, 79**; "The Washington Post," 85, 106; "Wedding March," 88
South Africa, 4, 129, 194n9
Spanish-American war, 157
Spanish flu. *See* influenza
Stackhouse, J. Foster, 19
Stanford, Charles Villiers, 20, 25, 59
"Star of Gold," 214, **215**
Starret, Lora V., 214, **215**
"Star-Spangled Banner, The," 89, 90, 226; performances of, 228; quotations of, 157, 210
Statue of Liberty, 118
Steinway Hall, 27
stereotypes: gender, 116, 119, 150; racial, 103, 119
St. James's Hall, 27
St. Louis, 80, 87

Stockman, August Cornelius, 191
St. Paul, 80
Stravinsky, Igor, 59, 61, 231
Stuart, Herbert, 6
Sullivan, Adele V., 155
Sullivan, Arthur, 117
Sullivan, Daniel E., 200
Sulte, Benjamin, 180
Sweet, Al, **205**
Swinburne, Algernon Charles, 191
Switzerland, 6

Tanguy, Charles, 180
"Tell Me, Pretty Maid," 109
Tennyson, Alfred, 184–85, **185**
Teyte, Maggie, 77
theater organists, 149, 152–63, 168–70. See *also* silent film music
Théâtre Chantecler, 180
Théâtre du Vieux-Colombier, 65
"There's a Little Blue Star in the Window," 205, **205**
"There's a Service Flag Flying at Our House," 204
"There's a Service Flag in the Window," 207
"There Was No One to Harmonise," 135
This Is the Army (*T.I.T.A.*, stage show), 98–99, 108–11
Thomas Dunhill Chamber Concerts, 27
Thompson, Gordon V., 4, 9n7
Three Poems of Fiona MacLeod, 231
"Thunderer, The," 85
Thynne family, 116, 127, 129–30; contributions to *The Longleat Lyre*, 133; musical performances, 134. *See also* Longleat House; *Longleat Lyre, The*
Tiersot, Julien, 66–68
Tin Pan Alley publishers, 104–5, 127, 137, 201–4, 208, 212–17
Titanic (ship), 19, 43
Tommy's Tunes, 117
"Too Late Too Late Blues (The Flu Blues)," 233
Toronto, 175, 176, 177; composers active in, 177, 190–91; music published in, 4–5, 17, **179**; wartime performances in, 90, 91, 183, 189
Toronto Symphony Orchestra, 191
Tosti, Francesco Paolo, 5, 16

Townsend, Natalie, 6, 10n14
Townsend, Yvonne, 6
Tracey, Cora, 158
transatlantic exchanges, 2, 17, 41, 98, 119, and
  passim
transnationalism, 1–4, 7, 74, 200, 218, and
  passim; and influenza, 115, 122, 234–37; at
  Longleat House, 115, 116, 136–39, 142
Treaty of Versailles, 242, 243
Trigon, George Marchant de, 7
Tsing-tau Symphony Orchestra, 77
Turcot, E. L., 7
Turner, Frederick Jackson, 225, 235–36
"Twins, The," 135

United States, 1, 2; and Allies, 4; and Britain,
  7–8, 17, 239n37; and Canada, 175, 186,
  188; Civil War, 9, 86, 167, 210, 227; entry
  into war, 3, 45, 80–82, 118, 149, 199–200;
  and France, 3, 6, 186, 218, 228–29, 232;
  German Americans, 7, 42; and Germany,
  18, 80, 118, 157, 175; Irish Americans, 7,
  75, 87–90; and League of Nations, 219,
  242; and *Lusitania*, 7–8, 17–19, 31n15,
  37–44, 53n1; military, 46, 48, 56n36, 82;
  music publishing in, 199–223 and passim;
  Prohibition, 103, 119, 219; war insurance
  debates, 43–50; women in, 21, 36n63,
  119, 154–56, 159–70; World Trade Center
  attack, 9, 37–38, 52–53. *See also individuals by name*
"Until," 135
"Up from Somerset," 136
U.S. Navy, 76, 77–79. *See also* Sousa, John
  Philip

Vallas, Léon, 69–70
Vancouver, 190, 192
Vanderbilt, Alfred Gwynne, 19, 42–44
Vanier, Georges-Philéas, 186
Varèse, Edgard, 235, 239–40n45
Varley, Irene, 166
vaudeville, 100, 101, 175, 202, 217; and silent
  film, 152, 159. *See also* "Dumbells" (vaude-
  ville troupe)
Vaughan Williams, Ralph, 17, 20, 25–26,
  30, 117; *Dona Nobis Pacem*, 242; "Pastoral"
  Symphony, 242
Verdi, Giuseppe, 156, 157

Versailles, Treaty of, 242, 243
Vézina, Joseph, 190
Vickers, Justin, 1, 2
Victoria, Queen, 117, 175, 178
Victory Loan Campaign, 57n43, 84, 91,
  94–95n23
Vietnam, 241
Villon, François, 60
Vines, Ricardo, 72n47
"Vive la canadienne," 178
"Vive la France!," 186, **187**, 190
Voluntary Aid Detachment (VAD), 129, 130,
  135
von Blon, Franz, 177
Vuillermoz, Émile, 61

Wagner, Richard, 60, 88, 138, 194n20, 231,
  242; and silent film, 153–54, 156, 157, 158
Wallace, Frances, 233
waltz songs, 158, 203, **205**, 205–9, 213–19
Ware, Helen, 163–64
Warren, Francis, 30
"Watchman, What of the Night?," 128
Watt, A. S., 163, **164**
Watt, Charles E., 229
"We Are Coming, Father Abraham," 191, 210,
  222n34
Weir, Robert Stanley, 178
Wells, J. Deane, 192, 198n71
Werrenrath, Reinald, 4, 10n8
"When the Ebb Tide Flows," 128
"When the Little Blue Star in the Window
  Has Turned to Gold," 207
Whitman, Walt, 230–31
Willan, Healey, 190–91
Williams, W. R., 213
"Will the King Be Proud of Canada," 6
Wilson, Clyde B., 89
Wilson, Jason, 175
Wilson, Woodrow, 7, 117–18, 219, 242; and
  influenza, 230, 232, 234, 239n37
Wimperis, Arthur, 10n10
Winters, Mary, 218
women, 3, 87, 88, 89, 226, 228; activists,
  116, 119, 121; in Britain, 4–5, 8, 21, 26–30,
  115–16, 172n35; in Canada, 5; as com-
  posers and songwriters, 121, 206, 208,
  211–17; impersonated by men, 101, 102,
  130; and the *Lusitania*, 15, 19–21, 28, 30;

and motherhood, 199–223; as performers, 8, 26–28, **27**, 128–30, 134–40 and passim; portrayed as sweethearts, 7, 99, 108, 137; and recruiting, 5, 115–16, 210; and silent film music, 119, 149–73; in the United States, 21, 36n63, 119, 154–56, 159–70. *See also individuals by name*

Wood, Henry, 28, 36n64

World Trade Center, 9, 37–38, 52–53

World War I, 1–5, 97–98, 109, 115–22, 241–44; Allies, 4–5, 15–16, 118, 133, 136, 190, 201, 235; connections to World War II, 9, 69, 97–98, 109–10, 241; and illness, 224–25, 234–36; and medical therapies, 29, 36n67, 229–31, 234–35; memorials, 193, 207, 213–14, 217–19; music early in, 3–11; represented in film, 157, 158; trenches, 7, 107, 117, 121, 131, 137, 140, 174, 227; veterans, 91, 118, 120, 218, 228, 242; *See also listings by country*

World War II, 9, 69, 97–98, 109–10, 241, 243

Yale University, 39, 42–43

Yip Yip Yaphank (stage show), 9, 97–111, 112n13, 113n31

YMCA, 106, 116

"Yorkshire Lad in London, A," 128, 135

"Your King and Country Want You," 4–5, 15

Ypres, Second Battle of, 18, 46, 120, 144n15, 184, 187

Zamecnik, John Stepan, 156

Ziegfeld Follies, 99, 100, 106, 111

Zimmerman Telegram, 57n47, 80, 118. *See also* Germany: and Mexico

The University of Illinois Press
is a founding member of the
Association of University Presses.

———————————————

Composed in 10.25/13 Marat Pro
with Trade Gothic Condensed display
by Kirsten Dennison
at the University of Illinois Press
Cover designed by Dustin J. Hubbart
Cover illustrations: Cover of "Over There" sheet music, 1917;
UK flag (Michal Bednarek / Shutterstock.com)

University of Illinois Press
1325 South Oak Street
Champaign, IL 61820-6903
www.press.uillinois.edu